Patricia and Robert Malcolmson are social historians who have edited several diaries for publication. They have edited three different volumes of the diaries of Nella Last, the inspiration for the award-winning drama *Housewife, 49: Nella Last's Peace, Nella Last in the 1950s* and the collected edition *The Diaries of Nella Last*. Patricia and Robert's other books include *The View from the Corner Shop: The Diary of a Yorkshire Shop Assistant in Wartime* (the diary of Mass Observation writer Kathleen Hey) and *Women at the Ready*, a history of the Women's Voluntary Services on the Home Front during the Second World War. They live in Nelson, British Columbia, Canada.

The Mass Observation Archive at the University of Sussex holds the papers of the British social research organisation Mass Observation. The papers from the original phase cover the years 1937 until the early 1950s and provide an especially rich historical resource on civilian life during the Second World War. New collections relating to everyday life in the UK in the twentieth and twenty-first centuries have been added to the original collection since the Archive was established at Sussex in 1970.

**Edited by
Patricia Malcolmson &
Robert Malcolmson**

A Nurse's War

A diary of hope and heartache on the home front.

Harper
North

HarperNorth
Windmill Green,
Mount Street,
Manchester, M2 3NX

A division of
HarperCollins*Publishers*
1 London Bridge Street
London SE1 9GF

www.harpercollins.co.uk

HarperCollinsPublishers
1st Floor, Watermarque Building, Ringsend Road
Dublin 4, Ireland

First published by HarperNorth in 2022

1 3 5 7 9 10 8 6 4 2

A catalogue record for this book
is available from the British Library

ISBN: 978-0-00-851915-5
TPB ISBN: 978-0-00-854191-0

Printed and bound in Great Britain by
CPI Group (UK) Ltd, Croydon

MIX
Paper from
responsible sources
FSC™ C007454

This book is produced from independently certified FSC™ paper
to ensure responsible forest management.

For more information visit: www.harpercollins.co.uk/green

'I like people who keep diaries: they are not as others, at least not quite . . .'

Henry 'Chips' Channon, *Diaries*,
11 July 1939

Contents

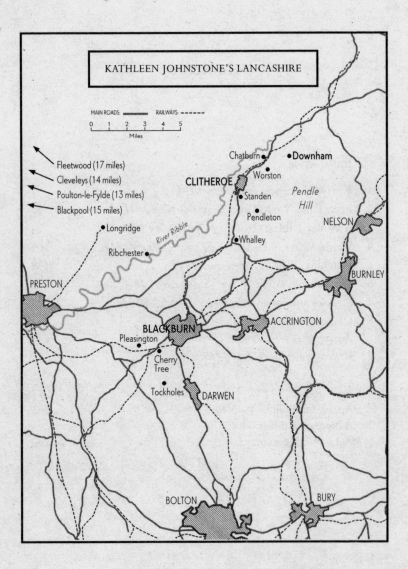

KATHLEEN JOHNSTONE'S LANCASHIRE

MAIN ROADS: ——— RAILWAYS: - - - - - -

0 1 2 3 4 5
Miles

Fleetwood (17 miles)
Cleveleys (14 miles)
Poulton-le-Fylde (13 miles)
Blackpool (15 miles)

Chatburn   • Downham
Worston
CLITHEROE
Standen
Pendleton   Pendle
             Hill
Whalley   NELSON

• Longridge
Ribchester •   River Ribble
                              BURNLEY
PRESTON
                    ACCRINGTON
        BLACKBURN
Pleasington
    Cherry
    Tree
  Tockholes   DARWEN

BOLTON   BURY

Introduction

How does a good diary come to exist? There must be many plausible answers to this question, some emphasizing circumstances, others the personality of the writer, others still a blend of both. Some good and now well-recognized diarists emerged virtually out of the blue. This was the case with Nella Last (b. 1889) of Barrow-in-Furness, the 'Housewife, 49' vividly portrayed on film by the late Victoria Wood. Nella Last's lovingly detailed and engaging diary, which she began at the end of August 1939, runs to millions of words and four books have now been published based on what she wrote.

Perhaps the same sort of surprised discovery can be linked with the diary of Kathleen Johnstone, a student nurse in Blackburn, Lancashire, who began her diary in June 1943. Like Nella Last, she, too, wrote for Mass Observation (MO), the social research organization launched in 1937 to foster a sort of social anthropology of contemporary Britain. MO wanted to collect evidence on a wide range of topics, often relating to the everyday life of 'ordinary people' – that is, aspects of life that had previously not been much studied. Diaries were seen by MO's leaders as one way of capturing these social realities, in the manner that a camera might. Hundreds of people signed up as diarists. A few proved to be

very good at it. Kathleen Johnstone was one of them. From
the start she revealed her talents as a diarist, drawing readers
into her life and times, her personal feelings and observations of public lives and events, all during the last two years
of the Second World War.

Kathleen Johnstone was born on 16 November 1913 in
Sharnbrook, Bedfordshire, the first child of George and
Ellen Johnstone. The couple had met while they were servants at Tofte Manor, a large house in Sharnbrook. He was a
footman and later a butler (when Kathleen was born), she a
housemaid. They had married in 1912. The Johnstones were
to have two more children, Phyllis (b. 1916) and Stanley (b.
1920). George Johnstone spent most of the First World War
as a gunner in the Royal Artillery and was discharged from
the Army in 1919. Once in her diary (2 September 1944),
Kathleen reflected on the struggles of her mother during
this war, caring for two young children and trying to get by
with little money. These were undoubtedly years of hard-
ship for the family.

George Johnstone spent most of his post-1918 adult life
as a butler in households in different parts of England. For
some fifteen years after the First World War, he was butler to Algernon George Lawley, 5th Baron Wenlock (1857–
1931), at Monkhopton House, near Bridgnorth, Shropshire.
The Johnstone family lived in Monkhopton; the children
attended the local village school, and Ellen was a post mis-
tress. George left this position in 1935, soon after the death
of Lady Wenlock, and probably served briefly in at least two
different houses during the following two years (one of them
Hungerford House, near Fordingbridge, Hampshire, a country home of the Bishop of Salisbury). Then, in later 1937,
George and Ellen moved to Downham, Lancashire, where

he took up a position as butler to Ralph Assheton at Downham Hall. George remained in this position for the following fifteen years, including all thirty-nine months during which Kathleen wrote her diary.*

Kathleen's life before the 1940s is thinly documented. It is virtually certain that she lived for all or most of the 1920s with her family in Shropshire, probably leaving school in or about 1928 – perhaps even earlier. Family members report that she was away from home in hospital for considerable periods of time in the 1920s, probably because of the rheumatic fever she had contracted. She is remembered by relatives as later walking with what seemed to some a limp, to others a certain stiffness of gait, and sometimes using a stick, a result of those childhood illnesses that had kept her away from school. This sickly childhood is never mentioned in her diary. Despite a disrupted education, Kathleen was a committed reader, and in adulthood many books of various kinds passed through her hands. She was interested in all sorts of topics. She spent at least some of the 1930s as a nursery governess, perhaps in London; certainly, she knew London reasonably well and had lived and worked there for an undisclosed period of time. Her other residences in the 1930s (as recorded in her sister's address book) include Bexhill in East Sussex and East Grinstead in West Sussex, and there were probably more. Family records indicate that she received a Red Cross certificate for anti-gas training in 1938.

* We are very grateful to Kathleen's nieces and nephews for giving us information about their families' history, including Kathleen's life both before and after the war: Elizabeth Newton Price, Peter King and Mary Jefferies, children of Kathleen's sister Phyllis; and Dene Shaw and Phil Johnstone, children of her brother Stanley. We are also indebted to our friend, Ann Stephenson, for her invaluable genealogical assistance.

With the outbreak of war in September 1939, Kathleen soon joined the Civil Nursing Reserve (CNR) as an auxiliary nurse and spent all, or almost all, of the following two years working in the Weavers Emergency Hospital in Poulton-le-Fylde, a few miles north-east of Blackpool. She then decided to train seriously as a nurse and in October 1941 entered the Blackburn and East Lancashire Royal Infirmary as a nurse probationer. It is possible that, in previous years, her slightly wobbly health had kept her out of nursing training, but with the war and the heightened demand for nurses, this barrier was removed. Kathleen's ultimate objective was, after three years of training, to take exams which, if she were successful, would allow her to become a State Registered Nurse (SRN). It was a little over half-way through this training that she began her diary for Mass Observation. Her reasons for becoming a diarist and sticking with it until September 1946 are never disclosed.

Kathleen's diary has many merits. One is the diversity of its subject matter. Her writing touches on an impressive range of topics: the trials and satisfactions of nursing, fatal accidents, April Fool jokes, bus travel, clothes rations, Italian prisoners-of-war, VD, dental work, country walks, the cinema, US soldiers, dances, feelings about death, children, hospital rules, penicillin (just recently available), packed trains, a beauty contest, wounded soldiers from France, battlefront successes and setbacks, food scarcities, toys, a murder-suicide, Lancashire Wakes Weeks, pregnancies, arguments about religion, holiday celebrations, Winston Churchill, wartime marriages, the blackout, amputees, and, not least, her POW boyfriend in Germany whom she had not seen since October 1939. Kathleen was an observant person; lots of different people and events attracted her attention.

Her tone, too, as revealed in her writing, varied: sometimes matter-of-fact, at other times more emotionally intense; often ironic; sometimes offering a sparkle of wit, at other times gloomily self-denigrating. Hers is a portrait of life that is colourful, absorbing, and full of incident. It is also a portrait from two of the most gripping years in modern British history, written at a time when the fear of invasion had greatly receded but all sorts of other fears and uncertainties remained, not least the uncertainty as to how much longer the war would drag on. While some people were optimists and others pessimists, nobody (of course) actually knew. So, much was still up for grabs.

* * *

Almost all of Kathleen's diary up to mid-1945 was written while she was in Lancashire. And in Lancashire she was based in both a city, Blackburn, and the countryside, in the village of Downham where her parents lived. In *Three Rivers: Being an account of many wanderings in the dales of Ribble, Hodder and Calder* (1946), a book that was written at the same time as Kathleen was writing her diary, Jessica Lofthouse reflected on the ties between city and countryside that were central to Kathleen's wartime life. 'Although most of this country is within easy reach of all the big industrial centres of the north, it remains surprisingly untouched and unspoilt. Thousands love it . . . In normal times it is the country of escape for the dwellers in the towns; it is a pastoral countryside of deep silences and vast solitudes' (p. 16). Perhaps this was to over-romanticize, though it is noteworthy that one woman born (in 1935) and brought up in difficult circumstances in Blackburn, in a working-class household, had similar memories of the country beyond the cities: in *Little Me*, Joyce Fielding wrote, 'The historic villages and lush countryside that surrounded the dark smoky towns did not go unnoticed by the children in Lancashire. They escaped un-chaperoned when they could, and walked, or rode their bicycles for miles. Whalley, Clitheroe, Darwen Tower. Castles to see, green hills to climb, soft clear streams to dip your feet in, were not too far away.'[*]

Kathleen experienced this duality virtually every week, working as she did in industrial Blackburn at its Infirmary, while enjoying most of her days off-duty and her holidays at her parents' home in Downham, a picturesque village some fifteen miles north-east of the city, at the foot of Pendle Hill. In Blackburn, while she often wrote about the town, her life there was consumed mostly by nursing and the various frustrations and satisfactions that went along with it. The Blackburn and East Lancashire Royal Infirmary (BRI for short) was a 'voluntary' hospital funded by private donations. As the Infirmary's surviving account book for 1939–40 shows, these donors were numerous and drawn from a wide range of local society.[†] They included annual subscribers, contributors to specific fund-raising events, and those whose relatively large gifts were linked to the naming 'in perpetuity' of hospital cots (£500) or beds (£1,000). One local woman (b. 1926) was told that her well-off great uncle, after a family feud, gave a lot of his money 'to the Blackburn Royal Infirmary, to pay for new wards to be built and more beds to be put into use'. Later, after a stay of some eight weeks in the Infirmary, her mother reported that the ward was full of beds with the great uncle's name on the end of them.[*] It is probable that the Infirmary was the most prominent charity in East Lancashire, taking in tens of thousands of pounds each year.

The most important source of funding, by far, was the East Lancashire Workpeople's Hospital Fund. This fund was supported by thousands of workers who contributed (usually) a penny a week to the work of the Infirmary. The fund was easily the most important financial contributor to the Infirmary, accounting for at least 40 per cent of its yearly revenue. Its annual report for 1943 acknowledged that 'the workpeople's contributions form nearly half the total Income and are an absolutely vital source of revenue without which it would be impossible to carry on' (p. 7), and the report the following year recorded the Board of Management's 'high appreciation of the splendid support they received from the Workpeople's Hospital Fund' (p. 7).[†] Here, then, was an example of a 'public' institution heavily dependent on proletarian backing.

The Infirmary's finances in the early 1940s were relatively robust,[‡] and there was a strong sense of the people in the region 'owning' the facility. Located on the southern edge of Blackburn, in the direction of Darwen, the Infirmary had grown incrementally since 1865; various buildings had been cobbled together over the decades. In the early 1940s it had 240 beds for patients and housed 108 nurses and

[*] Margaret Ford, with Jacquie Buttriss, *A Daughter's Choice* (London: Pan 2019), pp. 28–29.

[†] These annual reports are held in the Lancashire Archives (AC/24) and the Blackburn Central Library. Records of the East Lancashire Workpeople's Hospital Fund for 1944–5 are held in the Lancashire Archives, HRBK19/2.

[‡] *A History of the Blackburn and East Lancashire Royal Infirmary 1865–1965* (n.d.), p. 7, held in the Lancashire Archives and the Blackburn Central Library.

nurses-in-training. Its medical staff was made up of around 32 doctors.* All sorts of Blackburn's citizens, plebeian and otherwise, came to the Infirmary for treatment, some for just a few hours, some for weeks, others to die there.

In nearby Downham, by contrast, a short train journey and then bus ride away from Blackburn, life was conducted according to different codes and different rhythms. Its traditions had deeper roots than those of a gritty, smoke-filled cotton town that had fallen on hard times after the First World War. Farming was central to Downham's way of life. And since the whole village was owned by one man, there was little question as to where power lay and the character of social relations. Kathleen's father was butler to the head of this family, Ralph Assheton, and George and Ellen Johnstone lived in a tied house, at 2 Top Row (see image section), as did everyone else in the village.

Still, if certain contrasts between city and country were stark, one reality created a sense of commonality – the fact of war. Conscription for war service was near universal. War entered into rural life just about as much as it entered into city life, though of course often in different ways. And these were years when the war was reaching its climax. Germany was increasingly on the defensive. Its forces in the East were losing to the Russians. Anglo-American bombers were devastating German cities. Italy was about to be invaded. The Western Allies were preparing for a Second Front in France. After four years of near-relentless tension and conflict, Britain was on the cusp of – perhaps victory? But how many would die in pursuit of victory? How many families

---

* *Barrett's Directory of Blackburn 1942*, pp. 25–6; and the annual *Report* of the Infirmary for the years during the war.

would lose loved ones? And were there other grim things that would happen before the war was over? Kathleen's diary provides vivid testimony as to one woman's experiences of these tumultuous times.

* * *

Most manuscript diaries do not exist as 'natural' books. They need to be *shaped* into books, and this is what we, as editors, have tried to do.* We have created chapters out of what Kathleen wrote; selected those entries that testify to the wide range of her observations and her keen intelligence; highlighted the narrative strands of her writing; and sometimes composed a paragraph or two that sum up her thoughts and activities over a period of several days or even weeks. We have given prominence to those passages in her diary that speak in some detail to how life was lived in this particular part of wartime England and to circumstances and attitudes that were both specific to time and place and, in some respects, shared by millions of others. Individuals were embedded in a history over which most of them had little or no control. They were almost all aware of large forces at play; many were also conscious – indeed, proud – of the small roles they were playing is this vast drama. Perhaps taking up a pen to write was one way of asserting an element of personal control in a world that was otherwise so manifestly fragile.

---

* Some specific issues related to editing are discussed in 'A Note on Editing' at the end of the book.

1

Everyday Scenes

June–August 1943

Wednesday, 23 June 1943

I am starting this diary on my weekly day off, which I invariably pass at home. Blackburn may have its good points but beauty is not one of them and I always enjoy coming back to Downham, which has been described as one of the loveliest villages in Lancashire. It consists of a cluster of grey stone cottages at the foot of Pendle Hill, often mentioned in [William] Harrison Ainsworth's tale of *The Lancashire Witches* [1854; especially Book Three, Chap. 1].

I came home the evening before as I was lucky enough to be off duty at 6. My father and mother are both away on holiday so I had asked the village shop-keeper to keep me some bread and milk which, with three eggs given to me by a patient and some cheese we had in the house, I hope to keep body and soul together for a day. On reviewing the food situation this morning while having a late breakfast I decided that egg for breakfast, dinner, and supper was too much of a good thing and that a trip to Clitheroe for a meat pie and some potatoes was indicated. I was too late to catch the Downham bus, which runs every two hours into Clitheroe, so walked down to Chatburn to catch a Ribble bus [the major operator in the North West], which runs forty minutes past every hour, or so I thought until I found that this particular bus had been knocked off. However, there is also a privately owned bus service operating through Chatburn, a typical little country bus, the driver and conductor often being the same person, and a little bus came rattling along in fifteen minutes. I boarded the bus with another woman and as we both wanted 3d tickets we were presented with one 6d one between us, to save tickets I was told. I was much amused as it was the first time I had come across this form of paper saving.

Arriving in Clitheroe I found most of the shops closed. Being early closing day they had not bothered to open. I saw no sign of potatoes or meat pies and I began to think my journey had been wasted except for two No. 8 batteries I required in Woolworths. I thought I would pay a visit to the hairdresser's to inquire about the prospect of a 'perm' but even they were closed, and I was just returning to the square for a bus home when to my delight I saw meat and potato pies in a café window.

When I got home I pulled some lettuces and radishes, picked some gooseberries and stewed them, made some custard and had quite an enjoyable lunch with the meat and potato pie and some home-made chutney. The meat I might say consisted of one small cube of meat about ¼ inch square.

After lunch I retired to the top of the garden to stuff an elephant I have been knitting for my small nephew. It has been made from scraps of RAF blue wool which I had left over from various pullovers, gloves etc. which I had knitted for an airman who will not want anything else knitted for him. Having stuffed the elephant, mowed the lawn and weeded the onion bed, I adjourned for tea. After tea a laze with a book and back to the [Blackburn] Infirmary on the 8.40 bus from Downham.

Thursday, 24 June

When I walked into the dining room this morning for breakfast my attention was called to a notice marked IMPORTANT. On reading it I found that if I did not give three clothing coupons for uniform within a reasonable time I should be prosecuted. We have to give twelve clothing coupons a year for our indoor uniform and each quarter the powers-that-be have a hectic time extracting from unwilling nurses their coupons. There are long and loud arguments over this, some of them holding the view that if factory workers can get extra coupons for overalls, why should we have to give up twelve of ours. A great many of the staff are going about stockingless as many of them are without coupons for black stockings or anything else. Some of the nurses who still owe coupons for uniform have none to give, though in my case it was purely laziness that my name was on the list as I still have a few left. Accordingly I took my book to Matron at 9.30 expecting a slight telling-off for ignoring the previous notice. But she took them calmly, merely asking me if I had been to her about my summer holidays, so a little speech I had rehearsed in self-defence was not needed.

This evening myself, two other nurses and a lady doctor did the female VD clinic. These clinics are held here every Monday and Thursday evening and in the short space of time I have been doing this clinic (about three months) the number of patients has increased enormously. This is due to the increased campaign against VD and judging by a great many of the new patients we get I should think a blood test before marriage would do a great deal towards preventing the spread of this disease. Many of the new patients are young girls, newly married; some are already pregnant. What a heritage for the new generation.

Friday, 25 June

I was told today that I was being transferred from the Outpatient department to the Men's Surgical ward on Monday. I am sorry because I have found the OPD most interesting and you seem more in touch with the outside world than when you are on a ward. I shall miss the big surgical and medical clinics when the patients, poor things, sit in rows for hours on the hard benches, patiently or impatiently according to their natures, waiting to see the surgeon or physician. I feel very sorry for them but it is difficult to see how things can be improved under the present system. For example, in a big medical clinic I have been taking regularly, which is scheduled to start at 9.30, the patients are queuing up at the registration office at 8.30. By the time the physician comes at 9.30 the benches are crowded and even the late-comers are there before 10. There are usually about fifty-odd cases to see, some new, some old. Some are quickly disposed of but some have to be thoroughly examined and take anything from ten to fifteen minutes. The time passes very quickly and often at 12.30 there are still people waiting who came round about 9. You are often asked if you can get someone in before their turn because there is a baby to feed, children coming home from school, or work waiting to be done, perhaps a foreman from a factory who says there are twenty people idle if he is not there etc. It is difficult to sort out genuine reasons and you often feel that for one person who has asked there may be ten with more urgent reasons who have not asked; and if you do call a person in before her turn what a muttering and murmuring goes on from the crowded benches. 'I was here long before she was,' you hear them saying.

When the poor things have seen the doctor it does not mean they are free to go. Very often they have forms to take to the laboratory or X-ray departments for various tests, which often means another journey to the Infirmary for them if they cannot be fitted in that morning. It seems that reforms are needed but I cannot think of any constructive idea under the present circumstances.

Saturday, 26 June

Saturday, the day in Out-patients when we do the weekly spring-cleaning, wash walls, polish furniture, clean lights etc. Casualties who are waiting to see the doctor sit and stare at us, occasionally remarking that they thought we were nurses but did not know we mopped floors. The windows are all bricked up [because of the blackout] except for a few inches at the top where we catch a glimpse of the weather, and as I saw the sun shining outside this afternoon while I was washing the walls, I thought of my brother, the baby of the family [Stanley, b. 1920], who was being married in Kent today, and I almost shed a few tears of self-pity into the bucket of water. My own boy friend is a prisoner-of-war in Germany and I have only a few infrequent letters to keep me going. I was just thinking gloomily that some people had all the luck when suddenly the other nurse who was working with me slipped on some Lysol, skidded across the floor and knocked the bucket of water over herself, so I soon had something else to think about.

Sunday, 27 June

On Sundays the nurses from Out-patients and the theatre are sent on to the wards so I went on to C-1 ward, a big women's surgical ward in the newest part of the building. As the morning gave promise of a hot afternoon and as it was my half-day I skipped lunch and got changed quickly, hoping to get away before the Sunday afternoon crowds. Unfortunately lots of other people had the same idea and there were long queues for the buses and trains when I arrived down at the square in front of the station at 1.45. I managed to get away on the 2.35, reaching home about 3.30, but it was worth it just to get out into the country and as I lazed in a deck chair on Sunday evening listening to the church bells the war seemed so very remote and far away from this peaceful little village. Actually, though, it has touched quite a number of the families in the village. Most of the local boys joined the Territorials in 1939 in an Anti-Aircraft Company which got back safely from Dunkirk but were lost in Crete. Some of course are prisoners-of-war but quite a few will not come back again. A little later on I was talking to a typical old country-man who was telling me that on the job he was working on, laying water to some outlying farm, they had six Italian prisoners-of-war to help them. I inquired how he got on with them but all he seemed to be able to tell me was that they were 'lazy beggars'. Personally I see no reason why they should be anything else as they have no incentive to work hard.

Tuesday, 29 June

Apparently the heat wave has come to stay for a few days and how we people in the pre-war style regulation grey dresses with long sleeves and high stiff collars and starched cuffs envy the people in the wartime uniform. The new uniform consists of a blue dress opening all the way down the front with short sleeves and soft white Peter Pan collar and an apron buttoning on the shoulder. Much cooler this kind of weather. What makes the atmosphere of the wards so oppressive is the fact that so many of the windows have a permanent blackout and it is impossible to open more than a few of them. Most of the staff are going about stockingless except for a few of us whose feet blister very easily. That, I find, is the great problem because even when I am off duty and not running round as much as on the wards I very quickly get a blistered heel no matter how comfortable the shoe or what precautions I take. Some of the nurses are wearing ankle socks but they really do look a bit odd with uniform and it seems to me that woollen ankle socks are warmer for the feet than black silk stockings. One advantage I find on the men's ward is the fact that there is a wireless and I can now hear the news each day, though at the moment most of it consists of bombing and yet more bombing. There is much speculation in the ward about the invasion of Europe, some holding the view that it will come very soon, others inclining to the theory that we shall try a much more intensive bombing of Italy, hoping to achieve her capitulation without much invasion by land.

Wednesday, 30 June

At our mid-day meal today Matron asked for volunteers for blood donors. This is the first time this has been done as previously only under exceptional circumstances has a nurse been asked to give a pint of blood. Just before I came here all the nurses had a blood test and their blood grouped, and on one or two occasions when blood of a certain group was needed urgently for a dying patient a nurse of that group has given a pint. Otherwise we have not been encouraged to offer ourselves as blood donors. I don't quite know why there is this change of attitude unless it is that the public is losing interest in becoming blood donors. I know that the number of donors has been steadily declining of recent months and we have not been getting nearly so many as at the beginning of the war. We have a centre here every Tuesday and Friday afternoons from 1.30 onwards. The local WVS [Women's Voluntary Services] makes tea for the donors and some VADs [Voluntary Aid Detachment] come to help and eight nurses from the wards are also in attendance. There are two rooms holding four couches each and there is a nurse in attendance at each couch and a doctor in each room. I went to this centre for five months and the biggest number of donors I ever had on my couch in one afternoon was seven; sometimes I only had one. We used to get people up in batches from the factories some afternoons following an appeal for blood donors. In their working overalls, some in clogs, they used to come in, most of them treating it as a big joke, others so nervous that they would faint before we had time to get going. Once you have given a pint and you have been put on the list of blood donors you are sent for about three times a year. Some of the donors have given six or seven pints in all. Most of the blood is dried but a certain amount is kept for use in the hospital.

The really big event of the day, though, was receiving our wage packets for the month. The Sister or staff nurse goes down to Matron's office and signs for the wage packets for the number of staff on the wards. The Rushcliffe scale of salaries [recently set out] has been adopted here and as a second-year nurse I get £45 per year instead of £35, which was the original rate of pay for a second-year nurse; third-year get £80 now and first-year £40. What hampers me considerably is the fact that in my more prosperous pre-war years I took out an insurance [policy] in one of the big insurance companies of £12 a year. As I was then earning about £80 a year as a nursery governess I felt I could well afford it but when I started nursing at £30 a year I found it very hard to balance my budget. Especially because you have to provide yourself with various text-books, none of them very cheap, and pay 2 guineas entrance fee for the Preliminary State examination out of your first-year salary. My reason for taking out this insurance policy was the fact that as there is of course no pension scheme for nursery governesses I felt I had better make some provision for my old age. At the age of 60 I can draw out a lump sum or take an annuity for the rest of my life. I can also, if I do not wish to continue payment as long as that, draw out the sum of money I have paid in plus a bonus. How the Beveridge scheme will affect this kind of insurance I am afraid I have not had time to find out. But it seems pretty obvious that it is going to be a long time before it is going to be accepted, except 'on principle'.*

* The Beveridge Plan, published in early December 1942, laid the foundations for a welfare state. Its proposals were widely supported, though Churchill and other Tories wanted to steer clear of debates about post-war social reform, even while most of them endorsed it 'in principle'.

Thursday, 1 July

The first of July and we are already half-way through 1943. It does not seem possible that six months have passed since New Year's Day. The time does go quickly when you are busy and each day passes all too quickly before you have had time to do one half of what you intended to do. The hot weather seems to be continuing longer than usual up here and each afternoon on the lawn in front of the Nurses Home you see rows of nurses sunbathing in every possible kind of garment. If any of the gardeners happen to stray into that particular part of the grounds they look most embarrassed and beat a hasty retreat.

As it is my day off tomorrow I managed to get off duty promptly, at 8.30, and rushed down to the station in time to catch the 9.13 home. When I got out at Chatburn I found that my mother and father had been on the same train. They had started at 10 in the morning [from Kent] and looked hot and tired. Fortunately an acquaintance of ours with a car and a spot of petrol [unavailable for private motoring since mid-1942] was on the train too so we were able to ride the distance between Chatburn and Downham instead of walking it. They had been to my brother's wedding and after hearing all about [it] I felt more disappointed than ever that I was not able to go.

Friday, 2 July

On waking round about 9 this morning I saw it was going to be another hot day and regretted having made an appointment for a 'perm' in Clitheroe for 2 p.m. I half thought of phoning to put it off but on thinking it over decided I had better not as some people have had to wait weeks for an appointment. I had quite a shock when I rang up last Saturday and they said they could take me today. Accordingly after lunch I went into Clitheroe and came out of the hairdresser's as the clock was striking 6. What a waste of a lovely summer's afternoon. I felt an awful freak until I got home and combed out the waves and tight little curls and made the whole thing look a bit more natural.* As I had had no tea I decided to have a tea and supper combined as it was then about 7 and I was catching the 8.30 bus back to Blackburn. I had my meal in the cool of the garden and then got ready to start back.

While I was waiting for the Blackburn bus in Clitheroe a woman came up to me and said that my face looked familiar and then decided she had seen me in one of the clinics at the Infirmary. I could not remember her but she sat beside me in the bus and told me about her complaints and a great deal of her life history. Apparently she had been in domestic service as head parlour maid in Kensington but the house was bombed in the Blitz and she found a job up here to get away from the air raids. The only job in domestic service she could find was as a work-general which she hated, being used to the bustle of a large establishment and the companionship of the rest of the staff. Then the poor thing had a nervous breakdown. After that she found another job but had to give it up on account of

---

* Perms may have been a laborious process but in wartime they were increasingly a social necessity as more and more women entered the workforce, particularly in uniform, which demanded neat, orderly hair. *Hairdresser and Beauty Trade*, a trade journal, noted in 1941 that women in the North were 'spending more on hair and beauty treatment than before the war' and that many holidaymakers in Lancashire 'had taken the precaution, before going away, of having their hair attended to' (27 June 1941, p. 5). More women were earning money and rationing limited expenditures on clothes. This meant that women during the war could and did spend more on their hair. (Patricia Malcolmson, *Me and My Hair: A Social History* [Gosport: Chaplin Books, 2012], especially chapter 4.)

the attacks of pain she now has. She is now living in a room for which she has to pay £1 a week and is waiting to be sent for to have an X-ray of her gall-bladder. Knowing how long are the lists for X-rays I could not hold out much hope that it would be very soon but, as said, she could not wait about indefinitely as she was having to draw on her savings to live. She was of course getting her panel money and her doctor did not advise her to find another job until the cause of these attacks of pain had been discovered and she was cured.

Saturday, 3 July

There is very little red tape here [at the Blackburn Infirmary] or sense of restraint which still characterises so many of the training schools, I believe, and the Matron is always ready to listen to any grievance we may have and try to remedy matters. I have just been reading *One Pair of Feet* [1942], written by Monica Dickens, a descendant I believe of *the* Dickens, in which she describes her experiences as a probationer in her first year in hospital. She does get the atmosphere very well and as you read it you realize she must have felt just exactly as you felt when you first started. You sympathise with her over the tiresome patient who will never let her pass the bottom of the bed without asking for something, the private patients who will keep on ringing their bells, having experienced it all yourself. It certainly does not present a glamourised picture of nursing. In fact, I think it rather errs on the other side and makes a nurse's life appear too drab and repressed.*

* Dickens's book is a humorous account based on her own experiences as a junior nurse. It exposes the petty tyrannies of nursing training and offers keen observations of hospital life that closely mirror many of Kathleen's accounts. (See also 28 November 1943.)

Monday, 5 July

On Monday morning we each take a plate and jar or tin marked with our name on to the ward for our butter and sugar ration, and it is the job of the most junior nurse on the ward to take the plates and jars down to the storeroom where the housekeeping Sister doles out our ration, 4 ounces of margarine, 2 ounces of butter, and 6 ounces of sugar. My fat ration soon goes but I don't take sugar in my tea, so I usually have some sugar over each week which I take home and my mother saves to make some jam to bring back with me. We have quite a few gooseberries and damsons and currants in our garden so we are not short of fruit for jam-making.

For the last two or three years my mother ran a Jam and Fruit Preservation Centre in the village. She took a special course at Hutton Agricultural College outside Preston and a lot of the jam made and fruit preserved at the Centre was bought by the village grocer so that the people knew exactly how their jam was made and lots of them had helped to make it. The grocer said that had it not been for the jam made at the Centre he would not have had enough jam in the first couple of years of war to keep his customers supplied.

Last year, though, the Centre did not do so well. It was not a good year for fruit for one thing and many people made their own jam with the sugar ration they were able to take out instead of jam; consequently there was very little surplus fruit for the Centre. Then of course there was the vexed question of helpers. The first year being a new thing there were plenty of helpers and people's time was not so fully occupied as it is now. Last year my mother did the whole thing practically on her own in addition to a whole-time job she has taken on. She does not enjoy very good health and she found it too much for her because there is a whole lot more to jam-making and fruit-preserving than standing in a crisp white overall daintily labelling jars of jam. She said she would help this year if someone else would run it but so far no one has volunteered. Of course quite a large percentage of the population around here is engaged in farming, which is a very whole-time job, especially during harvest time, and there are few who have time for anything else.

Tuesday, 6 July

The weather has well and truly changed and today it has simply poured down the greater part of the day. I was off duty at 6 so changed hurriedly and rushed down to the Town to catch my bus at 6.35. When the bus came in there was a long queue of people so the inspector said 'Workers First,' which was fair enough in its way but he made no attempt to see if they were really workers, such as asking for contracts etc. The result was that a whole crowd of people from the end of the queue surged forward and some of them looked suspiciously like people who had been doing an afternoon's shopping. Everyone got on, so it did not matter very much, but if they are going to take the Workers first they should arrange two queues and just check up on them. There were quite a few boys in hospital blue on the bus from the military hospital outside Whalley. They were part of a convoy of wounded from North Africa which had come in about a fortnight ago. They were all in great spirits at being home again, even those who had lost a limb, but poor things, it will be the long weary years afterwards which will test their fortitude, after they have got over the excitement of being home again, when the glamour that surrounds the wounded from a victorious army has faded and they have to settle down to leading an everyday life handicapped by their lost limb. Even the most marvellous modern science cannot replace that even though artificial limbs are so much better than they used to be and I have no doubt that big improvements are still being made.

Wednesday, 7 July

It is a lovely feeling waking up on your day off and knowing you can turn over and go to sleep again and that for one morning out of seven you do not have to force your reluctant body out of bed before you are really awake. I think the Double Summer Time is really to blame for the difficulty I have in waking up in the mornings these days. I seldom get to sleep before 11.30 or 12 at night however early I may be in bed and however dark my room may be. Consequently I never get more than 6½ or 7 hours' sleep and I am one of these people who do need a lot of sleep.

When the clocks were put back again a few weeks later, on 14 August, she remarked that 'I must say I like Double Summer Time. It does give you such lovely long, light evenings and of course does away with the trouble of putting up the blackout for a month or two if you go to bed at a reasonable hour.'

Friday, 9 July

There is a dance here tonight given by the Student Nurses Association, and the day nurses take it in turns to relieve the night nurses until 11 p.m. I am doing my spell of relief now and, as for a wonder everyone was quiet in the ward, I decided that I would scribble a few lines in my diary as I shall not feel like doing it when the dance is over. They are quite jolly affairs. Refreshments are provided and you can ask as many boy friends as you like and for those whose boy friends are away Matron usually sends an invitation to the Entertainment Committee of one or two of the companies of soldiers we have around here so there are usually some unattached men at the dances.

Her dance plans, however, were upset 'by the fact that my nose bled for the greater part of yesterday evening so I had to go to bed early instead' (10 July).

Sunday, 11 July

Every other Sunday we have a half-day but as it was my half-day last Sunday I had the morning off this Sunday from 9.15 to 12.40 and as it was pouring with rain, and my own particular friend with whom I usually spend my Sunday morning off-duty had unfortunately got the opposite Sunday off duty, I went up to my room and did all manner of odd jobs – cleaned shoes, darned stockings, did some washing, altered a dress and last but not least swept and dusted my room. I have the misfortune to be in one of the rooms on the third floor known as the horse-boxes. They are in the new part of the Nurses Home on the top floor and are the only bedrooms in the new part which have not hot and cold water in them. In addition they are about 12 feet by 10 feet with a built-in wardrobe and just enough space for a bed, chair and small chest of drawers and linen basket. The ceiling slopes and the window is back a little in a recess and when I want to open or close it I have to leap across my bed or pull it out, according to how I feel. The view from the window is non-existent as about 18 inches from the window is a pointed piece of brickwork extending well above the window, which decorates the front of the Nurses Home. The plan of my room is something like this. [She sketched a plan of the room.] It is not (as you must admit) a very spacious apartment and is definitely not one of the bedrooms Matron shows to prospective nurses. These 'horse-boxes' are the only rooms which are not cleaned weekly. The maid does them for some reason every other Sunday morning and being so small they soon get dusty. In between the weekly or fortnightly cleaning the rooms are never touched by the maids and it is very difficult to get hold of a brush if you want to sweep them in-between whiles. I managed to do it this morning but it was only because the maid was off duty. It has always been the custom here that the nurses' rooms are only cleaned weekly and it is not due to a wartime shortage of staff. There does not appear to be any compulsion for us to clean them ourselves, though, in between the weekly polish, but they certainly get very dusty.

Monday, 12 July

There seems to be cause for cautious optimism in Sicily [which the Allies had just invaded] with three airfields in our hands and a substantial landing made. The old men in the ward gave grunts of satisfaction when they read their papers. We get in very few patients between 18 and 50 years of age as of course most of them are in the Forces. Our free week is over [every fourth week all emergency cases were sent to another ward] and the emergency cases are trickling in – one appendix, one peritonitis and one parotitis during the day we had. I was off duty in the afternoon and when I had to leave the ward at 5.30 to go to the VD clinic it was terribly busy with cases coming back from the theatre.

The clinic was not as busy as usual owing to the fact that it is Darwen holiday week and lots of people are away, most of them at Blackpool, the Mecca of all holiday-makers in Lancashire. It is Blackburn holiday week next week and there are already queues of people outside the advance booking office on the railway station, and on some trains to Blackpool it is impossible to get a seat. Why people struggle to get to Blackpool for their holidays I cannot imagine. It is crowded, difficult to get meals, the places of amusement are packed and during the season very expensive, and the smell of sweating humanity in the Tower and Winter Gardens on a hot summer evening is quite enough to put one off dancing. I spent a couple of years at a little place called Poulton-le-Fylde about 4 miles from Blackpool so I consider I spent quite enough time in Blackpool to put me off from ever wanting to spend a holiday there.

'Blackpool looked much the same as it always does,' Kathleen wrote almost two years later, on 8 June 1945, 'lots of different uniforms, and a great wind blowing which nearly blew me off my feet as I tried to struggle across the road from Central Station, across to the promenade, where I knew I should get a train for Cleveleys.' A week later (15 June 1945) she wrote again of the huge summer crowds in Blackpool. 'Once the "Wakes Weeks" start for the various towns it is a case of the survival of the fittest at Blackpool. The whole town seems to transplant its entire population to Blackpool and they say it is easy to tell whose holiday week it is by the dialect heard at Blackpool.'

Friday, 16 July

Blackburn holiday week starts tomorrow and the buses were more crowded than usual with people who had finished on

Friday evening, when I started home this evening. I had to stand the greater part of the way to Clitheroe, which was not very pleasant as my feet were aching more than a bit. It is Clitheroe's holiday week too and both places have Holiday-at-Home programmes. Band concerts in the park, children's sports and tennis tournaments and dancing in the park, weather permitting.* The weather does seem as though it may be better this year than it was last. It simply poured for the greater part of the Holiday Week last year and most of the programme had to be cancelled. On Sunday there is community hymn singing in the grounds of the old castle at Clitheroe. It starts at 3 and my mother is thinking of going in to listen to it. I would like to have met her there as it will be my half-day but in view of the crowds there will be travelling on Sunday, I don't think I would get there before it is over.

It was a lovely peaceful summer evening, and as we wandered round the garden after listening to the news, which was good, I felt it was one of those times which I would like to continue indefinitely.

Sunday, 18 July

Not a very nice Sunday morning, windy and cold and dull, and several of us who had arranged to have a picnic tea together in the hospital grounds decided we had better

* These heavily promoted Holidays-at-Home were designed to discourage people from travelling at a time when the needs of military transport were to have priority. Recreational plans were published in great deal in the *Clitheroe Advertiser and Times*, 16 July 1943, p. 4, and in other papers. Still, massive queues formed in Blackburn of people booking tickets for trains to Blackpool, Morecambe and Heysham (*Northern Daily Telegraph*, 12 July 1943, p. 5).

change our programme. The weather improved slightly about 1.30 so after much discussion we decided to take our tea out and go for a hike. I had found an old book called *Rambles by Highway and Field and Lane, Round Blackburn* and we thought it would be fun to try one of them and we picked one called 'Over the yellow hills to Pleasington,' and very enjoyable we found it. When we had pooled our resources we found we had enough eats to keep us for several days, never mind just a picnic tea, so leaving some of the tea behind we started off by bus to the outskirts of Blackburn. We looked anything but a conventional Sunday crowd in pullovers and shirt blouses, slacks etc., and before we had gone far the sun came out strongly, though it was still windy. We took the book along with us to guide us and it was most useful even though it was over twenty years old. It took us across the fields where men and women were busy haymaking [and] over some heather-covered hills from where on a clear day you can see Blackpool Tower. We found a nice sunny sheltered spot for our tea, where we ate so enormously that we felt disinclined to move afterwards. Then after tea we dropped down into Pleasington Priory and then by way of a contrast we crossed the road and went into a small pub as we were all very thirsty by this time. Most of us had soft drinks and then we started on our return journey across the fields to Cherry Tree where we were getting a bus back to Blackburn. Before we reached Cherry Tree we had another halt and finished up the remains of the tea, though we still had a whole cake untouched. We were lucky enough to get a bus immediately we got to Cherry Tree and as soon as we got in we said goodnight and went to bed as there was not one of us that was not feeling sleepy with all the fresh air we had had.

Tuesday, 20 July

I have been hearing today that on Saturday 18,000 people left Blackburn for Blackpool on thirty trains, twelve of them 'specials'. It seems a large number to be going to one place in one day from a town the size of Blackburn [population c. 115,000] but the *Northern Daily Telegraph*, Blackburn's evening paper, has headlines saying the public is getting the right spirit and reports long lists of entrants for the competitions and large crowds for all attractions arranged for Holidays-at-Home [week of 17–24 July]. Tomorrow the Holiday King and Queen are supposed to be paying a visit to the Infirmary amongst other places.

Things seem to be going fairly well in Sicily. I must say the bombing of Rome [though not the historic centre] took me by surprise. Personally I thought we should be over-scrupulous and not bomb it and leave Mussolini sitting there in comparative safety. Needless to say I am glad this is not the case and if bombing Rome will shorten the war and save the lives of the Allied forces, by all means bomb Rome. What are bricks and mortar, however beautiful and steeped in tradition and culture, compared to human lives.

Wednesday, 21 July

The Holiday King and Queen did a tour of the wards of the Infirmary today, escorted by the Assistant Matron and one or two other big-wigs connected to the Infirmary. They arrived about half an hour after the [patients'] visitors had gone and held up the routine of the ward quite a bit. In fact when I came off duty at 6 o'clock we had not caught up with ourselves. The 'Queen' [employee in a laundry] was quite a pretty blonde dressed in some heavy satin material with trimmings of gold. The dress I believe was given by one of the townsmen and the 'Queen' did not have to give up any coupons for it. The 'King' [a local comedian] was portly after the style of Henry VIII and was dressed in velvet trimmed with gold braid. Before coming to the Infirmary they had put in an appearance at the Children's Ball and also the Baby Show. All ages have been catered for in the attractions for Holiday Week from infancy upwards. I am so glad they have had a fine week this year. In some mills they are working such long hours and they do look forward to this week the whole year. The only snag against holidays at home seems to be the fact that not only do the mills close but all the shops too, including most of the food shops, so that housewives find catering a bit difficult.

Friday, 23 July

I was awakened this morning [in Downham] by the sound of voices singing an unfamiliar song. I was curious enough to get up and have a look out of the window as it seemed a bit early in the morning for that sort of thing. I found it was the six Italian prisoners-of-war who are helping to lay water from Pendle Hill to some of the farms. They were seated in the back of a ramshackle looking lorry, apparently waiting for the old retired farmer who lives next door to us and who is supervising the work. I was talking to him later in the day and he was saying that they still firmly believe that the German and Italian flags will fly over Britain. I asked him whether they knew that Sicily was being over-run by the Allies. He said 'yes,' that one of their number could speak and understand English very well, and he was shown the daily paper, but it did not seem to damp his optimism. The old farmer was sporting a crimson silk kerchief around his neck, a thing I have never seen him wearing before, and I asked him whether it was the company he was working with that made him wear such a gay scarf.

Sunday, 25 July

A very sultry Sunday morning and another nurse and I went to Matins at the Cathedral. It was very pleasant to hear all the church bells ringing as we walked down.* It was too early for any trams to be running and except for an occasional car everything was quiet. I don't think I shall ever hear church bells again without offering a silent prayer of thankfulness for the great dangers from which we have been saved. I think that most people will agree now that I am not being too premature in saying that [i.e., that the risk of invasion was over].

The Cathedral was being rebuilt partly when war broke out and looking at it from the outside one might think it had been bombed as the rebuilding has been suspended for the duration. Inside where the services are held one often had to sit under the scaffolding. I don't quite know how extensive the rebuilding was to have been or what it looked like before it was started as it is only since I came to the Infirmary [in later 1941] that my knowledge of Blackburn has extended beyond the railway station.

Friday, 30 July

I am sure today has been the hottest day of the year so far. Not a breath of air in the wards, which are packed with

* Bell-ringing had been prohibited from the spring of 1940 to November 1942, reserving it for warnings of invasion.

emergency cases, and grilling in the sun on the balcony which is also packed. If it started to rain I don't know where we should fit all the beds but there does not seem to be much likelihood of that happening at the moment. I was off duty this morning and had to attend my first doctor's lecture in preparation for my Finals which I sit a year in September.

During the morning I had heard rumours that I was going on night duty, which was unhappily confirmed by Sister when I got back on to the ward. I was supposed to be starting on Saturday night but as my day off for the week was Saturday I did not see the fun of coming back at 8.30 p.m. and going on night duty, so I went to Matron and have got a reprieve until Monday night. I thought I had better ask for another thermometer while I was there [hers was broken] and Matron looked at me in horrified amazement to think I had broken two so quickly. Had she known it was really three, I don't know what her feelings would have been. It fell to my lot to take the temps this evening, about thirty of them, and every patient seemed to hold the thermometer in his mouth so awkwardly that I expected it to fall out every minute. However, I got round without a mishap but was not sorry when 8.30 arrived and the night staff came on duty. I hurried over to my room and got changed and caught the 9.13 train home. When I got home my mother produced from somewhere some very welcome Tanzaro Grape Fruit Squash, which I love and which tasted almost pre-war.

Saturday, 31 July

At 8.30 p.m. as I was ready to start back [to Blackburn from Downham] the rain came – a torrential downpour.

Fortunately I had left my umbrella behind at home several weeks ago so was able to set off with an umbrella, which at least afforded a little protection. There were crowds of people at the station, mostly women and children in cotton frocks, some of them already drenched to the skin [weather forecasts were not made public]. When the train came in and we all packed into the carriages the atmosphere inside resembled a Turkish bath more than anything else. We sat there in this awful damp heat in semi-darkness while outside the thunder crashed and the gloom was occasionally broken by flashes of lightning. At each station crowds of wet holiday-makers made a dash for the train from every available cover. All the glass has been removed from the roofs covering the platforms at the stations along the line [to lessen damage from air raids] so that even if the people were fairly dry to begin with they get wet dashing along the platform looking for seats. When I got to Blackburn there was a terrific scramble for the buses as the storm seemed to have started again with renewed energy. I was fortunate enough to get one fairly soon and was not sorry to find myself once more at the Infirmary.

Monday, 2 August

I am sitting in the ward kitchen and it is just before midnight. My dreaded night duty has begun. I came off duty at 2 p.m. and did a little packing and general clearing up in readiness for moving on to the night nurses' corridor tomorrow morning. I also gave my successor in VD clinic a little unofficial instruction in how things were done in the clinic. In nursing you seem to be continually faced with something fresh which you have never done before and I find a few tips from someone who has done it very welcome. It can be quite an ordeal going on to a new ward, and you can feel as awkward as the day you came if you are put on to something fresh without warning. I shall never forget my first visit to the centre for blood donors. I had no idea I was going there so had no time to gather any information about what one did down there. I was just handed a sphygmomanometer by the Sister on the ward and set straight down. I did not even know how to put a 'sphyg' on, and it was one of the busy afternoons when we had a lot of blood donors and no one had time to show me properly. I muddled through somehow but it would have been much easier if I had known a bit about it beforehand.

Seeing that I was new on night duty on this ward the patients were full of helpful suggestions about what was usually done, telling me which light was left on during the night, which chair the night nurse took into the ward kitchen for the night, and so on.

Wednesday, 4 August

I cannot say that I care very much for night duty. You seem so shut off from everything and everybody and just live in a little world of you own. Being on this small ward alone [of around seven to nine patients] makes one seem even more isolated, I find, with most of the patients sleeping soundly, and those who cannot sleep are not in the mood for any conversation. I went out this morning for a short walk but was almost sleeping on my feet most of the time. I envy those people who come off night duty wide awake and ready to go out and enjoy themselves or those who can get up in the early afternoon after two or three hours' sleep and feel no ill-effects. For myself I have fallen asleep between spoonfuls of pudding, standing up in church at the Morning Service, and over coffee in a café. Yet if I want to get up early in the afternoon and go to bed as soon as I come off duty in the morning, I seldom get any sleep that day. The mere fact that I am getting up early – and if I am going to have any sleep at all it must be in the morning – seems to keep me awake.

Thursday, 5 August

Last night there was a meeting of the NCM (Nurses Christian Movement) and a Miss Russell, who I think is the organising secretary, paid us a visit. The night nurses who are members, only five of us in all, had a talk with her before she left this morning and discussed why our branch was not as enthusiastic as it might be. It was rather awkward because the nurse who is the leader of the branch and has done all the business concerning it could not be there, and we felt as though we were criticising her behind her back. One of the troubles is, I think, that it has been too much of a one-nurse show – this one nurse doing everything and the rest of us rather reluctantly attending the meetings when they were called. The NCM is non-denominational but no one ever expects the Roman Catholics, which comprise about 65% of the staff, to attend and it has certainly not been run on the lines to encourage them. The leader has been running it on Evangelical lines and anyone who has voiced an opinion contrary to her ideas, which I find appallingly narrow, has just been ignored. For instance, I was taught – and I attended a Church of England school up to the age of 12 – not to take much of the Old Testament literally, that it was a collection of more or less folk-lore intended to teach us some great truth. The story of the Creation, which if one takes the Bible word for word tells us that the world was made in a certain number of days, was written to teach us that God made the world and that instead of days one should substitute aeons. Any ideas such as these she regards as rank heresy and I doubt if she has ever heard of such a controversy as the one over the Virgin Birth.

Nurses who are not RCs but who have High Church leanings seldom come twice to the meetings. To give just one reason, someone wanted 'Lead kindly light' to be sung at one of the meetings but this was squashed because it was written by Cardinal Newman just before his conversion to the Roman Catholic faith. I was not present at this meeting, I am sorry to say, or I should have had something to say about that. As a matter of fact, I have not been to the meetings lately because at the last one I attended I had a great argument over the opening of Sunday cinemas. There was at the time a big drive by the Sunday Observance Society to close all places of entertainment on Sunday, and Matron had been sent some post cards in support of this for the nurses to sign and send to the Home Secretary and the local MP. This was brought up at the meeting and I would not sign one, as I hold the theory that it would not prevent people from going to church if cinemas were open on Sundays as those who went to the cinema would in all probability not go to church in any case. It would give young girls and boys somewhere to go instead of promenading up and down the streets on Sunday trying to 'click,' as they say, and generally getting into mischief, and on the long dark evenings it would be better for boys in the Forces than spending their Sunday evenings in the pub as they do so often when they are away from home and have nowhere in particular to go. I pointed out a few of these things but instead of getting a reasonable reply was asked what I would say on Judgement Day when I was asked why I encouraged people to commit the awful sin (?) of going to a cinema on Sunday. I replied that as I did not believe in a specific Judgement Day when we were brought to book for our sins I was not unduly dismayed at the prospect. Needless to say this did not improve matters and as I felt by this time I was being regarded as an out and out atheist I did not bother to attend another meeting. The leader I might say has never been in a cinema in her life. It seems unbelievable in this year of Grace 1943.

Friday, 6 August

Things seem to be going a bit quicker now, with the capture of Catania in Sicily and Orel in Russia. I still say, though, that it will be at least a couple of years before peace is signed, and that is an optimistic estimate. We have still to meet the full force of the German Army and they will have the big advantage of short lines of communication. It seems to me that starting from Sicily is rather a round-about way of reaching Berlin from here and reach Berlin we must before the war is over.

To come back to things a bit nearer home, I had a lecture from 12 to 1 so consequently was rather late going back to bed. I might just as well have been in bed for all I learnt from the lecture. All my energy was directed to keeping my eyes open and in spite of all my efforts am sure I must have dozed as the lecture seemed to be over in a suspiciously short space of time. The lecture was on diseases of the heart but as the lecturer did not get any further than variations of the heart beat I don't think I missed much of importance.

When I came on duty this evening it was to find that two of my patients had gone home. One of them was a girl in the Land Army with a fractured femur who had been in some time. She originally worked in an office in Liverpool but says she never wants to go back to office work again. The other patient was an elderly man who had fractured his pelvis but who also had a TB chest and as his fracture was better he was transferred to a local sanatorium. There is a very chatty little boy of 8 on the ward who was in a state of great excitement tonight because he had received a parcel from the American Junior Red Cross containing some sweets, a small trumpet with which he intends to wake the ward in the morning, a pencil with the sender's name on it, Marjorie Rochlla, and also a letter from the little girl. He says he is going to write to her and tell her he will go to see her when the war is over.

Saturday, 7 August

The night nurses had been asked to sell Alexandra Roses today [in aid of Blackburn Infirmary Week] so accordingly most of us turned up at the depot in uniform. A great many people had already bought their roses earlier in the week but we did a fairly brisk trade in spite of the weather which was very damp and inclined to rain. We are not provided with outdoor uniform and except for about half a dozen medieval-looking cloaks of navy blue with a hood and lined with navy blue, which one is allowed to use on very special occasions, we have nothing to wear over our indoor uniforms on occasions like this. The result was this morning that we all had our mufti [civilian] raincoats or top coats on, with uniform dresses and aprons hanging below, as most of our uniforms are much longer than our off-duty clothes. No one looking at us would have been attracted to the profession for the smartness of the uniform – in fact rather the reverse.* I know that the attractiveness or otherwise of the uniform should not have much influence over anyone thinking of joining the nursing profession as needless to say there is a great deal more in nursing than just looking glamourous. But the consciousness of well-fitting uniform which you feel you look pretty decent in gives you a feeling of well-being and confidence which is bound to react favourably on the patient, whereas badly fitting uniform which you look a fright in, and may be uncomfortable, such as tight neck bands, stiff collars that chafe your neck and so on, makes you irritable before you even start coping with the difficulties of the day.

Tuesday, 10 August

When I had had my meal this morning and gone on to the ward at 8.45 to give the report to the Day Sister, I got changed and went into the Town with two or three other nurses to change library books etc. I took out *Journey for Margaret*, which I have a vague notion has been filmed. It seemed strange to read of those awful days during the Battle

* By contrast, the Infirmary nurses who collected money at a cricket match on the Bank Holiday Monday (2 August) were reported to have appeared 'in their attractive uniforms [and] did a brisk business as collectors' (*Blackburn Times*, 6 August 1943, p. 5). See also 20 June 1944.

for Britain [July-October 1940].* They seem so near and yet
so far away when the thought of an invasion of this country
seemed as though a few days might turn it into a grim reality.
I have been very lucky so far where bombing is concerned.
If there has been any in the locality where I have been living
it has invariably taken place when I was away for a night or
two. Even when the village next to my home was bombed
[Chatburn, 30 October 1940] I came home the following day
and was not there when it happened. This village has a small
cotton mill where most of the inhabitants work and I suppose the solitary Jerry thought he might as well have a shot
at it. He missed the mill but got a row of cottages. It happened in the early afternoon and as luck would have it there
were few people at home at the time. The men were at work
and children at school and most of the women do part-time
work at the mill in the afternoon so that there were only two
killed, a retired postmistress and a petrol lorry driver from
Yorkshire. He had the misfortune to be driving down the hill
at the time and the lorry overturned and caught fire. There
were numerous injuries from flying glass etc. but none were

---

* This 1941 book by American journalist William Lindsay White reported on a visit
to England, mainly London, in 1940. The 1942 film directed by W.S. Van Dyke, a
loose adaptation of the book, starred Robert Young and Laraine Day and featured
5-year-old actress Margaret O'Brien as Margaret, the child in the title. While the
book highlights war reportage, notably the Blitz, as well as the author's mission
to adopt an orphaned child, the film, understandably, is more concerned with the
personal story and associated emotions. *Journey for Margaret* was an unexpected hit
on screen.

Other wartime books also appealed to Kathleen. The following spring she finished reading *Anger in the Sky* (1943) by Susan Ertz, 'a tale of the London blitz. It
is a tale not of any particular person but of a number of people in London for one
night, all coming from the comparative safety of a country house and each of them
spending it apart from the others. It was a good book because it made you think'
(2 April 1944). Kathleen's taste in books, as the diary shows, was remarkably eclectic.

fatal except these two. The people who had lost their homes were soon accommodated in neighbours' houses and various local relief funds started to help them replace their furniture and so on. Needless to say it brought crowds of sightseers from miles round and the local people found it difficult to get on the buses so packed were they with curious people. That happened nearly three years ago but there is still the row of ruined houses to remind one of it.

Wednesday, 11 August

You seem very cut off from life and the world in general when you are on night duty, and even the Infirmary, which during the day seems such a big place, appears to contract. You come on to the semi-darkened wards at 8.30 and your main object is to see that all the patients get some sleep and once the Night Sister and Doctor have done their rounds you seem to be isolated for the rest of the night, especially on a small ward like this [for fractures] where you are on your own. When you come off duty in the morning, even if you go out you never feel sufficiently awake to take much interest in things.

Kathleen regretted her proneness to fatigue and inability to get by without a lot of sleep. 'I wish I was one of those lucky people', she wrote later this month (28 August), 'who could wake up fresh and bright after an hour or two's sleep, but unless I get about seven hours' sleep I never feel right. Some of the nurses are often out at dances until the early hours of the morning with or without permission and they don't seem to bother about their lack of sleep, whereas one late night for me is enough.'

Thursday, 12 August

I admitted a little boy of 8 tonight who had fallen off an
8-foot wall and fractured his leg. Considering that his mother
wept noisily the whole time she was in the ward, the little
boy has been surprisingly good and settled down to sleep
without a murmur. With two new patients admitted during
the day, my ward is almost full again and I look like having a lively night. The first two or three nights are always
bad ones for fractured patients with their limbs strung up in
unnatural positions, which however good it may be for them
in the long run are very uncomfortable at first. The simple
fractures never find their way to Fracture Ward; they have
their plaster-of-Paris put on in the Fracture Clinic and go
home by ambulance. The ones we get on the ward are com-
pound fractures or those needing manipulation where the
bones have to be pulled into position before the plaster is
applied. Once they get their plaster on they are soon on their
way home with instructions to attend the Fracture Clinic on
a certain day.

*Several weeks later, on 25 September, she wrote that 'it has been a
perfect nightmare groping about Blackburn in the blackout, especially if you are not very familiar with the streets. The fractures we
get in during the winter through people just slipping off the kerb are
enough to justify some form of lighting.' On 22 April 1944 she came
out of a cinema in daylight and was glad not 'to stumble round
Blackburn's cobbled streets in the dark'. (See also 26 November
1943.) The hazards of the blackout could be experienced by anyone
almost anywhere. One who recorded such an incident was Lancashire writer Jessica Lofthouse, then in her mid-thirties. On a winter
night in 1942 she was walking to Pendleton 'and as I left Standen*

my torch flickered and went out . . . I entered the long, black tunnel,
which is a lane hedged-in by high thorns and hollies, stumbling over
fallen branches, thorns tugging at me when I lurched into the hedge.
Two things told me when I had reached the village: first a shower of
gold sparks blown across the sky as a cottager fed her fire with dry
sticks; secondly, the voice of the brook. I never appreciated the iron
railing till that night. *

Monday, 16 August

It was pouring with rain this morning so there was little
inducement to stay up and I was soon in bed. I am very fond
of reading in bed and seldom miss [it] before I go to sleep.
I had finished *Frenchman's Creek* by Daphne du Maurier and
was rather at a loose end so started to read Jane Austen's
Pride and Prejudice again. At one time I read quite a lot of her
books. They have always had a certain quaint charm, and
especially today with their great contrast to the grim realities
of life in 1943. I was soon lulled into sleep and awoke at
5.30 to hear the raucous strains of the maids' gramophone,
'Dreaming of a White Christmas'. I wished I was doing the
same – dreaming. But as I find that if I wake about this time
I can seldom go to sleep again, I got up and went for a walk,
getting back in time to change and have breakfast before the
lecture at 7.30 p.m. It was rather a nuisance waking as early,
as I have a lecture at 12 tomorrow – or rather today I should
say – as it is past midnight, which means that I shall be late
in bed again.

* Lofthouse, *Three Rivers* (1946), p. 56.

Tuesday, 17 August

I see in the evening paper that Sicily is completely in our
hands. Another step towards the end of the war. I wonder if Italy will be the next. I don't see how she can surrender with so many Germans in the country even if she
wanted to. In fact, even when Mussolini resigned I could
not see Hitler allowing the Italians the choice of surren-
dering or carrying on. If we invade Italy I can see us having to fight every inch of the way. I do hope we shall not
allow ourselves to be influenced in our bombing policy by
the Italians declaring Rome an 'open city'. It seems to me
a crazy idea altogether, this 'open city' business, in any
country. How can a place let alone the capital of a country
be cleared of all military objectives? The very fact of its
having a big railway centre used for the passage of troops,
ammunition etc. makes that an impossibility. In any case
if they wanted Rome to be treated as an open city they
have had plenty of time to declare it before the end of the
fourth year of the war. I suppose the whole fact is that they
never expected us to bomb Rome. Probably thought we
should still be regarding it through the mists of Munich
[1938 appeasement].

Wednesday, 18 August

When I came on duty tonight the usually calm Fracture Ward
was in a state of upheaval. There was an extra bed in the
middle of the floor, an operation bed ready for an arm ampu-
tation that was in the theatre, and a man with a fractured
spine on a trolley waiting to go down to the fracture clinic
for a plaster cast. I was not feeling too bright as I had been

out all the morning and had not slept very well either so I viewed the whole scene with great distaste and wished myself back on day duty.

Wednesday morning is market day in Blackburn and most of us enjoy a wander round the stalls to see if there are any bargains (?) to be had. There is one stall which is a great favourite with us all. They sell remnants of silk etc. for dresses and underwear in bundles, usually priced at 5s a bundle for one coupon. Each bundle consists of 2 yards of material in three pieces so I guess they are strictly within the law as not one of the three pieces is 1 yard long. Often there are a couple of bundles of the same material and last year I managed with a bit of contriving to make a dress out of two bundles of blue flowered crepe I got there. There was nothing on the stall we liked this morning so we moved on to some haberdashery stalls as I wanted some buttons for a jumper that I have been knitting for my niece. I had tried Woolworths for some buttons but the only ones I liked were 3d each and as I wanted eight decided against paying 2s for a few buttons. I did not have any better luck on the market [and] was offered miserable little white things at a penny each so decided to wait until I went home and have a look in my mother's button box, which contains buttons of every shape and size and rarely fails to produce something you can make do with.

Saturday, 21 August

One of the men on this ward with a fractured spine is very ill tonight and needs a great deal of attention. If he does not soon improve I am afraid he won't stand much chance of recovery. If he is no worse by morning I think he may pull round. It is surprising how detached one can be over the possibility of death. The first two or three you see upsets you very much but after a time you get used to the idea and rarely think about it when you are off duty. Of course personally they mean nothing to you and it is their friends and relations who you feel worst about. It is a terrible job having to break the news to them if a patient happens to die suddenly before they can be sent for, though sometimes I think it is not so wearing for the relations that way than if, as happens sometimes, they spend one or two weary days and nights beside the bed while the patient lies in a semi-conscious state and slowly passes away.

Monday, 23 August

My very ill patient was slightly better when I came off duty this morning so I hope the improvement will be maintained.* It was very stormy this morning with bright intervals and in one of the bright spells, which looked as though it might last a little while, I set out for a short walk. I was too optimistic and got caught in a terrific storm on some bleak ground at the back of the Infirmary up above Blackburn. It is a very bare expanse of ground with a few stunted trees dotted sparsely about it. But the air always feels very fresh up there after a night of being enclosed in stuffy blacked-out wards and you get a wonderful expanse of sky. You look

---

* During the night of 23/24 August 'The doctor on his last round ordered some sleeping tablets for my very ill patient which don't seem to have agreed with him. After falling into a very deep sleep he came round and did not know where he was. At least he thought he knew where he was, and that was in "The Swan" at Fleetwood playing Ludo. He keeps on trying to get out of bed every minute or two. I have to jump up and put him down again. He will be O.K. when the effect of the drug wears off but until then he is going to be a bit troublesome.'

down on Blackburn, enclosed in a dim blue haze, with its myriads of factory chimneys and there is a certain grim fascination about the scene. That line from 'Jerusalem' about 'England's dark satanic mills' always comes to my mind. It seems to fit the scene so aptly.

2

Free Time, Work Time

August–October 1943

Thursday, 26 August

After [breakfast] I got changed and with another nurse walked into the Town. It was a grand morning. The sun was shining brightly for once and we thoroughly enjoyed our walk. On our way down we pass an old mill used by the Army for billeting and other purposes. The soldiers were all walking around in gas masks looking hideous. I think Thursday must be their day for gas mask drill as last Thursday when we passed they were doing the same thing.* Talking of soldiers, we had a man brought in a day or two ago, a Home Guard instructor. He was demonstrating how to throw a hand grenade, I think it was, and it exploded while he was

---

* Three days later she saw more soldiers during a walk from home with her mother. 'We walked past an old searchlight camp and found a lot of soldiers there with Army lorries demolishing it. It was erected just too late to be of any use in the blitz on Manchester and Liverpool and to my knowledge has never been in action at all.'

holding it, blowing his hand off and making a terrible mess of his leg. They are trying to save his leg but it hangs in the balance whether to amputate or not. I think if I were a soldier I should feel far worse about anything like that happening to me in a demonstration than if it happened while I was under fire from the enemy.

I am reading a book [on] pre-war Germany. It is written by an American Quaker, Nora Waln, and is called, very inaptly, *Reaching for the Stars* [1939]. If Germany of the 1930s was reaching for the stars she must have strayed a long way from the original path. The authoress appears to have found the Germans she met socially during her stay in Germany with her husband, who was studying music, a very charming, cultured people. She appears to differentiate between the People and the Party. Yet surely the Party is composed of the people. Of the people as a whole she says the majority kept cautiously out of the Nazi way, but lived, cheered, sang and marched to their orders, and now could be added, killed, tortured, and many other things besides, also to their orders. I find it very difficult to believe that the majority of the Germans are these kindly, cultured people of whom Mrs Nora Waln writes. I don't see how you can draw a dividing line between the people and the Nazis.* Personally speaking, the Germans I have met over here, both in pre-war and

---

* In this account of her four years (1934–8) spent in Germany, Austria and Czechoslovakia, Nora Waln (b. 1885) presents a full and often nuanced portrait of the horrors of Nazism and the Party's atrocities. She also writes about the pressures on the population to conform to Nazi ideology and political practices. At the same time, she explores very favourably other aspects of Germany, including the beauty of its countryside, its folklore, and the glories of its music and culture, even describing in considerable detail one family's efficient running of its vineyard. As a practising Quaker, Waln seems to have encountered many dissenters against Nazism; Kathleen obviously thought that she overdid her admiration for 'good Germans'.

also the refugees, German Jews and so on, have struck me as being very arrogant. I don't mean the Germans who have settled down here but my generation, who in pre-war days used to come over here for a few months in various capacities to learn the language. I used to meet quite a number of them when I worked in London in pre-war days.

Kathleen began a three-week holiday on Saturday, 28 August – with heavy rain. She had no better luck with the weather the following day. Her time off work began at home in Downham, though she had plans to travel south. In the meantime, on the evening of Sunday the 29th her brother and his new wife, Yvonne, arrived from London for a visit.

Monday, 30 August

Pouring again when I opened my eyes this morning, rather late I must admit. I had intended going into Clitheroe to get my emergency ration card [to use while travelling], but seeing the weather I turned over again and thought I would try a bit later in the day. I was lucky because it cleared up and the sun actually came out in the afternoon, though it was still very windy. I soon got my business done and prowled around looking for sweets but was not successful. In Woolworths I came across an ex-patient who renewed her invitation for me to go to see her. I said I would go to see her when she first came out of hospital but she lives just out of Clitheroe and somehow I never seemed to find the time. She has a son who is in the Royal Corps of Signals, like my brother, but unlike Stan he has been overseas for two years now and seems to have had one or two adventures during that time. He escaped at the time of the fall of Singapore. When the Japs got hold of Java he and one or two others put out to sea in a small boat and were lucky enough to be picked up and taken to Ceylon. He is now in the comparative safety and quiet of Ceylon. What hair-raising tales will be told when they all come home again, if they can bear to tell them, that is.

Tuesday, 31 August

A fine day for a change though not particularly sunny. As for once all the family was assembled at teatime we had a great debate as to whether we should go into Blackburn and those members of the family who had not seen *Gone with the Wind* try to see it and the rest of us go to see something else, or whether we should go to Clitheroe and see the best of a very poor choice of films at the local cinemas. There was much argument for and against both proceedings until I suggested that as it was a fine evening we should go for a walk and call at The Calf's Head [in Worston] en route. This seemed to suit everyone so accordingly we started off across the fields, keeping a lookout for mushrooms but finding none I regret to say. Arriving at The Calf's Head we found the lounge was closed with a 'Private' notice on the door so we went into a room opposite, not so comfortable but provided with darts and dominoes and we were soon in the middle of quite a fierce competition. The Calf's Head is one of those unusually good little places you do sometimes come across in little country villages which attracts people from the towns nearby. In fact if you are out on a country ramble it is one of the places you drop in at.

On the way back it started to rain again which gave Father a good excuse for hurrying us along. He had been on tenterhooks in case we should not be back at 9 to hear Churchill's broadcast so positively welcomed the rain. We got in just before 9 but unfortunately as reception was bad we only heard someone reading Churchill's speech [his first for over a month – after the Anglo-American conference in Quebec]. Some time after the news there was some programme on in which an officer was discussing a sortie with his Sergeant. The officer had the usual cultured voice, the other a pronounced accent. My brother observed that according to the BBC it was impossible for anyone in the ranks to know how to speak the King's English correctly. He said he had never yet listened to a broadcast which did not portray the average soldier in the ranks as ever having anything but the rudiments of an elementary education. In fact he was so annoyed about it that he got up and switched off the wireless.

Wednesday, 1 September

Another wet day. Weather always plays such a big part in a holiday that so many pouring wet days are, to put it mildly, very disappointing. I had an appointment at the hairdresser's at 10 for a shampoo and set so set off early, leaving the others in bed. I don't as a rule indulge in the luxury of going to the hairdresser's as 3s 6d each time one wants one's hair washed is quite a big item out of £3 14s 8d per month but as I am on holiday I thought I would be lazy for once. The dampness of the atmosphere was not ideal for a newly waved head and by the time I got back my hair was not as immaculate as it might have been.

My father's employer [at Downham Hall] sent us some books along in the afternoon, which were very welcome – one on biographies and some novels. One on modern China which I am reading now. It presents China at war from the townsmen's angle in contrast to Pearl S. Buck who in *Dragon Seed* [1942] gave us the country people's point of view. I suppose each is representative of the type of Chinese he is writing about but I must say that *Dragon Seed* seemed to get down to the fundamentals of life more than the other. But I suppose this is true of country people the world over. Their lives and minds are not so cluttered up with superficialities as the townspeople. Their lives are not so artificial; they are not so introspective. To them the important things of life are the grim realities, though grim perhaps is the wrong word. Birth and death, marriage, a good harvest, enough to eat, a warm house etc.

Amongst these books was a pamphlet entitled *Why I am a Conservative* [by David Stelling, published at Conservative Headquarters, July 1943]. We were much amused, wondering if it had been put in purposely or strayed there accidentally. Like all big landowners my father's employers are Conservatives* but I am afraid the pamphlet fell

* The head of the family was Ralph Assheton (1860–1955), who employed George Johnstone at Downham Hall. His son of the same name and later Lord Clitheroe (1901–84) was Conservative MP for Rushcliffe (Nottinghamshire) 1935–45, Financial Secretary to the Treasury, and from 1944 to 1946 Chairman of the Conservative Party. During the war he lived mainly in London. We are grateful to Hannah Carson at the Bodleian Library for helping us to get a copy of this sixpence pamphlet, designed to bolster Conservative support in the face of anti-Conservative sentiment.

There is evidence that the Assheton family took an active interest in the welfare of the village. In August 1943 Ralph Assheton, MP, presided over the first of a series of meetings in Downham on post-war planning. 'In the discussion which ensued almost everyone present took part' (*Clitheroe Advertiser and Times*, 20 August 1943, p. 7). His wife, Sylvia, was in charge of managing the estate. The often brutally opinionated Conservative MP and diarist 'Chips' Channon had kind words for Assheton just after war broke out (7 September 1939): 'I walked all the way to the House with Ralph Assheton, whose appointment as Parliamentary Secretary to the Ministry of Labour was announced this morning. What a warm-hearted charmer, and so good and honest. He will do well, and I have long urged his claims to office.' (Simon Heffer, ed., *Henry 'Chips' Channon: The Diaries: 1938–43* [London: Hutchinson, 2021], p. 203.)

on stony ground. My brother is an out and out Red like the majority of young servicemen I have met who think of these kinds of things at all. There are of course a proportion of them who don't bother very much as long as they are jogging along O.K. themselves but of those who are interested in the various problems of the world as it is at present and as they hope it will be in the future, and who think and discuss it, I have not yet met one who claimed to be a Conservative or Liberal, yet neither did they seem to think much of the Labour Party either. Most of them had a sympathetic attitude towards Russia and also a great admiration for her. Lots of them were for more State control, but none of our political parties seemed to be viewed with any great enthusiasm.

Thursday, 2 September

During the afternoon I took some bottles for fruit preserving to a farmer's wife. My mother had promised to lend these bottles a week or two previously but had forgotten about it. These bottles are very difficult if not impossible to buy now so the farmer's wife was very grateful for them. After stumbling around the farm and knocking on one or two doors and getting no response I eventually found the back door and the family all in the kitchen except the farmer and his son. There was the farmer's wife, his son's wife, his crippled daughter, an old lady vaguely referred to as auntie and last but not least the small grand-daughter. Of course I had to go in and was given a glass of home-made wine, not made in recent years I might say, and also a bottle of apple-wine to take home with me. We all sampled it during the evening and it tasted like very strong concentrated cider.

Friday, 3 September

The third of September and the fourth anniversary of the war and with it came the news of Allied landings on the toe of Italy. It seemed to me a typical Churchill touch to have these 2 dates coincide.

There was a parade this evening of the Downham Civil Defence workers and considering the size of the village they put up quite a good little show. They were led by the Girl Guides with their flags. Then came the Home Guard, fourteen in all, followed by four Civil Defence in navy blue. Then came the WVS and last but not least the Downham Red Cross contingent. I guess a good many people would have laughed at our little procession but when you think of the number of the population I guess the percentage of Civil Defence personnel is as high as any. They marched into church where the Girl Guides presented their flags at the altar and then we had the special service for the day.

When we got home and had eaten our supper we started to cut sandwiches for our train journey tomorrow. My brother and his wife were going to spend the last weekend of his leave at her home in Sevenoaks [Kent] and I was going to stay with friends in London so we decided to go as far as Euston together. We had plenty of tomatoes so we cut mostly tomato sandwiches as being the least thirst-making of anything we had. Then we went to bed early as we had to catch the 8.30 bus in the morning and we had been sitting up into the early hours of most mornings talking.

Saturday, 4 September

After an early start we arrived at Blackburn for the Preston train to find the platform packed with people. We stood at the end of the platform and managed to cram into one of the front carriages, but it was a squash. Arriving at Preston we had a few minutes to wait for the London train so went for a cup of tea – which we were given sweetened quite unnecessarily as none of us take sugar – in the refreshment room. The London train was a few minutes late and when it did come in there was the usual scramble for it. We managed to get a seat between the three of us so took it in turns to have a few minutes rest. We ate our sandwiches standing on the corridor as we decided to split up at Crewe and see if we could find seats. We were lucky enough to get a seat each then, though in separate carriages. At Blisworth [Northamptonshire], I think it was, a crowd got in. At the same time two people got out of our carriage. There had been a man and woman standing in the corridor from Crewe and they made a dive for the seats but a girl with a baby, who had got in at this station, in the confusion sat down in one of them. They had no hesitation in turfing her out, the woman saying that poor 'Larry', her husband presumably, felt faint after standing in the corridor for so long. Larry looked a little embarrassed but took the seat nevertheless, which left the poor woman with the baby standing, so I could do no less than give her my seat. The train by this time was crowded and I just managed to find enough square inches to stand on the corridor. It was a gorgeous day and when we arrived in London everyone was wearing summer frocks.

Sunday, 5 September

I woke with a sick headache which though I tried to stick it out got the better of me and I had to go to bed after lunch. My friends had planned that we should go to Richmond but it was very stormy and the trip had been called off before I had succumbed and retired for the day so my falling out did not spoil their Sunday. I always suffered from travel sickness when I was a child so I guess this sick headache was the aftermath of the journey. They usually clear up around about 6 in the evening but this one was very persistent and when the bombers [en route to Germany] went over at dark, the throb of their engines seemed to echo my throbbing headache.

Monday, 6 September

Fortunately I was O.K. this morning though I did not feel very energetic so spent a lazy morning doing nothing but in the afternoon as the sun was trying to shine I thought I would sit in the park and write a letter. I am staying in Chelsea, which is not very near to any park, so I took a bus to Hyde Park Corner and set off across the park from there, stopping on the way to admire the flower beds. I thought I would like to sit on the slope that looks over the Serpentine and found a chair and had just settled down to write a letter when I heard a voice say 'Do you mind if I sit here?' I looked up with the intention of saying something freezing but changed my mind when I saw it was quite a decent-looking Yank, and I thought of the 'Good neighbour policy'! He said he had been staying with relatives in Scotland and had travelled back during the night in order to have a look round London for the day before going back to his company. He said he found it very dull walking around on his own – had I any suggestions. Well, knowing London fairly well in prewar days I was not devoid of ideas and I soon found myself having tea at the open-air tea place in Hyde Park. I phoned my friends to say I might be late getting in and then we went to see *Heaven Can Wait* [1943 American comedy] at the Marble Arch Pavilion. When we came out most people seemed to be standing around looking up into the sky and above the noise of the traffic could be heard the sound of our bombers going over to Germany. We were told that they had been going over for at least an hour but though we also stood and looked skywards all I could see was an occasional navigation light. We then went up West and had a spot of something to eat and drink and then we bundled into a taxi to collect his kit from the Washington Club and arrived at the station just in time for him to catch the last train down and as I said good-bye I thought I had done my bit towards furthering Anglo-American friendship! Joking apart, it was a perfect evening and I hope he enjoyed himself as much as I did.

During her next few days in London, Kathleen shopped (with little success) and socialized and did a lot of walking – and recorded some observations. 'It brightened up considerably in the afternoon [7 September] and so we took the dog for a walk in Battersea Park. I often wonder what Londoners would do for exercise if there was no dog to take for a walk.' Public intimacies also drew her notice. 'One habit I notice which has increased in the London parks is the public petting parties for two which used to be the exception rather than the rule. I wonder whether the Americans are responsible for this. I remember my mother coming home from a holiday at Salisbury a couple of years ago full of disgust at this habit of theirs in the Cathedral Close.' (Since the United States was not in the war two years earlier, this recollection is partly inaccurate.) On Thursday the 9th she met her RAF cousin and they had such a fine lunch for 2s 6d each at a restaurant called The Salad Bowl that she described it in loving detail. Then, on the afternoon of the 10th, accompanied by an aunt, she visited her father's brother and his wife in Chiswick, where they arrived in time for tea 'to find my cousin, who is still in school, full of complaints because she had hurried home from school and we were not there. My father's brother and his wife are both deaf and dumb. Consequently I never go to see them without this aunt, who can talk to them on her fingers, though they do lip read as well. In pre-war days my uncle earned his living as a cabinet-maker but now he is in an aircraft factory and seems to be doing very well. They have this girl and a boy who is in the RAF but they can speak and hear perfectly and are both very intelligent. I think they feel very self-conscious about taking their friends home, especially the boy.'

Over the weekend Kathleen did more sightseeing. On the 11th '[I] thought I would have a look at the terrace where I used to live in London, which is not far from Paddington Station. Walking down I saw that half of a notorious terrace of private hotels had been badly damaged and I think few people would regret their going. I found the terrace where I used to live quite intact but I hardly think there was one house occupied. I went round to see a French woman I used to know who gave French lessons in pre-war days. To my delight I found that she was still in her flat and was actually in when I called. She, poor thing, has lost all touch with her relations in France, though she still hopes that when the war is over she will hear from them again. That is why she stuck to her flat – so that when the war is over they will be able to write to the address they knew of old.' On the afternoon of Sunday the 12th, Kathleen went with a friend to see the Army Exhibition in the basement of what had been John Lewis's on Oxford Street. It was very crowded; people were being 'crushed and children started crying and one or two women got hysterical . . . It seemed that some of the children wedged down amongst the crowd would be suffocated.' Eventually officials intervened, calm was restored, and Kathleen finished the tour in

*'the section belonging to the RAMC [Royal Army Medical Corps].
I found many things of interest but one of the exhibits struck me as
being very funny. It was a small lorry filled with such things as
hammers, axes, picks, saws etc. and on it was placed a notice saying
"Equipment carried by the forward Casualty Clearing Station".'*

On Monday the 13th she *'said goodbye to my London friends'*
and she went to Paddington to get a train to Wiltshire for a visit
with her younger married sister, Phyllis (b. 1916). *After two station
changes she arrived in Warminster. She tried to get a taxi 'as I knew
there was no hope of my brother-in-law [Reginald King, a certified
accountant and chartered actuary] meeting me with the car as he
used to do in earlier times, but I was unlucky and had to climb up
as my sister lives about a mile from the station and is not on a bus
route. There are two hills to climb and the sun was shining brightly
and I plodded on, my two small cases getting heavier and heavier
and I arrived in no very pleasant frame of mind and to crown all,
my small nephew of 14 months [Peter] gave one look at me and
burst into tears. A cup of tea and some lunch soon restored me to
a better frame of mind and I spent the rest of the afternoon in the
garden watching my niece [Elizabeth] of 4½ making sand castles
from burst sand-bags piled against the dining room window.'*

Thursday, 16 September

My sister seized the opportunity this morning as I was there
to go into Warminster to do some shopping without the children. She says she does not think the birth rate will ever go
up until there are more day nurseries for children or more
help available for looking after them in their own homes.
For almost five years now her only relaxation has been a very
occasional visit to the pictures and one summer before Peter
arrived a game of tennis at the club after her husband got

back from business. They can never go anywhere together as one of them always has to stay behind for the children. When my mother and father were down here earlier in the year she went to her first dance for five years. Of course when a young married couple live nearer their relatives they are not quite so tied if there is a Grannie or Aunt who will have the children for a little while. Before Peter appeared on the scene my sister was offered a post in her old capacity as school teacher [she had graduated from teachers' college] but she could not find anyone, old or young, to look after the little girl so she had to refuse it as there are no day nurseries around here.

I packed up a big parcel of my things this afternoon so that I should not have so much to carry on my journey home tomorrow [where she arrived at 7.30 p.m. 'ravenously hungry'].

Sunday, 19 September

Sunday, and I was awakened by the sound of the church bells pealing for the early morning Communion Service but I regret to say I turned a deaf ear, and rolled over and went to sleep again. When I did eventually get up I turned out a trunk and suitcase to find a Viyella blouse I had promised to give to my cousin in London. I could not find it and remembered afterwards that I had it at the Infirmary. But at least I managed to get my things sorted out a little and tore up lots of old letters and receipts for salvage and had a look at some of my old clothes and planned a few renovations. I found amongst other things half a bottle of Eau-de-Cologne, and a jar of cold cream, to say nothing of sundry belts for which one has to pay such a big price these days.

In the evening we went to church. It is a little grey stone church which looks as though it just grew of its own accord. It has few stained-glass windows. Most of the windows are of ordinary glass and I like to sit in church and watch Pendle Hill, which tonight was partially obscured by drifting clouds but some evenings is lovely in reflected colour from the sunset. There were few people in church but when we came out there was a long queue for the Clitheroe bus. The people of Clitheroe are having a long weekend. Everything is closed from Friday night to Monday night so that, I was told, the machinery in the mills can be cleaned, but as all the shop people take advantage of it too it seems to me it may be just an excuse. As I went to bed I reflected sadly that this would be my last night in bed for some time to come and it behoves me to make the best of it.

Monday, 20 September

The awful day has dawned and I am now back at work. I got up late this morning as I wanted to try to get a bit of extra sleep but no such luck. As the time crept steadily on towards 5.30 my spirits got lower and lower until they touched rock-bottom and I was actually glad to get started on my way back. When I reached the Infirmary everyone I met asked me how I enjoyed my holiday, which only made me feel all the worse. I went into my room on the night nurses' corridor and soon one or two night nurses trickled in with the latest news and informed me they did not think I was going back on to fracture ward but was going to do the senior nurse's night off. I hoped they were wrong but found on going to report back to Matron that the rumour was correct. The snag for me is that when relieving the night staff nurse there is often theatre work to do and through some oversight I have not even done my junior theatre work yet so I shall be hopelessly lost.

I cheered up considerably though when I went into the dining room and there was a letter from Bill, my POW. I had not heard from him for over three months and had been imagining all sorts of things that might have happened to him and he started off by saying 'here was another [letter] of the many' – another of the few I thought would have been more correct. He said another camp was supposed to be sending over a football team but did not think they would turn up as it was pouring with rain. It sounded so calm and matter-of-fact and I had been working myself up into a frenzy of anxiety at times over him. Imagining all kinds of dreadful things.

When I got on duty I found I was extra for tonight which means you get all the odd jobs such as casualty and seeing to the sick nurses.

Tuesday, 21 September

I passed the early hours of this morning sitting beside a man with very bad burns. He had been in one of these factory accidents and some molten metal had been blown over him in one of these explosions that sometimes occurs.

I was very sleepy when I came off duty and soon had a bath and went to bed but only slept until about 5 when I was awakened by the inevitable gramophone. There was an air of excitement about the hospital today as forty-four of our nurses are sitting their preliminary examination this month. Poor things. I sympathised with them but to me even worse than sitting the exam is waiting for the results.

When I came on duty tonight I had to go on to one of the wards in the new wing. It has two sides, a male and female ward each, containing about twenty beds and two semi-private wards holding two beds. The wards are full but fortunately no one is actually on the danger list at present, though we have several cases of cancer which are inoperable. It is the first time I have had charge of such a big ward and [it] is rather a formidable undertaking, especially because I never feel my brightest at night. Fortunately the two junior nurses are very capable and don't need much supervision. On these big wards at night there is just a junior nurse for each side and a senior nurse supervising both sides.

While this turned out to be a quiet night, she said that 'writing the report on these forty-odd patients was quite a job as I had not got all their names and complaints very firmly fixed in my mind'. The following night would prove to be more trying. 'There are two people dangerously ill with their relatives sitting with them and at the time I am writing this we have an emergency case in the theatre so I don't suppose there will be much more opportunity for writing during the night' (22 September). The following morning, 'Just as we were going off duty my nose bled copiously as it invariably does at times of stress' (23 September). The next night around 2 a.m. the phone rang and 'I had to go down to casualty. A man on night work had caught his finger in a machine and it was in quite a bad state. I sent the porter to call the house surgeon who was "on call" for casualty and he soon appeared in his dressing-gown and amputated the finger down to the second joint. The patient was remarkably quiet about it. Of course he had a local anaesthetic but even so it could not have been pleasant to watch part of your finger being removed' (24 September).

Monday, 27 September

This morning we had a lecture at 11.45 so my friend and I went out for a short walk beforehand. I went to the chemist to see if I could get a pulsometer but had no luck. My watch with the second hand has given up the ghost long ago and I have been managing without one as they are such a terrible price but I think I shall have to accept my mother's offer to pay half towards a new one for me. Moving about from ward to ward and taking sick nurses' temperatures and so on it is almost impossible to do without one. You can if you are lucky still get pulsometers at about 3*s* 6*d* but I don't like them very much. They do not seem to me to be as accurate as a watch.

We then went to the Post Office where my friend bought a 6*d* Air Mail letter to send to her brother who is at one of the Empire flying training schools in Canada and I bought a 3*d* Air Mail letter card to send to my POW.

When we got back from our walk we made ourselves some tea to keep us awake during the lecture. It was given by the pathologist on diseases of the blood and was really very interesting. Some of the lecturers are so dull that it is difficult to keep awake at the best of times and when you are on night duty it is almost impossible.

Tuesday, 28 September

It is my night off tonight so when I came off duty I threw some things together into a little case and after our meal went straight to bed so that I could get in some sleep before the lecture at 12. I was disturbed by a nurse bringing me in a couple of letters, one of them from the Food Office. I opened it and found inside my old clothing coupon book with three coupons still intact and a note from the Food Office to say it had been found in Blackburn. I had used it last Saturday morning and suppose I must have lost it then but it is not often you get anything returned to you before you know you have lost it. It must have been a very honest person who found it and I am duly grateful to whoever it was.

After the lecture I did not bother to go in for dinner as I already had eaten one and went straight off home. When I got to Clitheroe I found that I should have to wait 1½ hours for a bus to Downham but soon got one to Chatburn with one of the local land-girls. She does not belong to the WLA [Women's Land Army] but has been employed on the Downham Home Farm ever since the war started and is now waiting for a vacancy in an agricultural college as she wants to continue to work on the land when the war is over. On the way up we met the Italian prisoners who are now working on the farm. They seemed quite pleased with life and shouted 'Hello'. The land girl told me that five of them as far as she can gather are pleased that Italians and English are now 'friends', as they call it, but she thinks the sixth is a strong Fascist.

Wednesday, 6 October

There was a great discussion in the sitting room this morning about the 'little nurse'. The *Daily Sketch* had published a [BBC] post-script given by a VAD [Voluntary Aid Detachment] on September 19 for the benefit of those who had not heard it, which seemed to comprise the whole night staff. The majority dismissed it as sentimental twaddle but I am afraid from the nursing profession itself it would not be regarded in a unbiased manner because it was given by a VAD. On the other hand I very much doubt whether a nurse (and by nurse I mean someone who has taken up nursing as a whole-time career) would ever have written it in the first place. I have never heard anyone admit to feeling sentimental about a patient though no doubt some of us do judging by the number of nurses who marry patients. But to get sentimental over a patient's death is definitely not done.

But the feeling the trained nurse has for the VAD is I suppose the feeling the professional has for the amateur in every walk of life. I don't think we are hostile to those we meet personally but especially during a war the Red Cross nurse gets all the praise and publicity while touching only the fringe of nursing as we know it.[*]

Thursday, 7 October

It is the emergency week for the women's side of the ward I am on tonight and [I] was greeted by a ward chock full when I appeared on the scene. There was also an emergency case in a semi-private ward containing four beds known as the old board-room. He was coming round from his anaesthetic as we came on and was shouting 'Down to the beaches,' 'Blast the planes,' 'Quick march,' and so forth. We thought that

[*] The Voluntary Aid Detachment was made up mostly of women who had received little training as nurses; they functioned mainly as 'assistants'. This 'post-script', broadcast on Sunday, 19 September at 9.15, says little about the actual work of nurses and a lot about sentiments and feelings regarding male patients and doing one's duty. It is much more inspirational than empirical, with almost nothing reported about those realties that would have dominated the lives of hospital nurses. The talk probably reflected the way members of the public wished to think about nurses. (The typescript text is held in the BBC Written Archives Centre, Caversham Park, Reading. Archivist Samantha Blake kindly supplied us with a copy of it.)

he was perhaps one of those who came back from Dunkirk even though he was in civilian life now but our imagination carried us too far and we found he was in a reserved occupation and a Home Guard.

Friday, 8 October

My nights off for the fortnight and as luck would have it we were late coming off duty, which was only to be expected judging by the numbers of patients who are seriously ill on this ward. I managed with a bit of scrambling to catch the bus I intended to [get] and was home at 9.30 where I was greeted by the news that my cousin in the ATS [Auxiliary Territorial Service] was home on seven days' leave. I have not seen her for about ten years so it was like meeting a complete stranger. She was still in bed and I could hardly keep my eyes open. I had a meal and went to bed myself until the middle of the afternoon. She seems to like life in the ATS fairly well but does not like the place she is stationed in now very much. Her chief objection seemed to be the sleeping quarters, which is a large hut containing about thirty girls. Previously she said the biggest number she had to share a room with was four which she liked much better. She volunteered for the ATS and is now in her fourth year. She tells me that at the end of four years volunteers have the option of leaving the ATS which surprised me as I thought they were in for the duration.

Speaking of ATS reminds me of a nursing howler made by one of the members of our class when she had only been at the hospital a week or two. One of the honorary surgeons [i.e., unpaid or largely unpaid] appeared on the ward and asked this nurse whether there was any ATS (meaning anti-tetanus serum) on the ward. The nurse replied 'No sir but there are two WAAFs [Women's Auxiliary Air Force] on the Women's Surgical Ward.' The surgeon of course thought it was the best joke he had heard for a long time and the unfortunate nurse has never been able to live it down.

Saturday, 9 October

I woke surprisingly early considering I had very little sleep yesterday. Since I was wide awake and did not want to get up I found a book [a novel] called *The Sowers* by [Henry Seton] Merriman. It was written in 1896 but he was very prophetic about the Russian Revolution. He said that there would come in the future in Russia such an upheaval as would make the French Revolution pale into insignificance.

In the afternoon I went into Clitheroe with my mother and cousin. My mother had promised to pay half towards a watch with a second hand for my birthday [16 November] and I thought I would avail myself of her offer. There was not much choice at all. The only ladies' watch with a second hand was a little silver one costing £8 15s 0d and as I wanted one badly I decided to take it. My cousin and I had some tea in Clitheroe and stayed to the pictures but Mother went home. We saw a very pleasant little film of family life in 1913 America, called *The Last Virginian* [actually *The Vanishing Virginian*, 1942]. With no mention of war, no suspense, no great problems, it was a very soothing picture and we thoroughly enjoyed it. We came out a minute or two before the end to make sure of getting on the last bus home, the 8.18, but there was plenty of room.

Sunday 10 October

It was another lovely autumn day and we all went to the Harvest Festival this morning. The church was decorated with fruit and vegetables and a little corn, and some flowers. The lessons were read by the farmers, one old and the other young, both very nervous so that they rushed through the lessons at great speed. The preacher was a very venerable old man with a white beard who gave us a very mellow sermon on the harvest. After church my cousin and I went for a walk to get an appetite for dinner and in the afternoon the sun was so warm that we sat out in the garden. I tried to get a little sleep but without much success and it was soon time to have tea and get the 5.30 back again.

There was a long queue for the Blackburn bus when I arrived in Clitheroe and I did not manage to get on the first bus that came in so I was a bit later than usual getting back. I found when I got back that my friend had forgotten to send my store tins down on Saturday. She had forgotten her own too so unless we can persuade the Housekeeping Sister to let us have them tomorrow we shall be without marge, jam, butter and sugar for the rest of the week.

Monday, 11 October

When we came off duty this morning we took our store tins hopefully to the Housekeeping Sister who promised to put them ready for us tonight without any demur. Much to our surprise. It was a miserable morning and I was feeling terribly sleepy so I was soon in bed. I woke once or twice but only to see that it was still daylight and I could turn over and go to sleep again. It was a good thing that I had a good

sleep and was feeling fairly bright as there are eight operation cases on the ward I am on tonight. That always means a
busy night as they need a lot of attention the first night after
their operation.

Seven of the cases were in the women's ward; the eighth
was on the men's side. There was also a man very ill with
inoperable cancer whose son was staying with him during
the night. I was doing a round with the house surgeon on
the women's side when the junior nurse ran across from the
men's ward to say she thought this man was dead. I hurried
over to the other side to find she was right and his son was
sleeping peacefully in a chair at his bedside. It was a rude
awakening for the poor chap but it was a blessing for the
old man. So often these cases of inoperable cancer linger
on for weeks, having bigger and bigger doses of morphia to
relieve their pain, but there is no hope for them. The Night
Sister speaking from years of practical experience says she
thinks these cases of inoperable cancer are increasing and
that whereas it used to be only very old people who were
the most frequent victims it is found now in much younger
people.

Thursday, 14 October

I am relieving the night staff tonight and except for one or
two casualties I have had a very quiet night. The casualties
were not bad ones either – two or three were night workers
with particles of metal in their eyes, a girl on night duty at
one of the factories who had got a fish bone stuck in her
throat while having a meal in the canteen. I am sure it is very
bad in the long run for these men's eyes who are continually
coming up to have foreign bodies removed. At some of the

jobs such as the sheet-metal workers we have the men up very frequently. One would think that some form of goggles could be worn to protect their eyes against flying metal, though in all probability they would not make use of them even if they were provided. Like the girls with their protective caps who will have hair showing. I have seen one or two very nasty results of this when the hair has caught in machinery.

Monday, 18 October

I saw my friend off to Preston this morning with suitable promises regarding blacking out her room at night-time and arranging the inevitable pillow in the bed [her friend had not signed out for the coming night as she was supposed to] and then came back and washed my hair with Rinso [a laundry detergent] as I had no shampoo powder. It seemed to answer the purpose just as well and I don't suppose it really differs very much from shampoo powder except that it has scent, though in pre-war days I should have been horrified at the thought of using it and should have expected all my hair to drop out or change colour or something equally as tragic.

We have been having great discussions lately at the dinner table about believing implicitly in Adam and Eve and the world being created in seven days and so on. Of the eight at our dinner table three of us take the view that they are tales to teach us a great truth, three of us believe literally in Adam as the first man and Eve as his wife being made out of a rib and so on, and the other two don't seem to have thought about it at all. The three disbelievers, as they call us, are Church of England and of the other three, one is Church of England and the other two RCs [Roman

Catholics]. The other three seem to think that because we do not swallow the Old Testament whole we are denying the existence of God which is not our idea at all. One can be a good Christian without believing in a literal Garden of Eden. The arguments are very heated at times and it does not seem to matter what subject we discuss we always seem to work round to this particular one. I must say, though, that even so it is better than the inevitable 'shop' that is all some nurses seem to be able to discuss.

Tuesday, 19 October

I had quite a pleasant surprise when I came on duty this evening. I was going round to see if all the patients were comfortable when an old man said 'Would these be of any use to you, Nurse?' and he handed me a card of what appear to be pre-war hair grips. Needless to say I did not refuse and was most grateful for them. I heard a bit later that he had given one or two of the day nurses a card of them too, but where he got them from remains a mystery. They are much better than the card of four for which I paid 6*d* when I was in London which are really very little use at all as they have no grip in them.

Wednesday, 20 October

It was a real blustery autumn day, sun shining one minute and pouring with rain the next, but I was lucky and managed to evade the storms. The people with whom I was having tea have a lovely bungalow on the edge of the golf links. The lady of the house is a partial invalid and spends a lot of her time making string bags which she sells and sends the profit to the Red Cross. She only started them about three months ago and so popular have they become that she has orders amounting to forty-seven on hand at the moment. She said she had already made about 10 guineas [£10 10s] which she had divided between the Red Cross and the local Soldiers' Comforts Fund. Her son is in India at the moment after having had thrilling escapes from Singapore and Java.

I heard when I got home that a cousin of mine who was in Hong Kong when it was taken by the Japs and of whom nothing had been heard since has just been reported as having died of wounds in April. Maybe it is just as well for him. It makes one's blood go cold to think of the brutality of the Japs. Beside them the Germans appear to be fairly decent.

Thursday, 21 October

This evening [in Downham] was the monthly meeting of the Women's Institute of which my mother is a member. In the social half-hour after the demonstration, the grandmothers were entertaining – at least six of them were, the other twelve absented themselves. The demonstration this evening was on rug making but not the pre-war rug making on a patterned piece of canvas with beautifully coloured wool. We were shown how to make rugs out of sacks, out of old stockings, out of underwear and out of gleanings of sheep wool from the hedgerows. My mother has been making a rug out of stockings for some time but she does not seem to have had much spare time for that sort of thing and it is not making much progress. After the demonstration cups of tea were handed round for which we paid 2d and then the grandmothers started their entertainment which consisted of a charade. The first scene was very topical.

It consisted of a babies' clinic to which the grandmothers brought their grandchildren whom they were looking after while the babies' mothers went to work on munitions. The whole thing went down very well and the members all said the grandmothers had given the best social half-hour they had enjoyed for a long time.

Monday, 25 October

I got up too late tonight [24 October] to have any breakfast before going on duty but wished I had when I got on to the ward and saw a patient just about to go to the theatre to have a Caesarian done. By the time we had got everything ready a nurse had brought the baby back from the theatre, a lovely little girl. Mother was back before the baby was bathed and dressed and mother had to have a blood transfusion. I got the things ready and then the blood would not drip properly and just everything went wrong that could go wrong. The blood giving apparatus got blocked with a clot of blood and the Night Sister was bespattered with blood. We moved the clot and then we got an air lock but eventually it got going and long after midnight we managed to sit down for a meal.

Tuesday, 26 October

I was out bright and early this morning with another nurse and we were in Town for 9.30. I got a black dye from Woolworths to dye some more stockings I found at home last week. I also tried to get a shampoo but my luck was out and it seems as if I shall have to fall back on Rinso again. I bought a quarter [pound] of sweets for myself and my friend but Blackburn has very little choice and we were obliged to have ordinary boiled sweets. We passed quite a bit of time browsing round the book stalls at Boots and buying nothing I might say. After that we went round the Market Hall as my colleague wanted some tomatoes. She did not find any there but went into a greengrocer's for them and got some onions as well. Her utility bag was a fine jumble by the time she had finished, what with onions and tomatoes rolling around a couple of library books, and two tablets of soap belonging to me. We are given two loose coupons each month for soap and I find that if I get two tablets of soap one month and a tablet of soap and packet of soap flakes for stockings etc. the next month I can manage very well. Of course one does not have to be too lavish with the soap in the daily bath but on the whole I find it enough.

Wednesday, 27 October

I see the papers are full of the exchange of wounded prisoners-of-war. It must be a wonderful feeling for them to be back home even though some of the poor blighters are minus an arm or a leg.* For a fleeting moment I almost wished my boy friend had been wounded so that he would have been on his way home. I see that some of the division he was in, the 51st Highland Division taken at St. Valery in 1940, are home again. In common with the majority of people I shall never forget that summer, with the glorious weather and the terrible feeling of tension as the BEF [British Expeditionary Force] got back from Dunkirk. Then people started getting letters or postcards or even the boys and men themselves

* Some 790 of these wounded men arrived in Liverpool the previous day; around 100 were 'stretcher cases' (*The Times*, 27 October 1943, p. 2).

arrived home, but there was no news from my boy friend and I began to feel very despondent. Then when the news came through about the small British Force still left in France, hope revived again. I was on holiday in the early days of June, staying in the South near Weymouth, when we were frantically trying to equip another expeditionary Force to send to France and the days and nights were full of the heavy rumbles of Army lorries as equipment was rushed through to the embarkation port. Then came the collapse of France and the news that the greater part of the 51st Division were either killed or taken prisoner-of-war. My friend was reported missing and I had given up all hope when in November I got a letter from him. For me the great tragedy of the collapse of France was completely overshadowed by my own personal feeling of loss and looking back on that summer of 1940 makes the present time seem calm and peaceful in comparison.

3

A Winter's Tales

October 1943–February 1944

Thursday, 28 October

When we went into the dining room for breakfast this evening there was a large notice on the notice-board and we found it was more demands for clothing coupons. We were pleased to see that only six are required of us this year instead of the nine we have been obliged to give up previously. I shall give all mine in at the same time so that I shall not be bothered for the rest of the coupon year. Some of the nurses have already spent the first page of their clothing coupons so don't quite know what they will do.

Friday, 29 October

I was sitting in the sitting room this morning, supposedly waiting for the letters but in reality too lazy to move, when the Night Sister came in with the letters and there were two postcards from my POW posted on the 12th of last month; they have got here fairly quickly. If ever he gets a letter from me he wants to answer quickly, he sends a postcard and these postcards were in reply to a letter I wrote to him in May, so it looks as if letters from here take longer to get to Germany than letters from Germany to reach here. I see in the paper some vague suggestions that the Swiss Red Cross are suggesting repatriation of men who have been prisoners-of-war since the early months of the war, the snag about that being, however, that British prisoners-of-war during the first two years must have outnumbered the German prisoners-of-war by about 100 to 1, so I guess that we should have no German prisoners for anything like a big exchange. But one can always hope and things do sometimes happen the way you want them to.

The hoard of pre-war exercise books we accumulated at home, half-filled and collected from our school-days and various activities since, on which I have been scribbling this diary, have now become exhausted and I shall have to fall back on flimsy wartime paper. The last pad of notepaper I bought resembled toilet paper more than anything else.

Sunday, 31 October

[She wonders about taking] a staff post here [at the end of her third year of training]. These are falling vacant very quickly as so many of our nurses as soon as they are finished are putting on the grey and red, or black and red as it will be in the future, and going off to the ends of the earth [she is referring to Queen Alexandra's Imperial Military Nursing Service]. Two of our nurses were in a boat that was torpedoed but apart from losing their kit (which is I believe quite an expensive affair) they seem none the worse for their experiences. We get letters telling us of bathing in the Mediterranean, and eating luscious fruit, which makes us green with envy, especially now that summer is over and we are experiencing fog and blackout once again.

It was pitch dark tonight. We had several blackout casualties in, with cut faces, mostly through walking into things in the blackout. One of them I found quite fifteen minutes after we had stitched him and sent him away groping about the Infirmary yard, not able to find his way out. I was on my way to the Villa (an annexe to the Nurses Home) to see that all the nurses were in, lights out etc. It was pouring with rain and I was trying to hold up an umbrella, keep my cloak round me and find my way with the light of a dim torch.

Monday, 1 November

Monday morning and we thought a walk into the Town would be a good idea. Someone wanted to change a library book, someone else wanted to have a look round on the off-chance of finding one or two Penguin books to put in a last-minute Christmas parcel to her boy friend overseas and I wanted to send some cigarettes to my POW. The search for the Penguin books was almost a failure except for a couple run to earth in Boots. We are all great readers and we spent such a lot of time at the bookstalls in Boots and at another bookshop that we had to come back without the usual drink of coffee to help us on our way. I know that the patriotic thing to do is to send Saving Stamps but what a thrill children are going to miss on Christmas morning when there are no bulky brown paper parcels to open. I have cut down presents to a minimum but even so there still remains the family and one or two old friends who I do not like to overlook.

Tuesday, 2 November

We were so hungry after the lecture that we had to make some toast and cocoa before going to bed. Consequently the Home Sister on her daily after-lunch snoop round the night nurses' rooms to see we are all in bed caught us all sitting round smoking and eating. She was not pleased, to put it mildly, but words failed her when she met me coming back from my bath just before tea. I gave her no time to recover herself but promptly disappeared into my room. I was not bothered, though, as the worst she could do would be to send me to the Matron, who is quite an understanding old soul. It is very ironical that while on duty you have so much responsibility and a slight error on your part might have grave consequences for the patient concerned, while off duty you are treated like a cross between an imbecile and an irresponsible schoolgirl.

Thursday, 4 November

I went along to the [Downham] village shop after tea and there I managed to get an Evan Williams camomile shampoo, a thing I have not managed to get in Blackburn lately. In the days when powder was so hard to get I often managed to get a small box of Pond's face powder there when you could not get it anywhere else. It is not the small village shop of popular imagination though, dim and fusty with things that have been on the shelves for generations, but it is clean and bright and run by a young married couple who even in these days have quite a variety of groceries and, now that trades-men's vans no longer come out to the villages from Clithe-roe, supply most of the inhabitants of Downham and several other small places with their groceries.

One of the Women's Land Army was seen by the estate agent coming out of the 'local' with her arms full of bottles of beer the day after the capitulation of the Italians. On being asked what she was doing she said the Italian prisoners-of-war working on the estate wanted to celebrate the capitu-lation of their country.

Saturday, 6 November

I had a letter this evening from a friend of mine at the Emer-gency Hospital I was at [in Poulton-le-Fylde] before I came here. It is staffed by the CNR [Civil Nursing Reserve] and has thirteen patients and sixteen nurses. When I was there it was definitely needed. It was for minor infectious diseases and we took evacuees from miles round, and also the Forces from Blackpool and various camps around, and were we busy. At the time when London was bombed and mothers and children were evacuated to Blackpool [September 1940 to May 1941] we were packed with a mixture of infections and at one time had over 100 children under 5 and no more staff than they have now. To make matters worse a mild form of dysentery spread like wildfire, not only amongst the patients but the staff too. But now that the Forces have their own hospitals and sick bays properly organised they get no more of the boys and all the hospital blues [i.e., military patients] have been taken away, and most of the evacuees have gone back home, so in my idea there is very little need for the place now. It used to be the Weavers Convalescent Home and they stipulated when the County Council took it over that the Matron should stay on and there is of course the domestic staff and various men outside. It is a lovely place with parquet floors, huge windows, some of which open directly on to the garden, and it is centrally heated throughout. When I left there to come here it was like coming into another world [though the Blackburn Infirmary had generally up-to-date medical facilities, which attracted specialists to practise there].

Sunday, 7 November

When I came on duty this evening I was greeted by the sound of babies crying and I never realised that 4 small babies could make so much noise. They have been going at it hard ever since, if not altogether, one after the other. They are all Caesarean babies as we only take mothers who cannot have a normal birth. They are supposed to be more placid than those who come normally but it appears to be only a fallacy. These are the noisiest little things I have yet come across.

Tuesday, 9 November

I am relieving the night staff nurse tonight and have had quite a busy time with casualties and sick nurses but it is rather fun not being tied to one ward and to be able to wander about the building. I enjoyed my walk across to the Villa in the moonlight to see a sick nurse over there. You come across some funny things as you go about and tonight seems to have been more amusing than usual. The first thing I saw was the new House Physician, an Irishman, who only came a couple of days ago and who has certainly kissed the blarney stone, coming in from his evening off duty with one of the nurses. The nurse is engaged to a Canadian sergeant and is supposed to be getting married next month but she and the new doctor have not lost much time in getting together. The news spread round the place like wildfire and within about five minutes every night nurse knew all about it. A little later on I was walking along the basement with the junior Night Sister when we saw two figures flit across the corridor in the dim distance and disappear. The Night Sister was soon hot on their track and switching on a light in a little cubby-hole remarked 'You often find strange things in here' and there behind the door were a couple of nurses sneaking in from a dance. The Sister is a good sport and thought this a great joke and let them go.

Thursday, 11 November

I am often ashamed of these badly written scrawls, often I fear badly spelt scrawls I send in, but I write them in all sorts of moments and have no time to consider what or how I am putting things. I just cannot devote a regular half hour of the day or night to writing this. It depends during the night on pressure of work and during the day on lectures and sleeping time and how sleepy I may feel either day or night. In the early hours of this morning I had a rare spell of peace and shut myself in the linen-room and made a couple of collars for my uniform out of an old apron but when I came to sit down with a pen in my hand I could not keep awake. As I was still relieving the night staff nurse I had no ward and was not directly responsible for any patients so I had a snooze with a clear conscience.

The scraps of paper I write this on are always being thrown hastily into the small case amongst the rest of the paraphernalia I bring hopefully on duty with me every night, as I get a sudden call from the ward or hear some suspicious sound. The junk I collect in my case increases from one lot of nights off to the next. The case is a convenient size for taking a few things home in so I just have to empty it before I go home. First of all there is my cardigan, most important as the corridors are always draughty and sometimes I regret to say so are the wards. Then there is notepaper and envelopes, my knitting, my lecture book, stockings to darn etc. I pop them all into my case hoping always I may have time to write a letter, or darn stockings, and sometimes they stay in my case without ever being taken out until I am ready to go home again.

Armistice Day today and how little it seems to mean now. I remember when I was a child at school how important a day it seemed, with the Service at the War Memorial and all the gay red poppy wreaths, and the two minutes' silence. I went to the last Service at the Cenotaph in 1938 and then coming so soon after Munich, when we obtained a brief respite, it seemed to have a greater significance. It was a sunny November day, I remember, and as mild as spring. The tall guardsmen were going over like ninepins after standing in the heat in their heavy uniforms and during the two minutes' silence I watched the pigeons wheeling round overhead against the blue sky and the only sound was the click of the newsreel camera man on the roof of a building nearby. That year I was in a post where I had a good deal of spare time in the morning and I saw the Lord Mayor's procession and the King and Queen driving to the opening of Parliament. It was the first and will probably be the last time I shall see any of them.

A frequent theme in Kathleen's diary from mid-November was the bitterly cold weather. 'We seem to have leapt straight from summer to mid-winter,' she wrote on 15 November. Keeping warm was a challenge, though she was grateful that there was plenty of hot water for baths in the hospital. When walking in Downham on 19 November she found 'the ground as hard as iron', though adding that 'the sun was shining and there was no wind so I quite enjoyed my walk'. Bone-chilling temperatures were hard to escape. One Sunday in February she had been obliged to walk to Downham from the bus stop in Chatburn and had forgotten to wear a hat. 'With the wind whistling across the open road up the hill to Downham, by the time I reached home I had a real stiff jaw and earache. These swept-up hair styles', she added, 'may be neat and trim but they don't protect the ears much' (20 February 1944). 'Downham in the winter is so bitterly cold with usually an icy wind blowing': this was her overall feeling (12 February 1944), though occasionally the sun did shine and mild conditions prevailed.

Thursday, 18 November

When I came on duty tonight the staff nurse gave me the report and she told me that while they were having their mid-day meal one of the members of the Hospital Board came into the dining room and asked if there were any complaints about the food. He went to each table and was I believe almost deafened by the responses he got. Where food is concerned people are making war the excuse for giving us any old rubbish and I am sure that war is no excuse for giving us sausages that have been reheated three times and are so hard they jump off the plate when you try to cut them, and scrambled eggs made from dried eggs, which are definitely tasting bad. I have had some very eatable scrambled egg made from the dried eggs but the stuff we get here has no resemblance to the scrambled egg one gets outside.

Tuesday, 23 November

Last night one of the nurses on a quiet ward collected enough staff together to make a small cake so that we could have cake with our tea. My friend and I dallied about so much, though, that it was too late to be worth while going to bed. First of all we had an apple each – I had brought some back from home with me. Then we had a cigarette. After that we ate a quarter of peppermint creams from off my friend's sweet ration. And then we thought we would go and help with the big tea making for the gang.

There is a great deal to be said for living a communal life. You don't get much opportunity for moping and even if you do feel a bit depressed at times you soon forget about it when you are with the crowd. I do appreciate going home, though, where I get a bit of time to myself, but I know that I should be utterly miserable if I lived at home with nothing definite to do all day.

Wednesday, 24 November

Last night was a very hectic night for me. It started off with a blood transfusion which fortunately went O.K. When I came on duty Sister told me that she considered this man who was having a transfusion and another man [to be] on the danger list and that their relatives were ringing up at 10 to know whether they should stay the night. I hate having decisions like that left to me because if you tell the relatives to come unnecessarily it is upsetting for them and in addition the Night Sister is not too pleased, and if you tell them not to come and the patient dies everyone is upset, the relatives because they missed his last few hours and the Sister because she will have to listen to the relatives' reproaches, and yours truly because of an error of judgement. It is very difficult to tell, though, when you have only been on duty about an hour and have never seen the patient before what his chances of survival are. However, I told the relatives of one man to come and of the other to ring up early in the morning and by a lucky chance I judged correctly as the latter man is now improving while the other died about 4.30 this morning. I had a shock a bit earlier, though, when a man died about 2.30 whom, though we were not expecting him to live, no one anticipated him dying so soon. They were both very old men and incurable. One of them had been lingering on for weeks in great misery. In between the two deaths we had an emergency admission who might have been for operation but the RSO [Resident Surgical Officer] decided he could wait until the morning, for which we were truly thankful.

Friday, 26 November

When I went across to the nurses at the Villa it was freezing hard and as I came in I said to the porter that fracture clinic would do a roaring trade. Barely had I finished speaking than the first fracture came in, an old Irish man who had been fire watching and had been lying for an hour in the cold before he was found. He was admitted to fracture ward immediately and another casualty came in very soon afterwards who was sent round to X-ray and had not come back when I went off duty. It was a bright sunny morning so we went out but had great difficulty in keeping our feet as except where they had put down sand it was like walking on a sheet of glass. When we came on duty tonight we were told that ten fracture cases had been admitted and sixty treated in fracture clinic.

I went to the women's surgical ward to do the 10 o'clock dressings for the nurse in charge who had her septic finger opened. Matron said she could not put another nurse in her place as she had not one to spare, so many were off sick. After that I went to the round of the sick nurses. There are great tales going around about the flu epidemic, such as 800 off from the Bristol Aircraft Company, half of the employees at this mill and so many at that factory. I don't really know how much is truth and how much rumour but to take this Infirmary alone there are more nurses off with it than have ever been off before.

Sunday, 28 November

I did not waken until about 6.30 when I heard the choir singing 'Lead Kindly Light' in the women's ward and was soon asleep again. I should have been free tonight but one of the senior nurses is off with flu so I had to take over her ward. It is very quiet on the ward tonight and I have had time to write up my morning lecture for tomorrow and I hope to get a few letters written too. I should have time as we have no seriously ill patients and it is an emergency week on either side.

I have just been reading about the film of nursing life, *The Light Still Burns*, supposed to be taken from the Monica Dickens book *One Pair of Feet* [see 3 July 1943]. From the title one would suppose it to be one of those sentimental

films that glamourises nursing and makes all nurses out to
be selfless individuals, with no other reasons for becoming
nurses except love of suffering humanity.* The unfortunate
fact is that it is not always the nurses with the highest ideals
who make the best nurses. One nurse who was here when
I came and who I think was absolutely devoted to her profession was to my idea a positive menace on the ward and
she was heartbroken when the Matron would not allow her
to stay.

Monday, 29 November

Our number of sick nurses seems to be increasingly steadily. Matron is talking of cancelling holidays if the sickness
becomes any worse. Fortunately the cold and flu epidemic
we are going through now does not seem of a particularly
virulent type. They run a sore throat and a high temperature for a couple of days but after that they soon get over it.
Much quicker, I might say, than some of us who keep going
though if all nurses went off sick who had a bad cold the staff
would be cut in half. Young people have been comparing
this epidemic to that of the flu epidemic during the last war
[1918–19] but I have not yet heard of anyone being seriously
ill with it this time. I should imagine the blackout to be a

---

* The correct title of this 1943 British film is *The Lamp Still Burns*. Its portrait of
hospital life is not unlike that in Katheen's diary: the air of calm efficiency offset
by petty tyrannies, strict hierarchy, and suffocating rules and discipline, as well as
long hours of work, fatigue, and the determination of nurses to be unemotional in
their interactions with patients. The film, which was made with the assistance and
collaboration of the Ministry of Health, was both a tribute to the work of nurses and
a plea for better training conditions in hospitals. The central character in the film,
a nurse-in-training who had been educated as an architect, was, like Kathleen, an
older probationer. See also below, 31 March 1944.

contributing factor with so many people shut up together at night during night work in places with very little ventilation. Another thing I should imagine, especially in Lancashire where we have rain six days out of seven, is the lack of umbrellas and rubber footwear for keeping people dry. Then of course one cannot jump into a nice hot bath and dry one's things in front of a nice hot fire as we could in pre-war days. To be continually wet and cold must lower people's resistance to infection.

One of the cases we admitted to fracture ward on the morning of the great Frost died today. I suppose it must have been from exposure as his fracture was quite a simple straightforward one.

Thursday, 2 December

I heard today on the wireless about the meeting between Churchill, Roosevelt and Chiang Kai-Shek in [Cairo] North Africa. It seems to me we had better get Germany finished off before we start talking about knocking out Japan. I am sure we shall not be able to beat them both simultaneously.

The release of Sir Oswald Mosley seems to have produced a great deal of controversy and I do not see why his [medical] condition could not have been treated just as well in prison as anywhere else. According to all accounts his prison life was not very rigorous and he is just as likely to die from his complaint in his own home as in prison.*

---

* Sir Oswald Mosley, leader of the British Union of Fascists, had been arrested and imprisoned on 23 May 1940. He had just been released from Holloway Prison after (it was said) his phlebitis had flared up and he needed better treatment.

Sunday, 5 December

There was a great commotion in the Infirmary in the early hours of this morning. The House Physician, who had been looking quite seedy yesterday evening, about 4 a.m. this morning became delirious and walked round the hospital with nothing on but his pyjamas, smacking the nurses' faces. The staff nurse had the worst fate of all. He broke her glasses and knocked her over before anyone could get the porter and other housemen to deal with him. He was put back to bed and was horror-stricken when he realised what he had been doing. One of the honorary physicians came in to see him and diagnosed it as pneumonia.

My friend who had been at home on her two nights off duty and the House Physician had been to a dance with her on Friday night and [he] stayed the night at her home. When she got back this evening and heard how ill the HP was she was horror-stricken too because she had thought on Saturday when he had complained of not feeling well that he was being soft and had persuaded him to go to Blackpool. At Blackpool she had told him he needed more fresh air and had taken him for a brisk walk along the Front – rather vigorous treatment for anyone in the early stages of pneumonia.

Monday, 6 December

So absorbed does one get in one's own particular job, especially on night duty, that the outside world is almost forgotten and the meeting of the Big Three, Stalin, Roosevelt, and Churchill, at Teheran in Persia aroused only the faintest flushes of interest. Actually when I can spare a minute to think about it I hope that it is the beginning of the end and that we shall soon be opening that real Second Front for an all-out drive in Germany. I am glad that Berlin is being bombed so heavily and that the arrogant Germans are getting a taste of what London endured. Germans are arrogant, I find, even though they are exiles from Germany and anti-Nazis. One German nurse we had here was heard to remark at the time that Rommel had pushed us back to El Alamein, 'No one can say that my countrymen are not fine fighters.' She was a stupid girl or she would not have made such a remark like that. She has left now as she failed to pass her preliminary examination but she was clearly the most disliked girl in the hospital.

Tuesday, 7 December

I had a smashing time this morning. First of all I broke a thermometer. As though that was not enough I knocked a patient's watch off her locker. It was true she had it hidden away in a fold in her bag and I moved the bag to put a tray down, but that did not make me feel any better about it. I said I would try to get it mended for her but she said her uncle was a jeweller and would mend it for her, so that lightened the situation a little. She is a private patient and has had a Caesarian done and has got a beautiful little boy. Her first child fell out of its cot and killed itself. Since then there were indications that she would not be able to have any more children so twelve months ago she adopted twin boys of 2 months. She is now appalled by the fact that she will have to manage these three children with the help of a girl of 15. The twins need circumcising so at the moment they are being conveniently cared for on the children's ward. The only woman relative she has to call on is her mother who is about 65 and very deaf so she is looking forward to a pretty picnic when she goes home.

Wednesday, 8 December

I have just come back from the Villa, the annexe to the Nurses Home, after seeing that the nurses were all in and the lights out etc. It was a beautiful bright moonlight night, unlike this morning when I went across to call them and it was pitch dark and pouring with rain. Unless it is actually raining I quite enjoy the little walk to the Villa. It is nice to get a bit of fresh air after a stuffy night in a blacked-out hospital. It is surprising how many people you hear about, at 6.30 in the morning. The sound of their clogs echoing on the pavement is a most familiar sound and the old trams clanging along at the foot of the hill is another sound you are most aware of as you stumble along the cobbled street. Cobbled streets I have found are most painful to aching feet which have been tearing around the ward for hours. As I came in a taxi pulled up at the door, and four or five anxious looking people tumbled out. Catching sight of me they crowded round me, asking how Mr _____ was now, was there any hope for him?* And so on. They looked most incredulous when I said I was sorry, I knew nothing about him, and directed them to the porter's desk. They could not understand that a relative of theirs could be dying and a nurse in the Infirmary not know anything about it. It is surprising how often one is stopped on the corridor and asked for Mrs _____'s ward.

Thursday, 9 December

It is amazing how quickly the fortnights pass, both for sending in this diary and going round the Infirmary during two

---

* This blank is in the text and reflects Kathleen's practice of not naming names in her diary (there are more such instances to follow), even when people are mentioned only matter-of-factly and not judgmentally. A degree of anonymity was observed by many MO diarists.

nights on each of the big wards in a fortnight. It is surprising how you can get to like doing things that you thought you would hate. I can remember how appalled I was when I came back from my holidays and heard I was going to do senior night's relief and now I thoroughly enjoy myself, going from ward to ward, and shall be quite sorry when I am taken off night duty.*

Today three of us were getting up to see *Cargo of Innocents* [entitled *Stand By for Action* in the US] and we went to bed early so as to get in as much sleep as possible. I was disturbed about 2 by the inevitable dust bins being rolled merrily around beneath my window but managed to get to sleep again. The film was well worth getting up at 4 o'clock to see and we all enjoyed it. Robert Taylor was most amusing as the executive officer of a destroyer in the US Navy coping with all kinds of situations including the 'Cargo of Innocents' rescued from a lifeboat adrift in the Pacific.

We were shown the momentous meeting of the Big Three at Teheran which was most surprising as usually the newsreel is at least a month old before it reaches Blackburn.

Friday, 10 December

There is a by-election at Darwen and of course the local papers have been full of it. Captain [Stanley] Prescott, the National Conservative candidate, is being contested by a

---

* 'There is such a nice crowd on at the moment', she wrote on 30 December, 'and we have had lots of fun and you get to know people better on night duty as there are fewer of you.' A few days later, on 4 January 1944, when she was about to return to day duty, she thought of how 'On night duty with twenty-odd nurses you form a cozy little circle, [whereas] on day duty, with a hundred-odd nurses, it is like stepping into an alien atmosphere, especially as I have not been on day duty since the end of July.'

Miss Honor Balfour, Independent.* The activities of both candidates have been rather restricted by flu but it is now in full swing. Darwen and Blackburn run into one another and the hospital is situated fairly near the boundary but close as we are to Darwen, a quiz by the Night Sister of the night staff showed that quite 50% did not know there was to be an election there and of the remainder few could supply even the name of one candidate. It does show how little interest we take in what is going on outside these four walls, though I don't really think nurses are the only members of the community who suffer from this fault [the campaign was very short: candidates were nominated on 7 December and the election held eight days later].

Mrs Prescott was nearly sent into the Infirmary as a patient tonight. Some kind (?) friends were just enquiring about the possibility of a bed in a private ward for her when Captain Prescott arrived back from some meeting and was most annoyed, as it was being done without his knowledge. She is suffering from pleurisy [which was preventing her from campaigning with her husband] but as he said he saw no point in her being moved from a warm room at that time of night – and we have heard no more about it. She would have been obliged to come into the ward in any case as we never have any empty private beds for emergencies.

---

* Wartime by-elections were not contested by the three major parties, except for the party holding the seat when it became vacant. In this instance, while no candidate ran for the Labour or Liberal Party, Honor Balfour, a Liberal Party activist and opponent of the wartime electoral truce, chose to run as an 'Independent Liberal' and lost by only seventy votes. The number of voters was well less than half the number who had voted in the general election of 1935. When wartime contests did occur, they usually involved Independents and/or candidates from small parties.

Saturday, 11 December

This morning we started off bright and early to do some Christmas shopping. It was a frosty morning but not the nice sharp frost with a blue sky and sunshine, but with the sun a red ball trying to penetrate the fog. I bought socks for my brother, two coupons, but they are for the rare occasions when he gets into mufti and does not want to wear the heavy Army issue, and some brushless shaving cream. I expended two more coupons on a very cute pinafore-apron thing for my sister, who I know is a bit short of them. I got a book for my mother and a bottle of shampoo I know she likes, notepaper for an aunt, a torch for the friend I stayed with in London, an ounce of tobacco for my father of an expensive brand he had to give up smoking long ago. My nephew and niece I had already dealt with and except for some Christmas cards and one or two calendars that is the sum total of my present giving this year. To my boy friend in Germany I have sent cigarettes, through a tobacconist of course, but I ordered them weeks ago so that they hardly seem to count as Christmas presents.

We were going to the YWCA for a cup of coffee and something to eat because we have found that you are allowed more cakes and scones there than you get in a café but there was a Bring and Buy sale in progress so we had to go elsewhere.

By this time in the war many consumer items were hard, if not impossible, to obtain or, if available, very expensive. On 27 November Kathleen had been able to get from a stall in Blackburn a wooden truck for her nephew for 5 shillings. 'It is a real bargain because with toys the atrocious price they are I should have had to

pay about 15s for it in a shop.' A week later, 3 December, after
shopping with her mother in Clitheroe, she remarked on 'the exorbi-
tant prices people are asking for unrationed goods'. The best buys
were often found at charity sales. Given the austerity of the times,
it is noteworthy that with every fortnightly submission of her diary
to Mass Observation, she enclosed as a donation stamps worth ten
pennies, a not insignificant sum out of a wage of around a pound
a week.

Monday, 13 December

I rang up the dentist when I got in and made an appointment
to have my tooth out. It has been troubling me ever since I
came on night duty but this cold weather has really started
it off in real earnest. Every time I open my mouth when I
am outside now it starts aching so I have to pluck up courage
and arrange to have it out.

Wednesday, 15 December

I went to have my tooth out this morning and my dentist
seemed decidedly pained at the thought of taking out this
tooth he had filled last year. However, the nerve was exposed
and I had gas and it was out very quickly and no further
trouble. What I like about gas is that there are no painful
after-effects such as you get with cocaine when the effect of
freezing is wearing off.

Friday, 17 December

The party [with fellow nurses] went off with a great swing
even though we had nothing but tea and soft drinks. Everyone

seemed to have the Christmas spirit and we laughed till our sides ached and though we did not know it a few doors away a nurse was sobbing her heart out because she had just heard that her boy friend, a Canadian air-gunner, had been killed in action. She is a refugee from Occupied Europe and has lost her parents, which makes things doubly hard for her. She has no home and no parents. Her relatives may or may not be alive. No wonder she is taking it so badly.

Monday, 20 December

I got back [from the Post Office] before the tea was all finished and had something to drink and then went off to hunt for a bath. Several of the bathrooms are being redecorated so one wanders all over the building looking for an empty bathroom, a practice frowned upon by the Home Sister who likes us to keep to the night nurses' corridor where we have a bathroom between about twenty-four of us. It is rather a slow business if there is a run on the bathrooms and you are about the third on the list but with only one bathroom in use we should be waiting indefinitely and the Home Sister cannot be on five floors at once so it is 5 to 1 odds that she catches you having a bath away from your own quarters.

Wednesday, 22 December

I changed hurriedly as soon as I had given the report and went down to the rehearsal [for the Christmas concert] in mufti. As soon as we had finished I rushed off down Town to the dentist to get another tooth fixed on to my plate to replace the one I had out last week. It is amazing how differently you feel about going to the dentist when you are not having a tooth filled or out. Instead of sitting in the waiting room in fear and trembling, watching for the receptionist to come and say 'Your turn next,' you settle down quite happily with a book. As it happened I did not have to wait long and was soon sitting in the dreaded dentist's chair, having a great lump of wax rammed into my mouth. I was told that I would have to wait until Friday for it to be fixed on to my plate but fortunately I have another one so shall be spared going about for a couple of night with a toothless grin. My old plate is not a very good fit and feels very insecure. I am told I am talking as though I have a plum in my mouth but it feels much worse than that.*

Friday, 24 December

It is Christmas Eve and everyone on night duty seems to have been infected with the Christmas spirit in the early hours of the morning. We played innumerable practical jokes on one another and it is a wonder that the patients managed to get any sleep at all on one or two of the wards there was so much laughing going on. One thing, though, explained it – the Senior Night Sister was away for the night and her deputy enjoys a joke as much as anyone.

We went to Town this morning after rehearsal to get our library books changed and I went along to the dentist and arranged to meet the other two for coffee at the County. I was very late arriving as the dentist kept me waiting longer than I thought he would and when I went to the library it took me much longer than usual to find a book.

* Diaries and other sources from these years show that many people had false teeth by the age of 30. Kathleen had four and, two and a half years later, on 25 June 1946, broke one of them after chewing a Mars Bar, a post-war treat to herself.

They had already had one cup of coffee when I arrived but started off again when I got there. When I came to get up I found to my horror that my stocking was caught on a nail in the chair. I was wearing one of my pair of fully-fashioned silk from Canada too. I don't usually wear them for ordinary occasions but put them on this morning in honour of Christmas I suppose. After coffee we dashed frantically round the music-shops looking for copies of songs we were still needing for the Christmas concert. We managed to get a couple of them after much searching and then hurried back to the Infirmary as it was well after 1 by the time we had finished.

When we came on duty this evening the day nurses were just putting the finishing touches to the Christmas decorations – what there were of them. So we finished off and tidied up for them, gave the patients a cup of tea instead of the usual water and turned the lights out in readiness for the carols. About 9 o'clock we heard the nurses starting the carols on the ground floor and gradually working along. They should have been carrying lanterns in the old traditional style but instead of that they had more up-to-date torches, at least those of the nurses who had batteries for them. They just walked slowly round the wards singing as they went with their torches shining and it really looked and sounded most effective.

On Christmas Day the patients 'had an egg for their breakfast, just to make a little change for them'. The House Physician arrived as Father Christmas, 'wishing them all a Merry Christmas but not I am afraid doling out presents from a well-filled sack'. Kathleen's breakfast – 'or rather dinner I should say' – featured 'pork chops, apple sauce etc., followed by mince pie' and accompanied by a glass

*of port. She then went home to Downham and enjoyed a lunch of
'turkey etc.' and opened her presents, 'books and some cosmetics.
Before I left the Infirmary the post arrived and I had a Christmas
card from my boy friend who is a prisoner-of-war, amongst others.'
She rested and caught up on her sleep. On 27 December she recorded
one of the infrequent pieces of war news to appear in her diary in
late 1943/early 1944. 'The news of the sinking of the [battleship]*
Scharnhorst *came as a very pleasant Christmas surprise and certainly provided a little relief from the monotony of the news during
Christmas weekend.'*

Saturday, 1 January 1944

Big Ben had just finished striking when the main door leading into the hospital was thrown open and in dashed the
House Physician carrying a basket of coal closely followed
by the Sister Tutor carrying what looked like a small brush.
These they proceeded to distribute amongst the members
of the staff who had gathered to watch, kissing everyone
and wishing them a Happy New Year. I was quite unpre-
pared for the outburst of kissing which followed as everyone
kissed everyone else and wished them a Happy New Year.
Then we all went back to our respective wards and peace
descended on the Infirmary.

My friend who is on holiday but came back to go to a
dance with the House Physician slept in my bed so I got
her breakfast when I came off duty and soon various nurses
drifted in for a drink except for the Roman Catholics who had
gone to Mass. When eventually my friend had departed and
all the others had taken themselves off I made an attempt to
tidy my room a bit and opened the door and windows to let
the cigarette smoke out. While the room was clearing I went

along to the laundry to look for a missing cup and on the main corridor a military band was playing and some of the nurses were dancing. I got along in time to sing 'Auld Lang Syne', and then the band started on carols. I had forgotten that it was the custom for the band to come in on New Year's Day and it was quite by chance that I went along. Now except for the staff dance I suppose we shall have to settle down to the trivial round and some hard work. I must see about getting my text-books for the finals [in September] and get down to some studying. At the moment I feel I shall never know enough.

Sunday, 2 January

On a Sunday morning, especially if the weather is not too good, the old sitting room is crowded out so that if you want to get anywhere near the fire you have to be there early. This morning I was so early that the fire had only just been lighted but I managed to get my hair dried before the day nurses streamed in. I had a little bath then and got my laundry ready, made up a clean cap, put my collar on my dress and the buttons in, and I had thought I might tidy my wardrobe and drawers but the spirit was willing but the flesh weak so I got into bed instead. It was blowing a gale but I do so hate sleeping with my windows shut that I opened them wide as usual. They rattled so much I thought the glass was going to break and the catch on my door is not very strong so that kept blowing open too. Eventually at 3.30, after having leapt out of bed at least half a dozen times to close my door or wedge my windows, I gave up the struggle for fresh air and closed my windows and fixed the blackout and got some uninterrupted sleep.

Thursday, 6 January

I got up this morning feeling decidedly strange [she had just been put on day duty], especially as I am still on the night nurses' corridor though I heard the clanging of the bell which one of the junior night nurses rings round the Nurses Home at 6.30 a.m. to waken us all up. I went down to breakfast at 7.15. I had previously worked it out that if I went down too early none of my own class would be in the dining room and I should not know which table to sit at and if I was late going down there would not be room for me to sit anywhere. At breakfast we sit strictly in order of seniority, the newest arrival at the bottom of the junior table working up to the senior staff nurse at the head of the staff nurses' table. Naturally as nurses come and nurses go you gradually move on and I found that my place was two tables away from where I was sitting when I first went on night duty.

The work on the ward was very much as usual. Sister had been sent for and came on duty. The doctors came to do their rounds tied in barrier gowns, and one or two ministers and clergymen came in, also similarly attired [there had been a case of paratyphoid in the ward]. A few visitors for the patients got as far as the barrier of screens standing at the entrance to the ward and reluctantly handed over their little parcels for the patients, usually consisting of something for the patients' tea.

I caught Sister alone and asked her about my off-duty as no one seemed to have mentioned it and I was quite pleased when she said she thought I had better take an evening tonight – that is go off duty at 6 and have a day off tomorrow. So when I came off duty at 6 I hurriedly got changed and caught the 6.35 to Clitheroe. Mother was rather surprised when I walked in at 7.30 as I usually let her know when I am coming because otherwise she starts worrying about the bed being damp [she liked to air it beforehand].

Friday, 7 January

There was a concert in the village school at night but as I had to get back it was not worth while going for an hour so as soon as my mother and father had gone I had some supper and caught the next bus to Clitheroe. There was no one in it but the local roadman, a real character, a poacher, heavy drinker. He spends every night of his life in the pub. A query – black marketer? He can always get things that no one else can. And he is the church verger. He seemed to be having a great political argument with the driver and conductor, who were sitting in the bus, but it died down when I got in. They all agreed, though, that when any Labour man got a post of any importance he abandoned the working people and they cited [Philip] Snowden, [Ernest] Bevin, Herbert Morrison, Ramsay MacDonald etc. The driver and conductor also had a private grievance against their managing director who they called a b____ Austrian Jew and they seemed to hold him responsible for the fact that the driver and conductor, who did overtime at Christmas, got less in their pay packets than those who did less overtime. I was afraid the bus would be late starting and I would miss my connection in Clitheroe with all this grumbling going on but the conductor suddenly forgot his grievances and said to the driver that it was time to be starting so off we went though I only caught my bus in Clitheroe by the skin of my teeth.

Saturday, 8 January

Already night duty seems like a thing of the past except for
the fact that I am still sleeping on the night nurses' corridor
or rather I should say my things are still there but tonight
I shall be sleeping in my new room in the basement of all
places and directly opposite to the Home Sister's room. I
have been lucky up to the present in sleeping well away
from any Sister as they have an unpleasant habit of expecting your light to be out at 11 or soon after, whereas I often
have mine on long after that, especially if I have an interesting book, which I have at the moment, called *Fame is the
Spur* [a 1940 novel], by Howard Spring. It belongs to a friend
of a friend of a friend and as the original owner wants it back
soon I am having to read it quickly.

*Three days later, on her day off, she stayed in bed and 'had a long
read at my book* Fame is the Spur, *which curiously enough deals
with the same aspect of Labour men as the bus men on Friday night –
how they desert the working man and lose their ideals as soon as
they hold an important position'. It is striking that Kathleen spent
several winter evenings reading this book, which runs to 679 closely
spaced pages. Its Welsh-born author, Howard Spring (1889–1965),
was immensely popular in the 1940s and 1950s. He was known for
his good writing and terrific storytelling. This book may have had
particular appeal for Kathleen and her friends because of its setting
in the industrial North (mostly Manchester and Bradford) and its
vivid descriptions of squalid slums, immense mansions and glorious moorland vistas. The novel's hero, born poor, is a clever man
of great ambition, arrogance and stirring oratory who becomes a
Labour peer, Viscount Shawcross, and, clad in velvet and ermine,
attends the May 1937 coronation of George VI.*

Monday, 10 January

When I closed my window before I dressed this morning I saw there was a sprinkling of snow on the ground, the first I can remember this winter. It turned out a lovely bright sunny day too with a clear blue sky and for once Blackburn looked quite attractive as we looked down on it from the ward window with all the snow-covered roofs shining in the sun.

I went down to the laboratory this morning to find out if all the results of the tests on our ward were through and if so whether they were all negative. I was relieved to find that all the tests were negative except the nurse I mentioned yesterday but the ward will be in quarantine for another fortnight yet. The entire nursing staff is having a blood test done now for the paratyphoid bacillus just in case this nurse has passed it among the staff, except of course the nurses on C-ward whose tests were all negative. The people in the laboratory will all be working overtime with all these extra tests to do.

I went out tonight straight after duty to get some chips for some of the night staff to augment their scanty meal and also to get some for myself. I looked into the dining room as I came off duty but retreated hastily when I saw it was a peculiar-looking potato pie. It was a beautiful bright moonlight night, freezing hard, with the streets as hard as iron but not a breath of wind so that it did not feel as cold as one would expect. It was just the night for a walk with a suitable person, though.

Food was probably the most widely discussed topic in wartime, at least by women, including, sometimes, the nurses in the Blackburn

*Infirmary. Almost three weeks later, on 1 February in the evening,
'having found out that it was potato pie again for supper we decided
not to go in and we were going out for fish and chips when we realised that it was Sunday evening and that all the chip shops would
be closed in the vicinity so we had to fall back on toast again'. After
the war in Europe ended, Kathleen acknowledged that nurses had
not fared too badly (23 June 1945). 'Am beginning to think that
those of us who have lived in institutions with no catering wor-
ries have had a lot to be thankful for. At least we have not had to
worry where the next day's meals were coming from.' She had one
further post-war thought about food (16 June 1945): 'In 1939 we
should have thought it impossible to keep body and soul together on
our present meager rations.' In early 1944 the Infirmary's management, in an effort to respond to complaints, appointed a food
supervisor 'to take complete charge of the reception, cooking and
service of all food for patients and staff' (*Blackburn Times, 7
January 1944, p. 7), though she did not last long. Good cooks were
hard to find and hold on to.*

Saturday, 15 January

We had a very sad case in yesterday. A woman aged about
30 was sent in and she had a bullet lodged in her spine. She
was in bed with flu when her brother, age 19, just home on
leave, called to see [her]. He came straight from the station
with all his kit which he dumped at the bottom of the bed.
He bent down to pick something up and caught his button
on the safety catch of his rifle which being loaded went off
and shot his sister. The bullet went up between her legs,
ploughed straight through her intestines, shattering part of
the hip bone and stopped in her spine. There was practically
no hope for her. They gave her a blood transfusion and sent

her straight to the theatre but she died early this morning about twelve hours after she was admitted. Her brother was demented with worry and no wonder. It must be terrible to feel that you have killed someone you love apart from the fact that he had no business to be carrying a loaded rifle around with him.

Sunday, 16 January

We have been discussing Lord Horder's report today on the future of the nursing profession and his suggestions for raising the status of the student nurse by making her pay for her training and by having the wards staffed only by trained personnel and domestic helpers. I have not yet read the full report. The Sister Tutor has a copy of it but I have not seen it so I don't quite know how the student nurse of the future is to get her practical experience which is every bit [as] if not more essential than her theory. But by practical experience I don't mean scrubbing lockers, cleaning lights, etc. which is the lot of the student nurse now for at least six months and her time is so occupied with these duties that she has no opportunity of really doing much for the patients except making beds, taking meals round and attending to their toilet, which does not need any specialised training.* At most

---

* On 23 December 1943, when she first read in the press about Lord Horder's Report (Thomas Jeeves Horder, 1871–1955), she had also dismissed the value of these menial tasks in training nurses. 'The time could be better spent in giving the patients an extra bed-bath instead of the once a week sponge down they get at present, often given in too much of a hurry to be done properly as the nurses are expected to get them all in on Saturday and Sunday . . . To be a good nurse it is not at all necessary to know how to sweep a floor and wash walls. It is no more relevant to nursing than, say, to typing, teaching, hairdressing etc.' Traditionally, student nurses had been seen as a source of cheap labour; this Report recommended that the focus be on their professional training (*The Times*, 23 December 1943, p. 8).

training schools now there is a preliminary training school which nurses attend for the first two months before they go on to the wards and where they learn a great deal of their theory before they start their practical work. Here we start straight away on the wards so that our practical experience is often in advance of our theory and there is a discrepancy between what we are taught in the lecture room and what we do on the ward. No scheme is ever perfect, though, and in spite of all the drawbacks it is a great life and my only regret is that I did not start earlier.

Tuesday, 18 January

[A day off work for her]. The fog cleared in the afternoon and the sun came out for a while [in Downham]. I had to come back in time for a lecture at 7.30 so had to leave home at 5.30. Just before I left, a family friend, a girl in the ATS on radio-location [i.e., radar], arrived for her twenty-four hours' leave. She said that they had been working overtime for one of these inspections by some of the 'Big Chiefs' that every man and woman in the Forces loathes, when they waste a lot of time, energy and material getting ready for the Big Event which could be put to much better use. The worst case that I ever heard of was at an aerodrome where the floor of a hangar was cleaned with hundreds of gallons of petrol for one of these inspections and the boy who told me had actually been one of the people cleaning it so it was no rumour. It happened a couple of years ago and I sincerely hope though I very much doubt it that that sort of thing does not happen now. The boy who told me was very bitter about it and who can blame him.

Thursday, 20 January

After the fuss there was a few months ago over the food the [Hospital] Board decided to appoint a dietician for the Hospital. They did appoint one but she is a Domestic Science teacher at some school and the school will not release her so we are still without a dietician and with no hope of any improvement in the food. On paper I have no doubt our menus sound fairly attractive but things that I quite enjoy are almost uneatable here. Sausages for instance, even in their present almost meatless state, I don't dislike but the Sunday breakfast sausages here are so hard and dry that they jump off you plate when you try to cut them. Cheese is another thing I have always liked but the cheese they serve up here is so rank and strong that your mouth feels it for hours.*

Wednesday, 26 January

It has been one of those pleasant uneventful days when nothing very exciting happens and nothing very unpleasant. We have been fairly busy on the ward but not too busy and definitely not overworked. There are days when you come off duty feeling that bed is the only place for you and that your aching feet will not carry you any further. But today I came off duty feeling fresh enough to climb three flights of stairs, someone as usual having left the gates open on the top

---

* Just after Christmas (29 December 1943) Kathleen had noted that at the end of one festive meal the cook brought in 'the Christmas pudding, alight of course,' and said that she was 'a girl about 19 years of age and looking younger. In pre-war days she would probably have been just a kitchen maid and I must say she manages equally as well as some of the fully-fledged cooks we have had.' The latter may have been absent for this relatively palatable meal.

floor to give a nurse from the ward I am on, who was off duty this evening, her share of a lovely sponge sandwich filled with cream that one of our patients who has a confectioner shop had made for us. It was infinitely better than anything she sells in her shop I am sure or she would have women queuing overnight for her sponge sandwiches. It is strange how much I think about food nowadays. In pre-war days I never thought about food from one meal to the next, but now with a combination of food rationing and hospital fare it is seldom far from my mind.

Thursday, 27 January

Tonight we have had the staff dance. We usually have it the first or second week after Christmas but this year it was post-poned until the end of this month owing to the paratyphoid [and consequent quarantine measures]. We all go to it in uni-form and you are supposed to hand in to Matron a week or two before the dance the names and addresses of the boy friends you wish to invite and they receive a formal invita-tion. Actually if someone comes home on leave or you meet someone between the time of sending out the invitations and the dance it is quite a simple matter to ask him to come along. We usually have a few gate-crashers in any case but amongst a crowd no one notices them.

The dance is held in the nurses' dining room and the lec-ture room is where we have supper. The night nurses are able to stay until midnight as the day staff have to relieve on the ward in relays. My turn was from 10 to 11 which was rather an awkward time for me. The friend I had invited came into Blackburn early as I was off duty at 5.30. We went to see *Kings Row* [1942], a morbid picture I must say but nev-ertheless very good [the character played by Ronald Reagan has both legs amputated]. The shows are never very lengthy in Blackburn, just the big picture and the news, so we were out in time for a drink and then I came in and changed into uniform having left my partner in the care of a friend. I had about three dances and then it was time for me to relieve. My partner had supper with this friend and then he had to go as the last train was 11.13 so that by the time I had done my relief he had gone. The dance did not finish until 2 and the room got terribly stuffy but I had a really good time in spite of my partner leaving so early.

Saturday, 29 January

I was reading in the daily papers today of the atrocities committed by the Japanese on the Allied prisoners-of-war. It sends cold shivers down your back when you think what agonising deaths some of the boys have died. My cousin, for one, who was at Hong Kong and has since been reported as having died of wounds. We did not hear anything except that he was missing until the news came through about three months ago. I think it must be worse, though, for those who have sons or husbands alive in Japanese hands. The awful part about it is that until we finish off Germany we cannot do a great deal about a big offensive against Japan, and we seem such a long way off, starting on Germany, let alone finishing her off. In this little island of ours once the bombing stopped we seemed to forget about the horrors of war and grumbled about its minor inconveniences such as rationing etc. and really we have very little to grumble about.

Monday, 31 January

I woke up this morning with the feeling that I had something unpleasant to face and with the return of consciousness I

realised that I was about to start on a new ward (the children's ward) and I viewed the hours in front of me in a very
depressed way.

My worst fears were soon realised. I got on to the ward
where I was confronted with seven babies and told that I
was in charge of them. I spent the day bathing, washing and
feeding babies, the last named being the worst job of all –
two were on two-hourly feeds, three were on three-hourly
feeds and three were on four-hourly feeds so that there was
seldom an hour of the day when I had not at least two babies
to feed. The worst part of it was the little blighters would
not take their feeds so that sometimes the two-hourly's were
feeding almost up to the next round. To make matters worse
I could not find a thing to use and Sister seemed to take a
poor view of me. I was down in the off-duty book for a 2 to
4 and was looking forward to it when I was told that I had
to take an evening instead. By the time I came off duty at 6
o'clock I wondered why ever I came into nursing in the first
place and how I could ever have said I liked it and felt like
going to Matron first thing in the morning and asking for
my holidays – a favourite gag of ours if we get on a ward we
don't like.

Wednesday, 2 February

Wednesday is visiting day and on children's ward the visitors come from 2 to 3 instead of 2.30 to 3.30 as on the other
wards. It seemed strange to see them leaving their bags of
biscuits, sweets and occasionally apples and oranges on the
trolley at the entrance to the ward instead of giving them
to the patients themselves. It is the obvious thing to do,
though, as the tinies with bags of biscuits etc. would have a

glorious time. There was a row of plates each marked with a child's name and on these plates the visitors put the things they had brought for their child's tea. One visitor said 'Now you will be sure Elsie gets this. Last week she said she had a brown tea cake instead of a white one I had brought her.' We take children up to the age of 6 so some of them are quite knowing. Another visitor said to me 'Can Brian's grandmother come up to see him this evening? She is working nights at t'fuse and can't come any other time' – 't'fuse' being a [Royal Ordnance] fuse factory which employs a fair number of people locally [in fact, thousands].

What a noise there was when the visitors were going, with most of the children yelling lustily for their parents. It subsided somewhat when the tea trolley came round but for about half-an-hour it was pandemonium. Thank goodness it is not visiting day every day.

Thursday, 3 February

It has been blowing a gale all day. Every fireplace we have has been smoking and the draught has just whistled around the corridors and into the wards. The windows of the baby ward are bricked up except for about a foot at the top to allow for a little ventilation but even so there seemed to be a mighty big wind coming from somewhere. The ward is lit by the daylight lighting which seems to give a bluish light and is not supposed to be such a strain on the eyes. It is not too bad in winter but these permanent blackouts in Summer Time are very depressing and it does not seem to me that I shall see the blackout taken down here.

The end of my third year is up in October and I cannot see the war finishing by then. I suppose if my boy friend were not a prisoner-of-war I might not long so intensely for the war to end but it will be five years in October since I said 'Good bye' to him. It is a long time and I often wonder whether we shall find one another changed and even if our feelings about one another may not have changed when we see each other again. All these years in a prison camp cut off from a great many of the normal things of life, with no responsibilities, must make a difference to a man's character. I think sometimes that maybe I would have been wiser to have let someone else take his place as I was strongly tempted to. I know that sounds callous but perhaps when he does get home in the dim, distant future he may find me changed, as I am sure he will. I know the last five years have made me harder, more self-assertive and also much more self-sufficient.

4

Wards, Walks, Well-Being

February–March 1944

Saturday, 5 February

I woke up this morning [at home in Downham] to find a cloudless, blue sky and the sun shining and it has shone all day. It is surprising what a difference the sunshine makes to one's outlook on life. How much more cheerful and hopeful everything seems on a sunny day than on a dull one.

In the garden I found quite a carpet of snowdrops and as I was picking some to take back with me the sun felt beautifully warm on my shoulders. It must have been a very heavy frost during the night because in parts of the garden where the sun had not penetrated the ground was as hard as iron. The daffodils and irises were just showing green tips above the ground and in the afternoon when I went for a long walk I picked some catkins to take back with me for my room.

When I got in for tea my mother, to my great amazement, was debating as to whether she should put a tablecloth on or not. On my enquiring as to why it was necessary to think twice about it I was told that laundries are not allowed to take tablecloths now or little napkins. The only time I seem to read the newspaper now is when I am at home so I had missed all the bother about Churchill's letter at the Brighton by-election.*

I listened during the evening to a German news bulletin in which I heard of a great raid on London during the preceding night. In fact there were two raids and immense fires were burning over the target area when the second raid started. The Jerries lost fourteen aircraft, a small number, so the announcer observed, in proportion to the large number of aircraft employed. Actually I believe we claimed five aircraft down during the night and the two raids only touched Greater London.†

Monday, 7 February

Sister had certainly got that Monday morning feeling and passed it on to everyone else. It started over the Nestle's

---

* The Prime Minister had vigorously objected to the efforts of an Independent candidate in Brighton's by-election on 3 February both to profess personal support for the PM and oppose the official candidate of the government. Churchill saw this Independent as 'posing as a political friend' while at the same trying to injure the National Government that he led (*The Times*, 1 February 1944, p. 2; 2 February, p. 2; and 3 February, p. 2). A key assertion in Churchill's letter of 1 February (*The Times*, 2 February, p. 2) was that 'an altogether unwarranted optimism has taken hold of large numbers of our people. There is a vain and foolish belief that the war will soon be over, that it is now as good as won, and that anyone is free to push personal or party ends without regard to the common interest.'

† These weeks in the winter of 1944 came to be known as the 'Little Blitz', the first serious bombing of the capital since May 1941. 'London seems to be getting heavier and more determined air raids than it has for some time,' Kathleen remarked on 22 February. 'I suppose if they continue the children will be evacuated again.'

Milk. There was none for the babies' 9 o'clock feed. The dispenser with the keys of the cupboard where the Nestle's Milk was kept did not arrive until 9.30 and he is not very lavish with it as it is on points and [he] resents handing out an extra tin. Sister said she had got a double lot on Saturday to last the weekend and where had it gone, etc. As most of my off-duty had come at the weekend, Friday evening, Saturday day off and Sunday half-day, I had no idea, but as usual no one knew, so eventually that blew over. The next thing was that I committed the unforgivable sin of leaving a baby with a bottle in its cot when Matron did a round. As Sister had given this baby the bottle herself (an extra feed) and had asked me to take temperatures, give medicine and arrange about children going home, it was impossible for me to be feeding the baby at the same time. But apparently what I should have done was, on Matron's appearance in the ward, dumped the medicine and rushed to the baby in the cot and either fed the baby until Matron had gone or removed the feeding bottle until she had gone and then given it back to it again and continued with the medicines. Sister finished up her lecture by saying that Matron was most surprised at me and that there was no reason for making her think worse of me than she need. The last remark was too much for me and I retired to the kitchen with the offending feeding bottle and had a good laugh over the idiocy of the whole proceeding. I don't suppose for one minute that Matron even connected me with the feeding of the babies. She is very absent-minded and can hardly remember the names of nurses even in their third year let along connecting any one nurse with a particular job on a ward. She often forgets whether you are on night duty or day duty.

Friday, 11 February

Matron put in a late appearance about 11 to do the inventory and we all breathed a sigh of relief when she had disappeared and we had a drink of coffee to soothe our shattered nerves. The rest of the day passed off quietly and at 6 o'clock I went off duty and scrambled into mufti and off home.

As I went in at the front door I met my mother going out to a whist drive in aid of the local Prisoners-of-War Fund so I decided to go along too. I hastily tidied myself up a bit and got down to the village school where it was being held just as it was about to start. Half-way through there was an interval when a drink of tea and scones were provided. Sausage rolls could be bought for 3*d* for those who felt hungry and most people seemed to. After the whist drive one or two things were raffled, including a basket of eggs. The Vicar said he was sure it was highly illegal but hoped he would be bailed out in time for the Sunday Service. After the whist drive there was a dance which was great fun, though the floor was not all that one could wish for. I think country dances are fun because everyone knows everyone else and you get quite a variety of partners.

Monday, 14 February

We have been very busy on the ward today, with admissions and discharges and operations. This morning a little boy was brought in terribly burned. We did what we could for him but he died this evening. I always feel so hopelessly inadequate when it comes to consoling the relatives. I can never think of anything to say except that I am sorry, and to tell them to come up at 10 o'clock the following day for the death certificate always seems so cold and businesslike.

I don't quite know how he got burned. Someone said he had been left in his bed and found some matches and set himself alight. He rushed out into the street, his clothes ablaze, and a neighbour smothered the flames. He came into the Infirmary with the district nurse and it was not until about 5 in the evening that his mother appeared in a very upset condition. The trouble is that so many mothers are doing war-work and making no adequate provision for the care of their children. Wages are high up here now and after so many lean years of poverty and unemployment everyone is seizing the opportunity to make money whether they are obliged to do war-work or not.

Thursday, 17 February

I have had a sore throat all day and have been going around the babies wearing a mask, which did not seem to improve it. But if the babies get sore throats it will be just too bad for all concerned.

We were each given a couple of oranges this afternoon, patients and staff, and very nice they were too and not going bad in the middle as some people have been gloomily foretelling. This evening another nurse and I went to see *So Proudly We Hail*, the film of American Army Nurses in the Pacific. It was very good and we both felt like rushing off and joining the QAs [Queen Alexandra nurses] on the spot.* The trouble

---

* This 1943 film, directed by Mark Sandrich, starred Claudette Colbert, Paulette Goddard, Veronica Lake (her magnificent hair sometimes had to be pulled up under her nurse's cap) and George Reeves. The film follows a group of nurses sent to Bataan in the Philippines months after Pearl Harbor. The nursing portrayed appears glamorous. Patients and male medical staff are young, fit, and of course handsome, and there were few rigid rules of the sort enforced in British hospitals.

is one's enthusiasm is always strangled by red tape and front-line nursing only falls to the lot of a very small minority. For the majority of us it is a case of the 'trivial round etc.', though even for us nursing has its moments. It is surprising how different things appear to an onlooker than a participant.

This afternoon I was sitting in the middle of the ward beside the fire feeding one of the infants. The ward door was wide open and I vaguely noticed an elderly gentleman standing in the doorway looking in. He spoke to one of the cleaners and when he had gone she came in and told me that he had said he could not help stopping to admire the lovely picture I made sitting so peacefully in the ward surrounded by the children in cots etc. There was a low table with some daffodils and jonquils on between me and the doorway and I suppose it did make an attractive scene but in reality it was far from what it seemed. The baby I was holding would not take its feed and showed every sign of bringing back what it had already taken. I was late with it and two others were beginning to get restless and whimper. One of the bigger children had been sick on the floor and judging by the odour it seemed as if another was in a dirty bed. In the dim distance shut in the bathroom I could hear one of the juniors bathing a very reluctant new patient who was howling its head off, and just after the old chap had gone one of the new patients who had been silently struggling with its 'restrainers' broke free, tried to scramble out of its cot and fell on the floor with a resounding bang. He did not seem any the worse for his fall but the peace of the ward was rudely shattered for a few minutes.

Sunday, 27 February

I was just going to tea this afternoon when the phone rang and casualty informed us they were sending us a boy of 6 who had swallowed a halfpenny. By the time I came back from tea the boy was on the trolley ready to go to the theatre as the X-ray showed the coin was stuck in the oesophagus. His poor father, who had brought him in, was half demented. He was expecting an addition to the family any minute and was torn between a desire to rush back home and see how his wife was getting on and stay and see the boy back from the theatre. Eventually he decided that he had better go home, for which we were truly thankful as visitors fidgeting about are apt to get in the way. The boy came back from the theatre with the halfpenny safely removed and as soon as he came round from the anaesthetic wanted to know if he could have his halfpenny.

Tuesday, 29 February

It will be another four years before I shall write that date again. I wonder where I shall be and what I shall be doing.

The highlight of today was the fact that it was pay day and we were each presented with a very welcome little pay packet. Tonight there was a meeting of the Nurses Christian Movement and it was better attended than it has ever been. It seems to fluctuate. For weeks there are good attendances and then numbers of members just seem to dwindle away until sometimes there are only two or three members who attend regularly. A short time ago the attendances were at a very low ebb but the numbers have gradually increased again and tonight we had a record number of nurses there. Two nurses gave a 'testimony' about their conversion to a Christian life. It seems to me, though, that it is not really necessary for a Christian to have a definite sort of moment in their life when they turn to Christ. It is far more likely to happen gradually, which I am sure it does for a great many people.

One nurse spoke about Judgement Day when according to her the saints and sinners were going to be sorted out and it was very obvious which side she thought she was going to be on. Another nurse said she did not want to go to Heaven if there were going to be any Jerries or Japs there. She was serious about it too, having just read an account of German atrocities at Kiev.

Wednesday, 1 March

This afternoon the sun shone brightly but when I got out-side what an icy wind greeted me. There was quite a crowd of nurses waiting for the bus into Town this afternoon. A great many of them were tempted out like me by the bright sunshine, and of course yesterday was pay day and after existing for the last week of the month on about tuppence, £4 goes to your head and you spend like a millionaire. I really wanted amongst other things a present for my sister's birthday, but could not find anything. I also tried to make an appointment at the photographer's to have my photograph taken in uniform but without success. I did manage, though, to buy some blue woollen material to make myself an old jacket – 1¼ yards 54 inches wide [for] 5½ coupons, which took the last of my yellow page in my clothing coupon book. I also got two of my favourite shampoos in Woolworths and a couple of black dyes for future stocking dyeing, and got back in time to change hastily before tea. We were given another orange today, much to our surprise, and the patients all had an orange too.

Conditions on a ward varied from day to day, depending on the number of patients and the nature of their problems. On arriving for work on the morning of Saturday, 4 March, 'I found I had another baby,' Kathleen wrote, 'only 3 weeks and desperately ill, just hanging on to life by a feeble thread, which took up a lot of my time. Consequently the other infants did not get quite so much attention as usual and objected audibly.' This was a medical emergency she went on to describe in some detail.

Sunday, 5 March

This morning our weakly three-week-old baby went to the theatre for an operation for pyloric stenosis, which means that the muscles of the pylorus had become so thickened as to stop the passage of food from the stomach into the duodenum. Every feed the poor little thing had vomited back again immediately. Tiny babies for abdominal operations are bound to a well-padded cross and this baby looked so terribly pathetic swathed in cotton wool on this cross and she was vomiting continuously. When we came off duty for our half-day she was back from the theatre, miraculously still living. She was 6 pounds at birth but had dropped down to 5 pounds 8 ounces and was a in terribly poor condition so that it will be a real miracle if she does pull through.

I did not go home but a party of us went out to Ribchester, a quaint old place about 5 miles out of Blackburn. We went for a walk beside the river and then went in for tea at a hotel there. It was well after 5 and we were feeling very hungry so when we were offered chicken and chips we did not refuse and what a helping we got. Practically half a chicken and a great pile of chips and a plateful of bread and butter and of course a pot of tea and all for 4s 6d. Good thing it was the beginning of the month. We went to the Evening Service at the old church and then back to the Infirmary where, feeling thirsty, we made some tea and sat arguing about various matters such as should a boy and girl go away for holidays together, whether certain passages in the Old Testament can be taken as absolute fact or not, whether German prisoners-of-war are anxious to get back to Germany or not, and various other topics.

Monday, 6 March

A rumour has been going round and we are reluctantly realising that it is true that Matron is refusing to fix a date for nurses' holidays on account of the starting of a Second Front. Her argument is that if a Second Front is started she does not want her nurses scattered over the country and unable to get back at a time when they would be wanted most urgently. What grounds she has for thinking that a Second Front is imminent I don't know but she speaks as though it was likely to happen during the next few days. We had been promised a month's holiday this year under the Rushcliffe scheme [Committee on Nurses' Salaries, 1943] but if Matron won't give any holidays during the early part of this year I can see that we shall be lucky if we get three weeks.

Today has been a very 'routinish' (if there is such a word) day. Nothing of interest happened and I felt flat. Even the fact that Sister removed herself from the ward and I was left in charge did not lighten the atmosphere. I suppose we must all have had that Monday feeling.

Our baby who was operated on yesterday is still alive and even looks a tiny bit better. The great test is whether she will be able to retain her feeds. If she starts vomiting them up again then there is not much hope for her as no baby can be kept alive for any length of time by artificial feeding.

Tuesday, 7 March

This evening a crowd of us went to see *Jane Eyre* [starring Joan Fontaine and Orson Welles]. We wanted to see it very much and it was our only opportunity to go together this week. The snag was that we had a lecture from 7 to 8 and all day when we met we debated as to whether we should skip the lecture or whether we should attend the lecture and then rush madly off in the hope of getting into the last house soon after the picture had started. We had not made any decision when about 5 o'clock they rang round to say that the lecture was cancelled so we were able to go with a clear conscience. When we got down to the cinema the place was full so we had to stand in the queue, which was very small but which grew in a very few minutes to a considerable size. When we had waited there about fifteen minutes the booking-office opened for the stalls. We wanted the balcony as one member of the party said she could not see from the stalls so we stood on one side. There was no hope of a seat until the last house started and very soon the foyer was filled with a seething mass of people for the stalls, and people who wanted [a] balcony seat started to queue behind us but the tail end of the queue was soon obliterated by the people waiting for stalls. Eventually they decided to issue one row of *2s 9d* balcony seats. We did not want to pay *2s 9d* so I asked why there would be no empty *2s 3d* seats in the balcony when the last house started, so as a great favour they issued us the necessary number of *2s 3d* seats. Of course when the people came out at the end of the show there was a great stampede as there was no sort of queue, nothing but a mass of people with tickets for the stalls. Eventually we managed to squeeze our way up to the balcony where there was plenty of room before the lights went down but people who we knew behind us in the queue had to wait about fifteen minutes before they were issued with tickets and so missed the beginning of the show. Blackburn is not used to great queues for pictures and does not seem to know how to manage them.*

Jane Eyre hardly seems the type of picture to attract such big audiences yet I think they were saying it was years since this picture house had such packed houses. It was a well-played picture which seemed to re-capture the atmosphere of the book. It seems impossible that less than 100 years ago such inhuman treatment could have been meted out to children. It brought home very sharply too how hard life was for girls who had to earn their own living when there was so little scope for them, how unusual for them to be travelling alone or to do so many of the things we take for granted. It makes me feel thankful that I lived in a more enlightened era even though it is in the middle of a World War.

Wednesday, 8 March

I was off duty this morning and went out with my friends to do a spot of shopping locally where it is not necessary to change out of uniform. We thought as we were out we would drop into Mrs R _____'s for some coffee. She keeps a small

---

* In 1939 there were sixteen cinemas in Blackburn with a seating capacity of some 16,000, about an eighth of the borough's population (Derek Beattie, *Blackburn: The Development of a Lancashire Cotton Town* [Halifax: Ryburn, 1992], p. 160 and the same author's *A History of Blackburn* [Lancaster: Carnegie, 2007], p. 288). Film-going was central to most people's leisure. A year later, on Saturday, 3 March 1945, Kathleen wrote that 'Tonight another nurse and I decided to patronise the local flea-pit known as the Savoy. We had omitted to book anywhere and knew we would have no chance of getting in at any of the other cinemas on a Saturday night.'

general shop almost at the gates of the Infirmary and has a room at the back where she serves coffee etc. but which looks as though it is used as a living room when the shop is closed. At one time no one was ever seen in there but nurses, and she used to keep chocolate biscuits for us to have with our coffee but latterly it has been discovered by the officers of a company stationed down the road and it is sometimes impossible to get in. It is the only place where we can go in uniform so it is rather a nuisance to find the place taken over by the Army, where we used to take our ease in front of the fire. Of course some of the nurses like it better this way but the majority of us prefer to have the place to ourselves. This particular morning we were a bit earlier than usual and were ensconced in the two most comfortable chairs before anyone else arrived, but chocolate biscuits were off the menu and we were offered jam sandwiches which we firmly declined.

Thursday, 9 March

Today I have had neuralgia all day and have taken every form of dope we have available but without any relief. I think it must have been the result of washing my hair last night and going to bed with it still damp. When I went to the old sitting room with the intention of drying my hair in front of the fire I found a 'Keep out' notice on the door and remembered that we had a nurse with scabies and that the sitting room was reserved for her use. I was off duty this evening with my day off tomorrow so I came home. It was a lovely springlike evening after a very foggy day and I should normally have enjoyed the ride home but all I could think of was a pillow on which I could rest my aching head. I had some supper as soon as I got home and then went straight to bed but with the usual perversity of life the pain was easing by the time I was ready for bed.

Friday, 10 March

I went with a girl I know to look over an old house known as Downham Mill, though why it is called a Mill I don't know as there is no sign of it ever having been one [it had been, but not for many years]. There is quite a big stream at the bottom of the garden, which incidentally makes the place rather damp, so maybe they might have done a bit of gardening there at some remote date. It is really an old farm house but the farmer moved to another farm and the surrounding land is being farmed by the Estate. The house is well away from the road and there is only a rough sort of track leading up to it. As we walked along it, everything seemed so quiet and peaceful. The only sounds were those of the rooks in the trees above us and the murmur of the stream and I looked at my watch and thought this time tomorrow I shall be back in the hurry and bustle of the ward, working probably with one eye on the clock, hoping that I shall get off to tea fairly punctually so that I shall get a decent cup of tea and not dishwater. I thought how lucky people were who could go out for a country walk whenever they felt inclined and stroll home for tea at their own fireside; whose lives were calm. Barely had the thoughts crossed my mind when my companion said 'I do envy you, your busy life and all the fresh people you meet and the interesting things you must see and do every day. My life is so monotonous. I seldom meet anyone fresh and I always know exactly what is going to happen from day to day.' For health and family reasons she has not been called up and she was most amazed when I said that at that very moment I was envying her. I really know that I should get bored if I did live a life of quietness but I do enjoy it occasionally and I do love the country.

Saturday, 11 March

The little baby of 3 weeks who was operated on last Sunday is still very much alive in spite of our gloomy forebodings. She is taking her feeds well and keeping most of them down. It will be a great triumph for all concerned if she does recover. She is the first child of two elderly parents and it is unlikely that they will be able to have any more so it will be a great blow to them if she dies [but see below, 30 March 1944].

We had two children of 18 months admitted yesterday. One pulled a cup of boiling water over on itself, the other pulled a pan of boiling water over. The first one is doing quite well but the other was running a temperature of 107°F tonight, the highest temperature I have ever taken, though I do know it is possible to have an even higher one and still live. She has been put on sulphanilamide drugs, which in the majority of cases effect wonderful cures if the patient can take them.

Sunday, 12 March

Sunday once again. Sister started her holiday yesterday afternoon so I was in charge this afternoon and evening. The ward was full as usual but we did not have any admissions so we had a fairly easy time once the visitors had gone and the children had calmed down. Visiting hours on Sunday are from 2 to 3 for the children and it is quite long enough. The children get tired and over-excited and the howling there is when the porter comes in at 3 o'clock and shouts 'Clear the ward, please,' and the visitors depart, needs to be heard to be believed. Twenty children shrieking on the top note need to be heard to be believed. They are very sweet, though. I went quietly into the ward just before going off duty just to see that everything was in order and I saw a little figure in a long white nightgown going from cot to cot. I picked it up and found it was Judy, a little girl of 3, a lovely looking child with a heart shaped face, blue eyes, curly fair hair and a real Cupid's bow for a mouth. She has a badly scalded arm which just won't heal. I asked her what she was doing out of her cot and she looked at me solemnly for a minute and then said she was looking for her mummy. Poor little thing. I felt like crying but she went back to bed quite peacefully and was asleep before I came out of this ward.

Monday, 13 March

All our Irish nurses – and they form quite a high percentage of the staff here – are very perturbed at the restriction on journeys to Ireland [travel there had just been prohibited]. Quite a few of them are from Eire so things may be a bit difficult for them. It is strange when you come to think about it how little we bother whether the Irish nurses come from the North or from the South of Ireland and yet at the moment it really does make quite a difference. We just say they are Irish and leave it at that.*

---

* Eire, though officially neutral, was suspected of harbouring Nazi agents and sympathizing with the German cause, or at the least of undermining Britain's security. With plans for the Second Front well underway, the British government was intent on minimizing the prospect of harmful communications and espionage across the Irish Sea.

There is still a lot of bother going on over the food. The new supervisor seems to think her chief concern should be to cut down expenses. With that end in view one presumes we have been cut down to one sausage for breakfast, no milk pudding as an alternative choice to the 'stodge' or whatever it may be for dinner and she even wanted to cut down our margarine ration but here Matron put her foot down firmly and refused to allow her to do that. I must say, though, the food has been better cooked since she came, though Matron seems to think otherwise.

Tuesday, 14 March

Today I decided to see what I could do in the way of persuading Matron to give me a week or two's holiday, so accordingly at 9.30 I presented myself outside Matron's office with another nurse who wanted a note from Matron to the effect that she had had a shirt and one or two other things stolen so that she could claim a few coupons. A great deal of petty pilfering goes on here, especially since the issue of clothing coupons got so small. Stockings in particular go in the twinkling of an eye.* I wanted a fortnight's holiday in May so that I should have four clear months to swat for the Final exam but Matron had other ideas. She said every senior nurse wanted May and she could not fit us all in, especially with the Second Front coming along and we might have to be recalled at a moment's notice, and so forth and so on. Then I dropped my demand for a fortnight and said could she fit

---

* Coupons were required (along with cash) for all purchases of new clothes; this severely restricted additions to a woman's wardrobe, which was consequently likely to wear out. Clothes rationing had minimal effect on wealthy women with large wardrobes.

a week in and she has given me the third week in May. I am not intending to go away but shall relax at home for a week, then perhaps at the end of the summer when I get the rest of my holiday and have my exam behind me I shall be able to go away and enjoy myself.

Thursday, 16 March

Nothing of very much note happened today except that this afternoon a woman came to see one of the children and practically accused the nurses of walking off with two apples she had left in the boy's locker. One of the nurses had certainly collected them from his locker because it is a rule of the ward that the children must not have eatables in their lockers. All sweets, biscuits, fruit etc. are pooled and the children get a sweet and fruit after their mid-day meal and biscuits with their milk in the morning and their drink at supper time. The Sister or nurse-in-charge locks the eatables in a cupboard and they are given out daily for the children but some mothers don't see why their little offspring should not be allowed to eat how and when they like and trouble arises. We explained this to this woman but she said she would not have left them if she had known that, whereupon I unlocked the cupboard and fortunately the apples had not been used so I handed them back to her. Whereupon she climbed down and said she would not take them back, and so on. I know she thought the nurses had taken them for themselves and was taken aback when I produced them. They were two large green cooking apples and no temptation to anyone, I might say. I laughed about it afterwards but it is difficult to keep your temper sometimes.

Friday, 17 March

I did not do anything very much during the day [in Downham] as I had one of my appalling headaches. They are getting so bad and so frequent that I am beginning to think I must have a brain abscess or tumour or some other kind of intra-cranial pressure. I took quite a few tablets and it improved enough for me to come back to Blackburn early and see Bette Davis in *Now, Voyager* [1942]. It was very good. Bette Davis was quite up to her usual standard but I think it had an unsatisfactory ending. I suppose she might find some consolation in looking after her lover's child but if it was his child she also was his wife's child equally as much. She would have done much better to have made a clean break and married the other man, even though she did not love him in the same way. A clean break is terrible at the time but how much better in the long run when you have won through to peace and probably happiness again than to drift along in an unsatisfactory sort of way. In this kind of film there is generally someone who wants to marry the girl even though she is in love with a married man and it always maddens me when she refuses him and her chance of living a normal life.*

* The film's ending shows the 12-year-old child, unwanted by her mother, as the new emotional link between Bette Davis's character and the man she loves, the girl's married father (Paul Heinreid), with whom socially acceptable love is impossible. This unconventional threesome is portrayed at the end as committed to one another and in the process of forging deep emotional ties. Kathleen appears to have doubted that such abnormal arrangements could give a single woman much long-term happiness.

Saturday, 18 March

I have just found my old fountain pen after losing it for a couple of days and though the top has had first aid applied to it in the shape of a strip of strapping plaster and the ink filling lever has to be raised by a pin before I can refill the pen with ink, I have been most miserable without it. It is surprising how often one wants a pen on duty, for filling in temperature charts, writing labels on bottles etc., filling in the inevitable forms for X-ray, laboratory and so on, admitting patients, writing reports and a hundred and one other things. I daresay I could get a new fountain pen as I believe there are still a few to be had but I am fond of this one, temperamental though it is, flooding one minute and drying up the next, even though it has just been refilled.

The news on the 'Kitchen Front' in this Infirmary has been most stormy of late. The new supervisor has insulted practically everyone, not excluding Matron, who dared to set foot anywhere near the kitchen even though they were on a legitimate errand. I have been lucky enough not to come in personal contact with her though I have seen her tearing from kitchen to dairy or storeroom as though she had the cares of the world on her shoulders. Today she has not put in an appearance and opinion seems to be divided as to whether it is her weekend or whether she has gone for good of her own free-will or otherwise. In addition to the non-appearance of the supervisor several daily women did not turn up either which meant that those who did had extra work to do and one of the ward maids packed her bag and went off in a temper over something trifling. There are very few of the domestic staff living in and they have to rely a great deal on daily women for work on the wards as well as cleaning etc., and with all due respect to them it seems to take most of them all their time to put one foot in front of the other, let alone all the hard scrubbing etc. the poor old things get to do.

Sunday, 19 March

It is my Sunday half-day today and day off tomorrow, which is very nice when it comes together like that but not so nice when you think you have all the rest of the week and maybe until the end of the following week before you get another day off. My mother went down to Bucks yesterday to see her father. She thought it would be wiser to go now than to wait until the Second Front started and travel was restricted. It is surprising how sure we all seem to be that there will be a Second Front this year. People stare at you in amazement when you suggest there might not be one. I hope that we shall get on with it and yet I dread it when I think how many thousands will be killed who are alive and enjoying life now.

My father was quite pleased to see me when I arrived home. He was sitting in solitary state in front of the fire looking a bit lost when I got in. I dragged myself away from the fire after tea to go out for a walk with him. It was bitterly cold – at least I thought so. My father thought it was fresh and I was thankful when he suggested calling in at a pub for a drink. I rather think he had that in mind when we started out and I was quite ready to fall in with his suggestion. On the way home we met a girl who was a Nursing Auxiliary at the same Emergency Hospital as myself. She has drifted from nursing into cooking at an Emergency Hospital for chronic cases outside Blackpool and as she said she was not going back until Monday night I asked her to have tea with me tomorrow.

Monday, 20 March

When I got up this morning and looked out of the window and saw Pendle Hill swathed in mist and only the lower slopes showing I knew there was not much prospect of a fine day and I was right. Before 10 o'clock it started to rain just a fine drizzle, which kept on all day, so I did not go out until I had to, at 8.30 tonight to come back. I did not see anyone to speak to until my friend arrived just before tea, but the day simply flew by. I can never understand people being bored when they are alone. There always seems so much to do, and I must confess that I can sometimes feel very bored when I am with a crowd. I often think I would make a good hermit. I suppose it is the reaction from the communal life one leads in Hospital.

Tuesday, 21 March

I see in the paper this morning Germany has occupied Hungary. What a stir it would have made once yet now it seems to be regarded almost with indifference. I suppose we shall now have refugees, Hungarians and a free Hungarian Government set up in our country. We shall soon be the most cosmopolitan of all nations bar none, with all the different nationalities who seek refuge here as well as the Forces of the Allied Nations.* I see fighting is still raging in and around Cassino. It makes me feel very uneasy when thinking of the Second Front that we cannot dislodge the Germans from one small town in Italy.

* Wendy Webster, *Mixing It: Diversity in World War Two Britain* (Oxford: Oxford U.P., 2018).

To come back to problems a bit nearer home. There is the food problem still raging here. There was a special meeting of the Board of Directors this afternoon and one nurse from each year attended it, one staff nurse, one Sister and one doctor, and they each had their say. Matron and the Assistant Matron were there and now that the supervisor has gone they were on the defensive but I think the members of the staff got a fair hearing. The Sister Tutor who was there put her foot in it properly by remarking that when she was in training they only had jam twice a week, when the subject of teas was mentioned. We get it every day except Sunday when we get a sad-looking lump of dough supposed to be cake instead. I know that nurses never have been very well-fed but the awkward part of it is that now there is so little you can buy to supplement your rations. As we never see our ration books there is nothing much you can get except a few cakes if you are lucky and chips if the chips shops are open.

Wednesday, 22 March

Just an ordinary routine day with nothing of note occurring. One of my babies went home, which has brought the number down to three, which gives me time to take a little interest in the other small patients. The baby who had pyloric stenosis is doing quite well and putting on a few ounces in weight though it will be some time before it looks like anything but a little wizened old woman. We had a little girl of 2 brought in this morning who had drunk something out of a bottle labelled 'Poison'. Her people had not the faintest idea what was in the bottle, which they brought along with them. The bottle was empty and did not smell of anything; neither did the breath of the child and there were no signs of any burns in her mouth so we are hoping it is a false alarm and that the bottle did not contain its original contents.

Another little girl admitted today had been knocked down by a car and except for a few grazes did not show any visible signs of injury. She had vomited repeatedly since the accident, though, which normally indicates some form of head injury. Her mother told me in a very matter-of-fact way that she had lost her other child in here with meningitis. People do take things so differently, some calmly, some hysterically, others almost lightly. There is no doubt that a hysterical parent passes on his or her anxiety to the child, who is invariably more difficult to deal with.

Some of the older children had a very interesting conversation about Jesus. One little boy of 7 said that Jesus was with us even though we could not see him and that Jesus was making him better – was making all of them better in fact. 'Jesus not making me better,' said 3-year [old] Judith, leaping about in her cot. 'Who is then?' said the small boy. 'Nurse,' said Judith confidently.

Saturday, 25 March

I was off duty at 6 o'clock this evening and was thinking of doing a few odd jobs such as darning stockings, washing my hair etc. but was persuaded to go for a walk instead. The sun was shining and there was not a scrap of wind so I did not really need much persuading. It was just the right kind of evening for a walk and we walked out of Blackburn and across some fields to a village called Tockholes. Whichever way you go out of Blackburn you have to climb and when you look down on the Town all you see is a misty haze with factory chimneys projecting above it, especially on calm days when there is no wind to disperse the smoke. It was beautifully fresh on these hills and you really felt you could breathe properly after being shut up all day in a blacked-out ward with artificial lighting. I find that the pure light of day is very dazzling to the eyes after groping about in poorly lighted rooms most of the time.

We watched the sunset from the hills and listened to a lark singing above us and it was dark before we finally reached the outskirts of Blackburn once more. We knew we should be too late for supper so stopped to buy fish and chips on our way back. A woman who was serving behind the counter was an ex-patient and remembered me, though I could not recollect her, and she would not let me pay for my fish and chips. She said it was a small return for all I had done for her and I don't really think I could have done so much or I should have remembered her as she had been in fairly recently. Some people are grateful for what others take for granted.

Sunday, 26 March

This morning was bright and sunny and we walked down to the Cathedral for Matins. I must say I like the Service in the Cathedral much better than some churches where the atmosphere reminds me more of a mission-hall. I enjoy listening to the organ and choir-boys' voices, which I think have an unearthly sound and I always come away feeling uplifted. I expect, though, that it is more of a sensual feeling than a spiritual one. We walked back envying the people who had the whole day free and got in just in time to get changed. In fact I was not ready when the dinner bell sounded and tore along to the dining room putting on my cap as I went.

When I got back on duty I heard that Sister was ill and was not coming back for another week and that I was spending another week on children's ward, so that rules out the Women's Surgical ward for me for the time being.

After supper quite a crowd of us listened to Mr Churchill's speech. His review of the war situation up to date was quite clear but there was nothing in it that we had not already seen in the papers, and as for post-war planning, well we know that it will be necessary to have plans and that they cannot be improvised in a few weeks, but the war had been going on so long now that it is getting difficult to visualize the time when the war is over. One begins to feel that you have lived most of your life under wartime conditions and that the war will never end. Personally I think that if Mr Churchill resigns when the war is over he will go down in history as one of the greatest Prime Ministers of all times but that if he carries on after the war he will not be so popular. His policy as regards social reform and so on seems to be to add on a bit to the existing system.

Tuesday, 28 March

We have had the most wonderful spring weather this last day or two. If only it will last, but that I am afraid is too much to expect. It has been grand to go out without an icy wind nipping you and to feel the sun warm on your back. I had not really intended to go out in my off-duty today but when my friend appeared and suggested it I could not resist and there will be plenty of wet days in which to write up lectures.

We walked into the Town and round Corporation Park and had some tea before we came back. Whilst we were having tea my friend told me she had just been reading an article on the Prison Nursing Service and thought she would like to join when she had taken the necessary training. Personally it would not make any great appeal to me. If I want to do something outside ordinary institutional life I think I shall do industrial nursing. But she is quite interested in social reform so it might suit her quite well. I should think it might tend to make you take rather a poor view of human nature and suspicious of your fellow creatures.

Wednesday, 29 March

We are very busy on the ward and have six extra cots in and no children really ready to go home. One or two of them are seriously ill, one with TB meningitis and the other with peritonitis we are not expecting to pull round. The one with TB meningitis is an only child and her father is in Italy, which makes things very hard for her mother, who is quite young. The child is barely conscious. One can occasionally get a little response from her but she is too ill to recognise anyone and it is heartbreaking to see the mother standing beside the cot crying. But what can one do? It would be cruel to raise false hopes of a recovery which is a most remote possibility.

Thursday, 30 March

We have been busy again today and I have yet another baby in. It has had a club-foot from birth and has come to have it straightened. His mother walked with a peculiar lopsided gait I noticed so I should not be surprised if it is hereditary. We had a little girl in when I first came on the ward with a congenital dislocation of the hip and her mother had the same thing. It is strange that people should want to marry cripples. Do they never think of the possibility of having deformed children?

The baby with pyloric stenosis who no one ever thought would live was discharged today by the surgeon. But when I rang up the parents to tell them the glad news they said they thought their other child was developing whooping cough so would we keep her another day or two until they could arrange something.

I came home this evening. The day had been quite bright and I was amazed when I first caught sight of Pendle Hill to see it covered in snow. The mere sight of it made me shiver and decide the temperature had dropped several degrees. I was told that there had been a blinding snowstorm during the afternoon which must have been very local as we did not get one in Blackburn.

Friday, 31 March

It is amazing how one gets used to things. When I first came to the Infirmary I found the mattresses painfully hard but now I find I sleep better on them than on the softer ones at home.

I came back early and met another nurse and we went to see *The Lamp Still Burns*. Personally I thought it was good, but as a recruiting agent for the nursing profession, if that had been its aim, it would have been hopeless. Seeing it now as a third-year nurse with two years' previous hospital experience I could afford to laugh but had I seen it before I started it would have put me off altogether. All the things the new nurse does that are wrong – how many have I done too. Giving a telephone message direct to a doctor, wearing cuffs when I should not be wearing them and not wearing them when I should be, and lots of petty things that irked me because like Nurse Clark of the film I was older than most of the nurses. But thank goodness there is not all that talk of discipline, nor is the Matron the holy terror the Matron in the film appears to be, but as far as discipline goes things are definitely slack here compared with some hospitals I have heard about.

It is strange how dramatic things appear when you do them on the screen even if you are used to doing the same thing several times a week, e.g. taking a patient to theatre, getting another patient ready for operation and so on.

5

Watching, Waiting

April–June 1944

Saturday, 1 April

April the first but we were much too busy to have time for the lighter side of life on the ward this morning so there were no jokes played on anyone. The only indication was that a girl from the lab appeared for the *Grave Diggers Journal* and as we had been forewarned we sent her on to another ward. In fact the poor girl did a tour of the whole building in search of this elusive journal, each department or ward passing her on to the next. Personally I felt rather sorry for the poor kid. She is one of the youngsters that are employed here straight from school to do a few odd jobs such as going round the ward collecting specimens for the lab, and I daresay she had previously been sent on quite legitimate errands for things she had never heard of before. They said she was a cheeky kid and it would do her good but I sympathised with her.

A favourite joke on a new nurse is to send her to another ward for a glass hammer and a bucket of steam and I believe one of the night nurses got caught that way.*

We received the unwelcome news this evening that Sister would be back on duty tomorrow so there was a general swing round to get things a bit shipshape before she returned. I had to go to Matron to report that one of the junior nurses had a sore throat and Matron packed her off to bed to everyone's amazement, I might say, as she had no temperature. Usually you get no notice taken of any complaint unless you have a temperature of 100°F. This left us a nurse short to add to the general confusion so I guess things won't be as tidy as they might be. We have a grand excuse with the ward packed to capacity, though. We have four cots and two beds down the middle of the ward where normally we have nothing but the desk and tables with flowers on.

Sunday, 3 April

It is surprising how whatever you do just now, talk of the Second Front comes up. A nurse on the children's ward had a fortnight's holiday because her brother, who is in the Regular Army, is home from India after six years' service abroad. She started her holiday on Thursday and went down to the station in her off-duty this afternoon to book her ticket. At the booking office she was told that she got the ticket in advance at her own risk because if the Second Front started

---

* In 1945, 1 April happened to fall on Easter Sunday, and this, Kathleen wrote, 'rather curbed the annual April Fool's day custom but one of the junior nurses from our ward was sent along to the theatre for a "stainless dye". The theatre staff, who must have been half asleep, took her request in all seriousness and sent her round to X-ray to see if they had it there.'

all passenger trains might be cancelled. She was quite upset about it as she lives on the North-East coast and it is a long tedious journey for her, not like the short trips on the bus or train some of us take to get home. Personally I think she need not worry about the Second Front so soon. Some people seem to think the bombing of the Continent will be our only contribution to the Second Front and sometimes I almost agree with them. The Russians are doing so well and we seem to have reached a deadlock in Italy.

Tuesday, 4 April

There is a great air of excitement about the place today. The written part of the Preliminary State Examination has been held here today and the Final will be held tomorrow. About fifty-five candidates sat today. About twenty of them were our own nurses and the others came in from various other hospitals in and around Blackburn. I can hardly believe that the next time I shall be sitting my Finals. Three years seems such a long time when you begin but how quickly they pass, and I have the awful feeling that I shall never know enough to pass. When the hospitals all adopt the idea of letting the nurses go off the wards to swat for a week or two before their exam it will be a great improvement. It is terribly difficult to concentrate after a hard day's work.

Thursday, 6 April

I had a rotten night and felt awful when I got up. The night staff nurse was in the ward kitchen when we went on duty and she said I looked like death warmed up. They took my temperature, which was 100°, and said I was being a fool when I did not want to go off sick. The night staff nurse said she had no patience with people who made martyrs of themselves – look at Nurse M_____ who stayed on duty when she had a temperature and had now got rheumatic fever. That shook me somewhat, and then someone else said if it was flu I was spreading infection, so in face of all these arguments plus the fact that I did not feel capable of doing a day's work I said I would let it be reported. I was glad to get back into bed and presently the Home Sister appeared with soda-water and fruit drinks, gargle, thermometer and more tablets and by the time the doctor came to see me in the evening I had no temperature and was feeling quite fit and furious with myself for being persuaded into going off duty.

My friends dropped in to see me with various things to read, amongst them being *Grey and Scarlet* [1944], which is a collection of letters from the war areas written by Army Sisters on Active Service. There are letters from every one of the battle fronts, from France, Crete, North Africa, Malta, Singapore. There is nothing flowery about these letters, just plain statements, of work done, hasty evacuations, being bombed and torpedoed, going dirty and often hungry in some of these withdrawals where things change so quickly that one minute they are with an organised party and then they are alone fending for themselves.

Friday, 7 April

Good Friday. I heard the church bells ringing for Service as I lay in bed. The sun shone and I wished I was back on duty with the prospect of finishing at 4.30 and going home with my day off Saturday. I am feeling much better and am eager to be up and about again, though I guess a day in bed will do me no harm.

I sleep in the basement – an expression Matron does not like us to use – and it really does give a wrong impression as there is at least a 6-foot drop from my bedroom window and I look out on to a part of the garden with some trees and flowering shrubs and over a low wall on to a residential street. The Infirmary is built over the crown of a hill, which gives all these different levels which are so infuriating when you first come. The view from the bedroom I had on the third floor, a view I could only get by craning my neck round an ornamental gable, was very different from my present one. From the third floor you seemed far and away above the tallest factory chimney and look down on Blackburn lying in a haze of smoke. Even the trams that travel along the road beyond the hospital grounds look like toy ones.

Monday, 10 April

I had been told that I was going on the medical ward this week so I got quite an agreeable surprise this morning when I was read out for the men's surgical ward. They were not terribly busy on the ward. Being Easter Monday the surgeons only had a short list of operations and up to the time we came off duty the usual holiday casualties had not appeared. The [annual Easter fun] Fair usually provides a fair crop of them but this year I did not hear of any interesting ones. My friends tried to persuade me to go boating with them as we were all off in the afternoon but I really felt too limp to be bothered and laid down and had a little sleep instead. It is amazing how even the smallest illness can take it out of you.

Tuesday, 11 April

My worst fears were realized this morning when I was read out for the medical ward. It is a ward not one nurse out of ten really likes and nurses have been known to be so miserable there that they have gone to Matron to ask for a move. It is a ward everyone has to do as it is the only medical ward in the hospital. It consists of three wards and has male and female patients and is run by one Sister. As usual it is the Sister and not the work that the nurses dislike. I must say, though, that to be a popular Sister and to run a ward efficiently a person needs to have exceptional qualities, though I am sure it could be done. A great deal of the trouble here, I am sure, is that most of the Sisters are elderly. They cannot forget that they had to work much harder and longer hours than we do. They have been here for years and are very set in their ways. There is only one way of doing things and that is their way so what is right on one ward is wrong on another.[*]

However, I managed to get through the day without tripping up too much. Sister was off duty in the afternoon and I was off duty in the evening so I did not see too much of her. I had a lecture at 7.30 so was not able to go out. I wanted to see Irving Berlin's *It's the Army*, as most people say it is good, but this is my only [free] evening this week so I guess I shall not see it.[†]

Thursday, 13 April

Tonight we have had another dance in the Nurses Home. We have them in the nurses' dining room, which has a good

[*] 'There are popular wards and unpopular wards,' Kathleen had observed the previous month (24 March), 'usually depending on the Sister in charge.'
[†] The correct title of this 1943 film is *This is the Army*, a morale-boosting musical comedy.

parquet floor, but this time instead of having a band we had a radio-gram. I must say in some ways it was an improvement as the radio-gram does not need such long intervals for refreshment as the bandsmen appear to. It was a good dance (tickets 1s 6d) and for once there was as many men if not more than girls. The only snag about these dances here is that one has to relieve on the ward so that the night nurse can go to the dance until 11 o'clock. We each relieve for so long depending on the number of day nurses available on the ward for relief. In our case it was only for half an hour but it means that it is not worthwhile changing into mufti until after you have done your spell of relief. I relieved from 10 to 10.30 and by the time I had gone over to my room and changed it was past 11 and the refreshments were finished. However, I danced practically every dance for a couple of hours which I find plenty after tearing round the ward all day.

The dance finished at 1 and then volunteers among the nurses carry the tables in and set them for breakfast in the morning. They also want volunteers for washing up too so our dances are quite strenuous affairs for the nurses, though I must say there never seems any lack of volunteers. It is strange how you come off duty feeling dog tired and thinking that it is almost too much bother to get changed and go out and then once you are in mufti and at the dance you forget how tired you were feeling such a short time ago.

Saturday, 15 April

It has been a lovely spring day [in Downham]. It was grand to see the hedges and trees bursting into leaf again and all the daffodils in bloom. There is a kind of General Post going on in the village at the moment. About half a dozen families are moving round, some because they want a larger house and others because they want a small one. We are moving into a bigger house next door ['Hillcrest'] but we cannot move for a week or two because the people living in it cannot move until the house they are going into is empty. The reason why all these moves are possible is because an old lady who would have been a hundred had she lived another month or two died a few weeks ago, and as she lived alone that meant an empty house in the village and so the swap round started [all houses belonged and still belong to the Assheton family].

The people who will be occupying our present home have already started to dig the garden and plant seeds. My father has been offered the same amenities in the garden belonging to the house we shall be living in but so far he has not, I regret to say, started 'digging for Victory'. At heart I think he is pleased to have a break. He is a Londoner and does not really understand a great deal about gardening though he does manage to produce some quite decent potatoes.

When I got back to the Infirmary I found a parcel waiting for me from my brother. It contained a reading lamp he promised to make for me last time he was home on leave. He is not stationed where there are many facilities for recreation and in his spare time he has made a couple of reading lamps for my mother out of brass candlesticks and when I saw them I wanted one too for my room here. In common with most bedrooms in institutions it is lighted by one bulb high up in the middle of the room and is a very poor light for doing anything by.

On Sunday, 16 April Kathleen mentioned a new feature of the war for the citizens of Blackburn. 'In the afternoon I took one of my *friends home with me. We walked down to the station as I thought it would be best to go by train and saw the Americans who came to the Town last week getting acquainted with the local girls. Am afraid the West Kents will not get so much attention now.'* One local woman (b. 1926) recalled 'the welcome influx of glamourous American GIs' into Blackburn in 1944. 'They were so friendly and cheerful, which rubbed off on all of us. They loved to dance and had money to spend. Above all, I could hardly believe how polite and courteous they were . . . My friends and I couldn't help flirting with our American visitors, most of whom were great dancers, good fun, and very respectful of women.'* While some other recollections of US troops in East Lancashire have found their way into print,[†] their presence (most for only a few months) was almost entirely unreported in Blackburn's wartime press.

The facts of war were rarely far from Kathleen's mind, at least when she was away from the Infirmary, whether from sights or sounds or conversation. One evening (24 April) she saw a 1943 film, Chetniks, about guerrilla warfare in Yugoslavia. 'It was not as bloodthirsty as I anticipated.' On Saturday, 22 April, 'Coming back in the bus tonight [from Downham to Blackburn] the conductor sat down beside me and started to show me photographs out of his wallet of his sons in the Army, as though I knew them. I was a bit perplexed at first until I realised that his wife had been a patient on a ward I was on last year and he had recognised me. One of his sons is a prisoner-of-war, another was killed in Italy in February and the other one is in India. It is strange how misfortune comes to one family and how another may get off scot free.'

* Margaret Ford, with Jacquie Buttriss, *A Daughter's Choice* (London: Pan, 2019), p. 185.
† *Lancashire Evening Telegraph*, 22 February 1999, p. 14.

Wednesday, 19 April

When we went into the dining room there on each table was a bowl of salad, beautifully arranged with lettuce lining the bowl and various vegetables cut into neat cubes in the centre. We had barely recovered from the shock when a large slice of corned beef and another one of Spam was placed in front of us and then a bottle of salad cream left us speechless. Then I remembered reading in the *Northern Daily Telegraph* last week a paragraph about the Blackburn Infirmary being one of the first hospitals in the country to realise the value of a nutritious, appetising, and properly balanced diet, both to the patients and hard-working staff [15 April 1944, p. 3]. It went on to say we were temporarily without a supervisor but that we no doubt should have one within the next few weeks. It would have been more to the point to say that we were temporarily with one than without one. The one and only food supervisor we had a few weeks ago just disappeared and there has been no mention of one taking her place. But to come to the point in this paragraph, it said we were having a visit today from a dietician attached to the Ministry of Health and I remembered remarking at the time that we could be sure of a good meal today.

Sunday, 23 April

The ward I am on is open again now, no further cases of dysentery having arisen, so there was a record crowd of visitors. In theory only two visitors are allowed at a time for each patient but there are few wards where this rule is strictly enforced, though if we consider the ward is getting too full or that any particular patient is getting over tired we go round and remind them of this rule. On visiting days here the most junior nurse on duty goes round with a collecting box, the money being used for extras for the ward such as vases for flowers, covers for cabinets, crockery for the night nurses, cutlery for the patients and so on. It always seems to me a strange custom and I often wonder whether it is the same in all the voluntary hospitals. I should have thought that all these things should be provided by the hospital and not dependent on the generosity of visitors. This Infirmary is supposed to be comparatively well off as far as voluntary hospitals go and the Chairman of the Board seems to think that should the Government National Health Plan come into force the Infirmary will not be as well-supported [from voluntary donations] and consequently lose a lot of its income.

During the following ten days Kathleen recorded a number of events and outlooks. On 27 April she heard of the condition of the baby who had suffered from pyloric stenosis, whom nobody had expected 'to survive the operation let alone go home in good condition. Her aunt said she was thriving and had put on weight and gained 12 ounces during the last week. It is grand to know she is doing so well and makes one's work feel more worthwhile.' On Sunday the 30th she was in Downham. 'After tea we went for a long ramble across the fields and I picked a lovely bunch of bluebells and marigolds to take back to my room. The only snag is they don't last very long in water but they stood the train journey back quite well – and what a train journey. We were packed in like sardines and there were so many people standing in the carriage that it was impossible to move your feet. But it is worth it to get away from smoky ugly Blackburn for a half day and into the fresh country air.' On 1 May she touched upon what would soon become a prominent theme in her diary. Matron had heard that some of the hospital's State Registered

Nurses might be transferred to other places and Kathleen observed that she 'will be in a flap with this additional complication and the impending Second Front. She has got "Second Frontitis" and whatever you go to see her about, even a broken thermometer, seems to have some connection in her mind with the Second Front.' Three days later (4 May) she wrote about a matter of personal concern. 'My mother told me that she heard on the wireless there was a possibility of men who had been prisoners-of-war for over three years being repatriated. She said she did not think they were speaking of disabled prisoners-of-war. I do hope she was right because Bill has been a POW for almost four years now.'

Friday, 5 May

We have stopped admitting list cases and are only taking emergencies now. This means that all the chronic appendices, hernias and so on will have to wait, though I must say that quite half our beds are occupied by emergency cases. We are naturally taking it for granted that it is because of the impending Second Front and to hear some people talk it might be starting immediately. We are, I believe, allowed half our beds for civilians in an emergency and the other half for the Forces. It seems a strange idea at this point to be taking general-trained nurses for work in fever hospitals etc. when there will be such a demand for nurses with surgical training.

We had another lecture tonight at 9 but I think the lecturer must have been tired – he was not in nearly such good form. I must say that I should not feel in the least like giving a lecture after a hard day's work. I must say that some of the honouraries do work hard because apart from their work here they often have a large private practice.

Sunday, 7 May

Just as we were going off duty at 1.30 I suddenly realised that
I had mislaid the needles for aspirating chests and I could
not find the wretched things anywhere. I searched high and
low but there was no sign of them and eventually I left the
ward after telling the nurses who had come on duty to keep
a look out for them. They haunted me for the rest of the
day and I kept on thinking over in my mind where I could
have put them. Even when I was mowing the lawn at home
I could not forget about them. Usually if I lose anything I
just trust to luck it will turn up, so why these needles bothered me so much I don't know, unless I was feeling tired. I
brought some lilies of the valley back with me and consoled
myself with the thought that next time I came home I would
not have to come back the same day.

Monday, 8 May

When I got on the ward this morning I found the aspirating
needles were back in their proper place and I was told I had
left them on the slab which is where we often put them to
dry before putting them in their box. I suppose if I had not
been in such a frantic hurry to find them I should not have
mislaid them.

I had a letter today which brough a whiff of my peaceful
pre-war life to me. It was from someone I had known as a
girl in her teens asking me if I thought of going back to my
old job when the war was over – would I take on the post of
nursery governess to her two boys? She married very young
in her first season after she was presented at Court just before
the war. I was nursery governess to her half-sister's children

then and saw a lot of her. Actually the thought of going back to that sort of life when the war is over had never crossed my mind, but as I sat on the ward kitchen table reading the letter in the middle of all the bustle and rush, I had a feeling of nostalgia for that life. I thought of some of the lovely country houses I had lived in with their beautiful grounds, the comfortable leisured life. No getting out of bed at 6.30 to the clanging of a bell, scrambling into uniform, and rushing into the dining room to grab an indifferent cup of tea and a plateful of lumpy porridge or one hard cold sausage before going on duty. But neither was there any real companionship, no feeling that every day you were learning something fresh, no day off a week, no fixed time each day when you could definitely say that you were free to please yourself, nor did you get the same feeling of satisfaction out of your job.

Tuesday, 9 May

Today I received a reply from Queen Charlotte's Hospital [in London] where I had applied for particulars about vacancies etc. for midwifery training. I was not surprised to hear that there were no vacancies until the summer of 1946 but I think I shall apply and try to get my name down on the waiting list. By then if I am still nursing I shall probably feel more keen to do further training than if I went on immediately from here.

This evening I was off duty at 6 and played tennis for the first time this season. I guess I shall feel terribly stiff tomorrow. My right arm is feeling a bit queer now. Since the removal of the iron railings round the hospital [for war production], hordes of children are tearing about the grounds and we had quite a big audience. The little blighters run about the tennis courts in their clogs if they think there is no one about, which does not improve the not so good surface of the tennis court.

We had supper at 8 and a lecture at 9 on the urinary tract. This lecturer is the only one who lectures at this awful hour except the ear, nose, and throat specialist and he only gives us two lectures. I don't quite know whether there are one or two more lectures to come but I shall not be here as I start my precious week's holiday on Friday.

Wednesday, 10 May

I was off duty this morning and as soon as I came off the ward I dashed along to Matron's office to tell her, or rather remind her, that I was going on holiday this week. Having done that I went off to the Assistant Matron's office to ask for my ration book. As I came round the corner of the corridor I met the Night Sister, who stopped and spoke to me, and in the distance I saw the Assistant Matron walking away from her room with a pile of things in her arms. I got away from the Night Sister as soon as I could but the Assistant Matron had disappeared and though I looked in every place I could think of she was nowhere to be seen. I paid several visits to her office at intervals during the next hour and eventually ran her to earth in the sewing room. After that I went to the little café across the road with another nurse, where we had coffee and malted bread. When we came back I rang up a hairdresser in Darwen to see if I could get my hair permed there on Friday morning and managed to make an appointment for 1 o'clock. This means it will probably be about 7 or later before I get home on Friday so had to drop a line to my mother to say I should not be home Monday night after all.

Sunday, 14 May

Sunday morning [in Downham]. I got up and went to church though it was a bit of a rush as I did not wake up until 9.30. There were not many people at the Service. We have no vicar at the moment. The last one [Eric Reeves] found a better living. He had three girls under 16 and I think they found it a hard job to make both ends meet here. They could not afford a maid and had to take in paying guests or boys to tutor, and during the last part of his stay here the vicar taught at the local grammar school. He was a good example of practical Christianity. He would go and sit with the invalids in the village not so much for the good of their souls but so that the people who were looking after them could go out for a little while. He was particularly good to a farmer's wife while her husband was dying in the Infirmary. It was during the winter and while she was visiting her husband daily he would go up and light her fire and then meet her off the last bus and see her safely home. Everyone was sorry when they heard he had got another living but who can blame him?

Downham's clerical living was worth £350 a year, and Kathleen revisited the issue on 3 January 1946 when she remarked on the efforts of the Bishop of Blackburn to raise the stipends of all less well-paid vicars to £500 a year. It had been proposed that if Downham's parishioners paid £75 a year, the Ecclesiastical Commissioners would pay the other £75, and since the local landowner, Ralph Assheton, later 1st Baron Clitheroe (1955), the patron of the living, had guaranteed to pay £25 annually, £50 would remain the responsibility of the parish. The enthusiasm for this plan was apparently modest, according to Kathleen. 'Someone has hit on the bright idea of each household contributing 1s a month and little

*envelopes have been sent round for that purpose. The villagers con-
sist mostly of farm workers and people from the mills [especially in
Chatburn] and naturally they say why should they contribute 12s a
year to someone who is already getting more than they are.'*

In other passages Kathleen put on record some of the details of
housing in the village. 'At the moment,' she wrote after the war, on
10 July 1946, 'the only two houses in the village with proper sani-
tary arrangements are the Hall and the Vicarage. The war stopped
the plans for a Sewerage Scheme which is badly needed to replace
the primitive earth closets.' Downham was (and still is) considered to be a particularly attractive village and lots of holiday-
makers visited it. Once (6 August 1944) she remarked on the
'crowds of people in Downham, hikers, cyclists and family parties
picknicking on the green at the bottom of the hill beside a stream
which looks very picturesque but in reality what drainage system
there is in the village empties into it'. However, the picture was not
entirely grim, for, she said (10 July 1946), aside from these deficiencies in sanitation, 'the houses in the village are very up to date
compared to some country places. Every house has electric lights
and in spite of the war and the shortage of men and material the
owner of the village has managed to install a bath and hot water
system for the tenants who asked for a bath, whenever there was
sufficient room.' (Some of these tenants put up their own interior
bathroom partitions.) Kathleen's parents, given these deficiencies
of indoor washing facilities, paid for the services – as no doubt
did others in the village – of a professional laundry, whose van
routinely visited the village (25 August 1944). Almost all toilets
were out of doors.

Sitting by the fire was a common consolation in a wet environ-
ment. As Kathleen once observed (31 January 1946), 'these old
stone houses, picturesque though they may be, are all damp. We
notice that in this house [Hillcrest], the new part (built about 15

years ago) is dry but the old part, which may be a couple of hundred years old for all I know, is very damp. Great patches of moisture appear on the walls in stormy weather' – and it was stormy at this time. Whatever discomforts Kathleen endured at the Blackburn Infirmary, her bedrooms there were usually (it appears) dry and adequately heated.

Still, the Johnstones' roomy house in a pleasant village could make a favourable impression on city-dwellers. On 16 May 1946 some friends visited from Blackburn and 'were enchanted with Downham and also with my home. The village and the house was looking its best in the bright afternoon sunshine. The house faces southwest and does not get much sun until the afternoon and evening but the rooms are bright and airy and my friends, who live behind their shop in one of the busiest streets of dingy old Blackburn, thought it was ideal.'

Tuesday, 16 May

This afternoon I went into Clitheroe with my mother and went to the Food Office to get my Emergency Ration Card for the week. The Food Office is in a building just below the ruins of Clitheroe Castle. You get a wonderful view but oh! the wind. On the way up I met mothers coming down with bottles of orange juice and what looked like halibut oil. It must have been the free issue day at the Clinic.

I then joined my mother at the second-hand furniture shop where she was trying to find a little extra furniture for the new house. She had bought two bedroom chairs at 15*s* each when I got there and after that she got a rocking chair for 15*s* and another wooden chair with arms for 12*s* 6*d*. They seemed quite decent value for the money when you consider the exorbitant price of furniture these days and the scarcity.

After that my mother and I parted company. She came back to Downham and I went on to Blackburn where I met one of my friends and we made up a foursome with a couple of Yanks. They seemed quite decent boys but were not exactly in love with our climate. It was not to be wondered at. There was an icy wind blowing and every few minutes there was drenching downpour of rain. We had a drink and then went to see *The Lodger* [a 1944 crime film] at the Rialto. I had to catch the 9.13 back home and they came to see me off. Practically as soon as I got out of the station it started to pour and the wind was so rough I could not keep my light umbrella up. I was just giving up in despair when I saw a familiar figure in front of me, plodding along, with a large umbrella. It was my father on his way home from a British Legion Committee meeting so I got under his umbrella and put mine down.

Thursday, 18 May

Today I have paid a visit to the Fylde. I doubt if anyone but a Lancashire person would know what I meant, but it comprises the low-lying country district around Blackpool. I started off bright and early this morning. At least it seemed early to me after a week of staying in bed until round about 10. The sun was shining. There was not a cloud in the sky and I thought we were going to have a perfect May day but as I was on the way to Preston the sky became overcast and a cold wind blew up which continued throughout the day.

The bus was full of school children. It was Ascension Day and they had a holiday and were obviously going to spend it in the country. On my return journey they were all on their way home laden with flowers, bluebells, lilac and so on. Arriving at Preston I found the bus I had intended catching, though it had not left the bus station, was packed to capacity so I had to wait for the next. As they only run every hour I had a bit of time on my hands so I had a drink of coffee and then went and listened to the band playing outside the Town Hall for the 'Salute the Soldier' week.

I reached Poulton just after 1 and after having a look round the wards of the Emergency Hospital and paying my respects to the Matron, who is the same person who was Matron when I was there [in 1939–41], the nurse who I had really come to see and I went in to second dinner. After that a trip into Blackpool was indicated. We caught a train by the skin of our teeth and were in Blackpool in about five minutes. It looked just the same as ever except that a concrete pill-box had been removed from the station entrance. It was camouflaged to look like a kiosk and was built in 1940 when we were expecting to be invaded.

We went into the Savoy café for an after-dinner drink of tea. It was fairly empty then but soon filled up with members of the Forces. I should not think there was one of the Allied nations who was not represented there. Apart from the Forces stationed in and around Blackpool, I think a great many of them come to Blackpool to spend their leaves. The sun was shining by this time so after a walk along the North Shore we went on to the North Pier to listen to the band. After that we had some tea, a walk round the shops, and that big bazaar 'Hills', and then it was time for me to start back.

I got to Clitheroe in time to catch the last bus up to Downham and found my mother had gone to a Women's Institute meeting so I had to find her and get the key as I had forgotten mine.

Friday, 19 May

The last day of my holiday so I gave myself an extra bit of time in bed. Once I did get up I packed up all my belongings scattered around the house ready for the great 'move,' the date of which is fixed for Monday, when I shall not be here. I then collected a few things to take back to the Infirmary with me and then took my ration book to the shop to get my tea and points. I cannot think why as you have to get an emergency card – everything is not obtainable with this card. While I was in the shop I got a jar of vanishing cream of a reliable make for which I had been looking for some time. During the afternoon I decided to mow the lawn of the new garden but found it was too long for the lawn mower so I had to clip the wretched thing all over.

All too soon came the time for me to start back. The bus from Downham was crowded with girls and boys going to a Red Cross dance in Chatburn and consequently I nearly missed the last Blackburn bus. When I got back I reported back to the Night Sister and at the bottom of the stairs in the Nurses Home were my two special friends who had just made some tea to welcome me back. The burning question – Which ward am I on? – which everyone asks as soon as they get back, and was solved for me by one of my friends who said I was going back on medical ward and that she was on the ward too [which was only taking emergencies].

1. Kathleen Johnstone (left), her mother Ellen, and younger sister Phyllis, c. 1927. Courtesy of Mary Jefferies and Phil Johnstone.

An aerial view of the Royal Infirmary in 1938

2. Blackburn and East Lancashire Royal Infirmary, 1938. Courtesy of Blackburn with Darwen Library & Information Service.

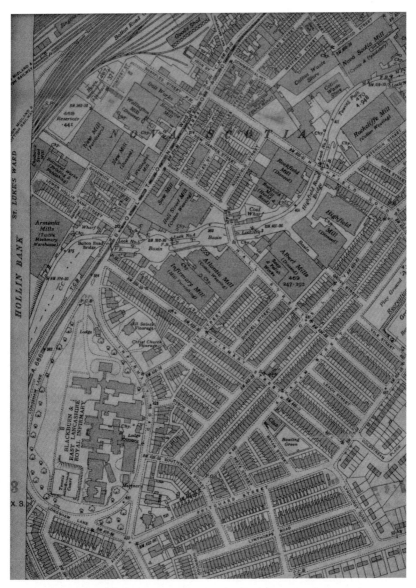

3. Ordnance Survey map of Blackburn, c. 1938. Bottom left shows the Infirmary's location. Courtesy of Blackburn with Darwen Library & Information Service.

4. Blackburn's train station and town centre, 1920 © Historic England

5. Top Row, Downham. In May 1944 Kathleen's parents moved to 'Hillcrest' (far left) from 2 Top Row (immediately to its right). These properties were owned by the Assheton family. © The Francis Frith Collection

6. Infirmary Hotel on Bolton Road, Blackburn. From this junction, just north of the Infirmary, Kathleen would have walked or taken the tram to the centre of town. Collection of the late Ray Smith.

7.   Kathleen Johnstone, 1944. Courtesy of Mary Jefferies and Phil Johnstone.

8. Fisher Street, Blackburn, 1930s: a typical residential street in working-class Blackburn. Photographer John Eddleston, published on cottontown.org

Sunday, 21 May

After dinner we made some tea for the thermos flask and started on our way [for a country walk]. We took a tram out to the other side of the Town. It is the residential part and one can hardly believe it is part of Blackburn after continually seeing the grimy streets of this part of the Town. We got off the tram at the terminus and in about five minutes seemed to be in the depth of the country going down a little lane towards a farm. No encroachment is allowed in Lancashire on the Right-of-Way which takes you through farmyards and over fields you would be chased out of in other counties. There is invariably a well-defined path and little stiles for you to use so that there is not fear of people leaving gates open. These so-called stiles are often two big slabs of stone placed upright so that people can squeeze through but not cattle. Often there is a smaller slab placed between them which you have to step over but I am sure these stiles seldom need any repair.

We went through a farmyard and across some fields over a stream with most solid stepping stones and through a lovely wood carpeted with bluebells. We found a sunny spot for our tea out of the wind and sat there until we heard some church bells ringing, when we thought it was time to move. At one spot our guidebook led us across a field that had obviously been left for hay. However, we edged round the outside of the field until we came to one of these little stiles so we knew we had not gone astray. We went down a rocky little lane into a place known as Alum Scar wood. In the old days it was an Alum mine but now it resembles more nearly a Scottish Glen with a stream rushing along the bottom and the deep tree-covered sides.

Eventually we worked back to the tram terminus where we were delighted to find a tram in. The guidebook said the

distance was about 6 miles but it was half past nine before
we got back and we felt as though we had walked farther
than that.

Monday, 22 May

We have had a very pleasant though very quiet sort of day.
No admissions or discharges and with Sister not back until
tonight from her weekend the atmosphere has been most
peaceful. I had time to read the daily paper through this
afternoon in the peaceful seclusion of Sister's sitting room.
My chief interest at the moment is the movement of 'Mercy
Ships,' bringing back home some repatriated prisoners-
of-war. Even though I realise they are sick or disabled and
my fiancé is neither, yet there is always the faint and utterly
unreasonable hope he may be on it.

There is also this ghastly business of the forty-seven Air
Force officers shot while presumably trying to escape [from a
POW camp in Silesia in March] and that combined with the
fact that I have not heard for three months [from him] gives
me some uneasy moments. Reason tells me that he is in the
Army, not the Air Force, and that I have gone almost as long
as this before without hearing from him but the fear still per-
sists when the hope of his return is not present. It is times
like this that I am thankful that I have a job that demands
so much time, energy and concentration. It is always in my
off-duty that I worry more.

Friday, 26 May

Tonight we had a dance and just before that a lecture. Owing
to the fact that the dance is held in the nurses' dining room,

we had supper early in two relays at 7 and 7.30. As I had to go to a lecture at 7.30 I had to go to first supper but Sister said I must wait until she came back from her supper before I went as there was no one else to leave in charge of the ward. It was 7.20 before she arrived back and when I got to the dining room the maids were already cleaning for the next supper. I asked if there was any supper left and was politely (?) informed that I should be in the dining room at the proper time. Fortunately at that moment Sister Tutor popped her head through the service hatch and asked if everyone had had supper. So the maid who had previously told me there was none left had the pleasure of proving herself a liar by having to get me some. The rudeness we need to put up with from the maids needs to be heard to be believed and if we complain there is nothing much that can be done about it with the domestic problem so acute.

The dance was a great success. About forty American officers turned up and there was actually more men than girls. The dance was in aid of funds for the library and we charged 1s 6d admission. We all have to pay to go to the dance but no other girls are allowed in except the nurses and the office staff. It is surprising, though, what a number of girls try to get in.

During these weeks Kathleen mentioned from time to time her resolve to study for her final exams and her frequent lack of will to do so. 'I had made up my mind that I would do half an hour's swatting each day but somehow something always seems to come along and stop it' (27 May 1944). 'When I think of how little I know for September I get really frantic' (31 May 1944). There were clear grounds for worry, she thought. On 1 June 'We had another coaching class this evening. It is strange that when you think you know a subject

*how often you are floored by some simple question.' 'I am denying
myself reading matter at the moment,' she remarked on 10 June. 'If
I have nothing to read then I am more likely to do some swatting
for September.'*

*There was also money to think about, for 'Next month we shall
have to pay 3 guineas entrance fee for the September Finals' (2 June
1944); this was about three-quarters of her monthly wage. Saving
money was virtually impossible. Spending it was a different sort of
challenge – because of the scarcity of so many goods and some services.*

Saturday, 3 June

It poured with rain all day and this morning I went into the
Town to spend some of my princely salary. At first I met with
little success. I have a small travelling clock and the hinge
had snapped so I have not been able to prop it up. I took
it out with me thinking I might be able to get it repaired
but no such luck. No metal workers left, I was told. To do
jobs like that I was advised to have a wooden support made.
Then I went to Boots where I tried to get a fountain pen and
a certain text-book but here again I had no luck. Next I went
to the photographer's to try to make an appointment for next
week. They were booked up to the end of June.

I then went to the library to change a friend's book. She
had given me quite a long list of books she wanted but not
one of them was in. I was feeling thoroughly annoyed with
things by this time because not only was I unable to get anything I wanted, but it was pouring with rain and I was feeling
cold and wet in spite of mackintosh and umbrella. At last
my luck turned. In another bookshop I found the text-book
I wanted and also a fountain pen. This cost me 12*s* 10*d* and
I only hope it writes well. It feels most odd after my other

one and is not nearly such a nice nib. I tried another photographer's and arranged an appointment for next Saturday and after spending some sweet coupons I came back having spent over a pound of my salary already.

Monday, 5 June

It has been my day off today and as I was sitting in solitary state in the dining room having a late breakfast one of the maids informed me that we had marched into Rome last night. I had gone to bed fairly early so I suppose that is why I had not heard about it last night. It was grand news to be greeted with first thing in the morning and made me feel that we had taken a step forward. I am very glad that the Germans [are getting] out of Rome without making a stand there. It would have been terrible from every point of view had Rome been turned into a battle area. Later on in the day I heard our troops had a marvellous reception when they entered Rome. For myself I went home after breakfast and went to Nelson with my sister-in-law. It was a stormy day but it was a lovely drive over the moors, though Nelson itself was very disappointing. We had only about a couple of hours there as the last bus to Downham was at 2 o'clock so we had a very nice meal in a British Restaurant, which was beautifully cooked and nicely served. It was my first experience of one and I must say I was really impressed.* After that we did a bit of shopping and got back home in time for tea.

---

* British Restaurants were designed to serve a hot and nutritious, full-course midday dinner for around a shilling. Their service was commonly cafeteria-style (not the norm then in restaurants), and while the cooks were paid, most of the rest of the staff were volunteers, such as members of the Women's Voluntary Services. It

Tuesday, 6 June

Well the Great Day has dawned. The first thing I knew about the Invasion was when a nurse rushed out of the ward on to the corridor where I was getting the dressing trolley ready for the morning's work and said 'The Second Front had started'. She is usually full of mis-information so I was a bit sceptical and when I went into the ward the announcer was telling us what the German News Agency was putting out. It seemed almost unbelievable that the long looked-for Second Front had started. An air of excitement pervaded the place and Matron was hopping around looking as though she expected a convoy of wounded to descend upon us at any moment. I was brought down to earth by a summons from the Assistant Matron to produce my identity card, otherwise I should not get a new ration book. Then the Sister Tutor sent for me to fill in my form for the Finals exam and asked me to produce my 3 guineas before the 17th of the month.

My friend and I were off duty at 6 and just before then the telephone operator rang round the wards to say that an intercession Service was to be held at 7.30 at the parish church so we decided to go. The church was packed and everyone seemed to have the same sort of feeling we had when war was declared. It was a very touching service and the congregation seemed strung up. Lots of people were crying and an ATS in front of me sobbed for the greater

was expected that most patrons would be people unable to eat dinner at home or in some institutional setting, such as travellers, people lacking kitchen facilities, evacuees, and various urban workers. Eating in a British Restaurant did not require the use of ration coupons, an important attraction. The British Restaurant was one of the war's great success stories on the home front.

part of the service. I did not hear anyone say they were sorry the Second Front had started but we all know there will be a tremendous loss of life before it is over and there must be very few people who have not got someone they love involved in it.[*]

* A few days later, on Sunday, 11 June, Kathleen was returning by train to Blackburn from Downham: 'A number of soldiers got in at one station loaded with equipment. They were being seen off by a crowd of their friends and one wit said he would send them a postcard from Berlin.' The confidence in victory was often combined with fear of the expected loss of life.

6

Warriors and Wounds

June–September 1944

Wednesday, 7 June

Our enthusiasm for the Second Front has been tempered today by the fact that Sister will be returning tonight. All Sisters on holiday were supposed to return if the Second Front started so our brief time of respite will soon be over.

I met my sister-in-law and her mother and small brother in Blackburn today. They said that the people in Downham seemed very little stirred by the opening of the Second Front. They were wondering if they would be able to get back to Sevenoaks in Kent next week when my sister-in-law's sick leave will be over.

We have got five medical students attached to the Infirmary. They were being showed round the wards this evening and we viewed them with marked disfavour. It is a well-known fact that in training schools where there is a school for medical students the students do all the skilled work that would otherwise fall to the lot of the senior nurses.

Thursday, 8 June

Today some of the nurses attended a lecture given by the pathologist on penicillin, the new wonder drug. I must confess that most of my knowledge about it has up to the present been gleaned mostly from the newspapers. It seems that though it is such a specific germ-destroyer in some cases, for certain germs it provides a marvellous breeding ground and these germs multiply so rapidly that they kill the patient. It has to be given under the most aseptic conditions and all appliances used in the giving must be absolutely sterile. If it is to be used extensively the nursing staff would have to be doubled or trebled so that certain members of the staff could devote their entire time to it. It cannot be given by mouth as it is destroyed by the gastric juices so it would have to be given by the continuous drip method or by intermuscular injections. It decomposes rapidly at room temperature so that only small amounts can be used at a time. I have no doubt though that we shall see it in use here very shortly [see below, 4 July and 21 and 27 August].

Friday, 9 June

Everyone seems to be settling down again after the excitement in the early part of the week. There is no longer a frantic rush to hear the latest news bulletins, which seem much of a muchness now. Our troops in Italy are quite out of the picture at the moment instead of being front page news and Russia does not seem to have made any striking advance for some time.

On duty things are very quiet. As we are only taking emergencies, our wards are just comfortably full, not crammed to capacity as they are in the normal course of things. I shall think I am killed when I have to rush round again instead of taking my time over things. Sister arrived back on duty yesterday after five days' holiday instead of fourteen. She is sorry she came back as things are so quiet but Matron only let them go on the understanding that they came back if the Second Front started. All our emergency beds are made up all over the hospital. In the empty wards they have already got them [the emergency beds] in the wards but ours [are] standing in the corridor. Each day we have to put fresh hot bottles in them. Rumour says that casualties have already arrived in Manchester, which is the distribution centre for the North-West.

Saturday, 10 June

This morning my friend and I had our photographs taken in uniform. We could not make an appointment at any of the better-known photographers' – they were booked up weeks ahead – but we are hoping they will not be too bad [see image section]. We had to pay in advance so we shall have to take them whether we like them or not. After that ordeal was over we went and had some coffee and cakes. My friend changed a library book but I am denying myself reading matter at the moment. If I have nothing to read then I am more likely to do some swatting for September.

These were mostly unremarkable days for Kathleen, as she and others waited for casualties to arrive from France. On 13 June she had to de-louse a man and was not pleased. 'He is over 60, a labourer, *and looked as though he had never had a bath in his life. Some of the patients who come in, when we proceed to give them a blanket bath, say that they cannot be very dirty – they had a bath a couple of weeks ago, or maybe a month, as the case may be.' On 16 June she remarked on the 'pilotless planes' – V-1 missiles, aka doodlebugs – that 'the Jerries' had started to launch against southern England. 'I suppose Hitler will make the most of this "secret weapon" in his propaganda to the Germans to offset the Allied offensive in France.' On 20 June she volunteered 'to sell Alexandra roses at the picture houses' – this, again, in aid of raising money for hospital care. 'We came off duty at 5 o'clock and borrowed one of the hospital capes each as the whole idea is that we should go in uniform. These capes are very voluminous garments and I felt like Guy Fawkes about to set fire to the Houses of Parliament in mine. We went to the selling centre at the Crown Hotel and the three of us who had come from the [operating] theatre were sent to the Palace, a big picture house in the Station Square. It was very amusing selling these roses and by 7.15 we had sold three basketfuls. After which we were given coffee in the cinema café and a free seat in the front circle to see the show, so we were quite pleased with ourselves. We sold the roses to all and sundry including the Yanks, who seem to have no idea of the value of our money and would put in 2 half crowns in our collecting boxes where lots of other people only put in 2*d.*"

Tuesday, 27 June

Well the Great Day has dawned. Tonight we are expecting some of the wounded from the Second Front. Word came through this afternoon and the Infirmary has been in an

---

* A half crown was 2*s* 6*d*, so these soldiers were contributing 5 shillings, a substantial (and remarkable) sum for a charitable donation, equivalent to several hours' wages for many labourers.

uproar. Not only have the nurses who are on day duty on the wards reserved for casualties got to go back on duty but also some of the nurses from Out-patients and some of the theatre staff and various nurses who are extras on different wards. The funny part about it is that we are only getting thirty walking cases and they are coming in a bus from Preston so that there will be about two nurses to each patient.

I have not been asked to go back on duty as I was off at 6 before Matron started rushing round telling all and sundry to go back on duty after supper. We had a coaching class this evening, which was cancelled, and supper was at 8. The information that supper was early did not penetrate to me so when I sauntered along at 8.30 it was all over and done with. I was ravenously hungry, having had nothing but a slice of bread for tea, but before I could do anything about it I was dragged into a meeting of the Nurses Christian Movement. The speaker kept on talking about someone who was empty of pocket and spiritually empty. I was tempted to stand up and say I was physically empty, which seemed to me the greatest of three voids at the moment.

I saw in the Evening Paper that Cherbourg has officially surrendered. The Russians are sweeping on well too but I could rejoice much more whole-heartedly if only I could hear from my fiancé.

Wednesday, 28 June

As we thought, there was a great glut of nurses to receive the casualties last night. They looked worn-out; they said [they] had come up from Portsmouth that day. They are all minor cases, fractured jaws and toes, perforated ear drums and such like. There is another batch expected in tomorrow, I believe, so maybe Matron will take their arrival a little more calmly. Am rather sorry I am in the theatre just now but I have no doubt that the war will not be over before I come out. It must be interesting to hear of their experiences. One of the casualties is a Blackburn boy. His parents were told by a newspaper reporter of his arrival at the Infirmary so they were soon up here to see him.

Thursday, 29 June

It seems strange to see men in hospital blue walking about the corridors. Those of them who were fit have been into the Town today. The nurses who are on their wards say that it is most interesting listening to the tales of their experiences. They have most of them been out there since the Second Front started. Some of them say their landing on the beaches was difficult and they met with stiff opposition; others say they just walked in – there was nothing to stop them. I suppose it just depended which part of the coast they landed on. Most of them seemed to have found the French friendly and eager to help, warning them of danger points where the Jerries were likely to be. There does not appear to be anything physically wrong with one or two of them. They just appear to be dazed and one of them, a boy of 20, has made no attempt to get out of bed. He just lies in bed dozing and wakes up with a jump saying 'They can't send me back there.' These cases seem to me more pitiful than physical injuries.

Tuesday, 4 July

In the early hours of this morning we had another convoy of wounded from the Second Front. I thought when I came through the Out-Patients waiting hall last night and saw all the stands for the stretchers put out that we were expecting some more wounded. I did not see a soul to ask on my way in and when I got to the corridor where I sleep there was no one about. Every other door seemed to have a 'Day Off' notice stuck on it and I suppose the other nurses must have been on duty. The wounded did not arrive here until about 2.30 a.m. and it was 4 o'clock or even later before some of the day nurses got to bed.

The cases this time are worse and about eleven of them are on penicillin which entails a lot of extra work for the nursing staff. About 7 o'clock this evening I met a nurse from off one of the casualty wards. She was not in bed until 5 o'clock this morning and was up for duty at 7.30 with the rest of us. She was supposed to be off duty at 6 but had to stay on to give this penicillin and had only just come off duty. She looked absolutely done up and about to burst into tears at any moment but she was contemplating staying up for the coaching class we had this evening. I persuaded her to go to bed and took her a drink and explained to the Sister Tutor why she was not at the class. The unfair part about it is that the rest of the hospital is not very busy and one would have thought that at least something would have been arranged so that the nurses who were up most of the night could have had some extra time in bed this morning.

One of the nurses who trained here has gone to Normandy with the first batch of Queen Alexandras. She joined last year and her sister, who has just passed her Finals, has been bombarded with requests from reporters on the local paper for some information about her.

Wednesday, 5 July

Another convoy of wounded is expected tonight. Sixty this time. We have despatched most of our original thirty to a convalescent home so we still have plenty of beds. I spent most of the afternoon helping to get one of the wards ready for them. We were not busy in the theatre so I was only too pleased to lend a hand. A lot of the boys had visitors this afternoon – their own people I mean, not the visitors who come up bringing cigarettes, notepaper, stamps, toothpaste etc. We had a couple of the casualties in the theatre today having pieces of shrapnel removed and I am sure every person with the faintest excuse for being in the theatre was there.

No diary-writing by Kathleen survives for the rest of this month. It is possible but very unlikely that she ceased writing for these twenty-six days, for had this been the case she almost certainly would have referred elsewhere to such a gap, perhaps apologising for it or explaining what had happened to keep her from writing. Rather, we think that she did continue her diary but that what she wrote during these days was probably lost, either in the summer of 1944, perhaps in the post or at Mass Observation's headquarters, or much later, after the war, in the confusion of storage or when Mass Observation manuscripts were being shifted (perhaps carelessly) from one location to another. We will almost certainly never know the reason for this gap. Similar unexplained gaps are found in other diaries written for MO.

Whatever happened, Kathleen's once existing diary for most of July 1944 no longer exists. Consequently, we cannot know what she might have thought about such events as the large-scale movement of evacuees from London and other parts of the South-East, *fleeing North from the terror attacks by flying bombs, the V-1 missiles (*Northern Daily Telegraph, *10 July 1944, p. 5; 12 July 1944, p. 5; 14 July 1944, p. 3), or the attempted assassination of Hitler on 20 July. Her reactions to the Allied advances in France at this time are also unknown, as are details about the newly arrived patients at the Blackburn Infirmary.*

When Kathleen's surviving diary resumes on 1 August, the soldiers in hospital continued to be a prominent feature of her life. 'Tonight we had a concert for the men on one of the big wards,' she reported. 'It is a most pathetic sight I think to see them all together in bath-chairs, on crutches, hobbling along with sticks or with their arms in slings and plaster-of-Paris. However, they all seem very cheery and the knowledge that the end is in sight makes everyone more cheerful.' Two nights later, further entertainment was offered. 'Tonight we had the party for the boys. We had to go in uniform and Matron went around the wards saying she hoped we would all behave professionally. Don't know whether she thought it was going to be one big petting party. I know she viewed this party with great apprehension. We think the ward Sisters must have been stuffing her up with all sorts of tales about the nurses' behaviour on the wards with the soldiers.'

Friday, 4 August

Another hot day. The lovely weather seems to be helping our offensive in Normandy. Even pessimistic me is beginning to think that maybe the war will be over before October 1945, which is the date I have set.

I went home after duty, caught the 9.15 train and was met at the station by my relatives from London, who are having a fortnight's rest up here [no doubt from the threats from flying bombs]. They told me my mother had gone to my sister's home in [Warminster] Wiltshire. My sister is worse and her husband sent a wire to my mother asking if she could go. Apparently they cannot find anyone to help them for love or money. When my sister realised she was going to have her third child at the end of October she applied at the Employment Office for help for the housework and they sent her an unmarried girl expecting to become a mother in September. For some reason this girl only came for a week but when she stopped her mother came every morning and has been coming every week to help with the housework until this week when her daughter has been taken ill and she cannot leave her. If it was not so tragic it would be funny.

Tuesday, 8 August

I had a letter from my sister and my mother this morning telling me that my sister had been taken to a nursing home and Friday morning produced a baby girl christened Rosemary Gillian and weighing 2 lbs 6 ounces, which at the time of writing was still alive. There is a faint chance of it surviving but it will need an awful lot of special care before it, or rather she, can be treated in the normal way.

Thursday, 10 August

There was another concert for the men tonight but we had another coaching class so we were not able to go. Instead we trailed round the theatre with the Sister Tutor doing instruments. The only consolation was that we were amongst the few nurses who were in for supper and got some really decent ham and salad.

I have been reading about the uprising of Polish patriots
in Warsaw when they heard the Russian guns and how they
were left to fight it out with the Germans unaided by any
Allied help. The Russians either could not or would not continue their advance on the city. I often have an uneasy feeling about the Russians and wonder how they will cooperate
when the war is over.*

Sunday, 20 August

What a wonderful week this has been for the Allies. The
landings in Southern France and the wonderful advance on
Paris with so much of the German Army caught in a trap. It
seems unbelievable that in one week we have progressed so
well. My only regret is that I have been so busy that I have
not had time to write daily in my diary [unusually, she had
missed the previous six/seven days: see below, 31 August],
nor have I had time to do anything but snatch a glance at the
headlines as I rushed round the ward. Have been busy both
on duty and off. Why, at a time like this, with such exciting
things going on, do I have to spend so much time immersed
in text-books? How dry they seem too, with visions of peace
and all that it means to me; not a thing to be vaguely hoped
for, but something that is likely to happen in the next few
months. After four years of disappointment and setbacks,
it seems almost too good to be true. I wonder whether the
French in liberated France feel the same. Have just been

* 'Russia's policy seems to be just what I was afraid it would be,' she wrote months
later, on 6 June 1945, when Soviet troops were occupying most of Eastern and
parts of Central Europe, 'co-operation with the Allied Nations providing that their
ideas are the same as hers. But as soon as a difference of opinion arises she will not
compromise – it must be her way.'

listening to a broadcast from one of the places in France liberated by the Maquis [members of the Resistance] when the Americans were drawing near. They sang the 'Marseillaise' followed by 'God Save the King,' and I felt like crying. I know perfectly well that not every Frenchman is waiting to welcome us with open arms, nor Dane, Dutchman, Belgian, Norwegian, Czech and many others. There are still some misguided people who sympathise with the Germans in every country but I am sure they are a very small percentage.

It is my Sunday half-day today and I was going to take a 'busman's holiday' and show one of our wounded from Normandy one of the beauty spots of Lancashire but it poured with rain so I brought him home instead. His army days are over but he is thankful that all he has got is a picturesque limp. He is one of the lucky ones who has a job waiting for him in 'Civvy Street'. By bringing him home I am breaking two rules. One – the Army rule that hospital patients should not go beyond a certain radius from their hospital, and the other unwritten rule that nurses should not go out with patients, a rule which I am sure is broken more than any other rule in existence, judging by the number of engagements we have had already. More than 50% of nurses marry patients or doctors.

Monday, 21 August

One of those quiet days when there is very little to record. Our patient on penicillin is doing remarkably well and I should say that undoubtedly it has saved his life. He is a boy of 16 and came in with an acute mastoid. When he was operated upon it was found he had lateral sinus thrombosis and the surgeon intended to tie the jugular vein in order to prevent

blood clots from reaching the head but the patient has progressed so well that he does not think it will be necessary.
Penicillin has only just been released for civilians and we had
a little difficulty in getting it but it has worked wonders.[*]

Tonight there was a concert in the men's surgical ward
given by local talent – some of the wounded and nurses. I
went along when I came off duty and managed to squash
into the ward. Each item was uproariously applauded and the
Scotch members of the staff and casualties did an impromptu
Scotch reel as the last item. When the concert was over there
was the usual trek back to the other wards. Long lines of
bath chairs, trolleys and men on crutches queuing up for the
lifts to the other floors.

Tuesday, 22 August

I heard today that my sister's 2 lbs 6 ounces baby died on
Saturday. Perhaps it is a good thing in a way as who can tell
whether such a baby would have grown up into a normal
human being. My sister is now out of the nursing home and
she said in her letter that the specialist who attended her
was killed in [a] car accident the day she went home.

Thursday, 24 August

Paris is liberated and by the French themselves, which
makes it all the more exciting. There must be some very

---

[*] *Miracle Drug: The Inner History of Penicillin* (London, 1946), by David Masters,
portrayed it as 'the most wonderful drug hitherto discovered by man' (caption on
title page). It was still expensive to produce and its supply was limited. At this date
it was applied in various ways (p. 142), including by injection as Kathleen reports
the following week (27 August).

determined men in France now, and I only hope that after the war France will pull herself together and do away with her corrupt political system.

Tonight I had a letter from my mother saying she was coming home tomorrow. It is my day off tomorrow so I shall be able to clean the house a bit. It is in a very sorry muddle with only my father at home. I was off duty at 6 and went home after the lecture. It was getting dark when I arrived home and I did not glance at the garden but my father soon informed me that when he came home a day or two ago he had found two cart horses prancing round the garden. I went out to inspect the damage, which was quite extensive as one might suppose, especially as it must have been a wet day as they had slithered around the lawn and flower-beds, to say nothing of eating all the cabbages. I was quite upset, especially as my mother is very fond of gardening and I had worked quite hard in it so that it should look presentable when she came home.

Saturday, 26 August

The news from Paris reads like some exciting serial story each day. It is an exhilarating experience to be living in 1944 and though we are so far removed from the actual fighting I think the presence of the casualties from Normandy gives you the feeling that you are part of the great struggle. The tales they tell you of their experiences, in such a variety of dialects, would make thrilling reading if only there was time to put them down.

This morning we had another convoy in, a real mixed bag this time – Poles, Yankees, Belgians, darkies from Africa and one man who can only speak German. He is in a Polish regiment but I should think he finds the language problem rather trying. The nurses are finding it difficult but very amazing and the Sister has managed to acquire a Polish dictionary to help to understand the Poles.

Sunday, 27 August

This morning I was off duty and got down to some real hard studying. With only three weeks to go to the Final exam I must get some done. I seem to know nothing.

We have another patient on penicillin – an acute mastoid complicated by meningitis. He is in a very poor state. I doubt if even penicillin will save him. I hate giving the stuff and it invariably falls to my lot. It is given into the muscle with huge intra-muscular needles specially sterilised in the laboratory. I am sure there is no need for these colossal needles. A smaller size would penetrate the muscle equally as well. But the laboratory transfers the blame to the General Office, and the General Office says they cannot provide smaller needles in sufficient quantities, and so it goes on.

Tuesday, 29 August

Well the convoy of wounded was arriving as we came on duty this morning. Thirty wounded German prisoners-of-war, none of whom can speak English and amongst them are several SS men. Overlooking the entrance at which they were brought in are the bathrooms belonging to the men's surgical ward and one of the Poles was looking out of the window when the ambulance drew up. At the foot of each stretcher are placed the men's uniforms and when he saw the German uniform he nearly went mad. Leaned out of the window, shouting and spitting and had to be hauled back to bed by some of the other patients. When they got news from Preston that we were getting Germans they cleared one side of B-ward for them. The remaining patients on that side were hastily dispersed amongst the other wards. They grumbled about being moved around in the early hours of the morning but when they knew it was for Germans were they mad.

Wednesday, 30 August

Feeling is running high about the Germans and the unfortunate nurses on that side are not liking things very much. Matron conceived the bright idea of putting one of the German Jewess nurses on that ward to translate for them. The nurse in question was very upset about it and the whole staff was up in arms so Matron had to bow to public opinion and change her mind.

The nurses say when they go into the ward they are greeted by all kinds of catcalls and the Jerries jabber away amongst themselves and appear to be jeering. They are treated in exactly the same way as our own boys, even sharing in the free issues of cigarettes sent to the Hospital by various organisations and individuals. On the medical staff we have a female house physician – I believe she is a Russian married to a Czech and has lost her people in the fighting in Russia. She has absolutely refused to go into the ward and made a great scene in the theatre today when she went in and found the Jerries being anaesthetised to have their wounds attended to. Some of them I believe are in a terrible mess but there are a few who can get up and there is nothing to stop them from walking out of the ward directly into the grounds and away, except of course lack of clothes.

In our instructions sent to us through the EMS [Emergency Medical Services] dealing with POWs, it said that any company stationed in the district must provide an armed guard for them but so far the armed guard has been conspicuous by its absence.

Two months later, on 30 October, when she was on holiday, Kathleen heard that a few days earlier another convoy of German POWs had been admitted to the Blackburn Infirmary. 'Apart from all the other difficulties which arise with the Jerries, the language is the worst I should imagine. Although personally I don't feel strongly on the subject of nursing them, nevertheless I hope I am not put on duty on that ward when I go back.'

Thursday, 31 August

The last day of August, and our progress during this month seems to me almost unbelievable. Had anyone told me at the beginning of this month that we should clear Northern France so rapidly I should have regarded them as super-optimists with absolutely no reason for their optimism. As our troops approach the Pas de Calais area everyone seems to be looking forward to a cessation of the flying bombs. Lots of people seem to think that Hitler may have something else up his sleeve to launch upon us when things are desperate for him, and quite a few people I have spoken to seem to think that Hitler will yet use gas. I am sending in my diary monthly [rather than fortnightly] and much regret my week's lapse, especially at this time. I am afraid it was not only due to hard work but play also. During that week [13/14 August to 19 August] the only time I spent in the Infirmary, apart from the time when I was on duty, was when I came in to go to bed and that was not very early and somehow before I realised it a week had slipped by without one entry in the diary.

Friday, 1 September

My morning was enlivened by the appearance of the monthly pay packet, £3 19s 5d, but apart from that the whole day seemed nothing but a rush. We had ten cases for the theatre including one of the casualties from Normandy who had his tonsils removed just by way of a change. He turned out to be one of those unfortunate people who bleed a great deal and when I came off duty this evening he had bled so much that it looked as though he would need a blood transfusion before very long. I came home after duty and my brother (who is home on leave) and his wife met me at the station. It was getting dusk as I got out of the train and I was not relishing the thought of my walk alone. Of course had it not been for the fact that we still have Double Summer Time it would have been quite dark. My brother told me on the way up that the Canadians were in Dieppe. What a contrast to their last visit.*

Saturday, 2 September

This morning I woke to a pouring wet day and my brother bringing me a cup of tea and saying cheerio. He and his wife

* The Allied raid on Dieppe, 19 August 1942, was carried out mainly by Canadian forces, who suffered severe losses: two-thirds of them were killed, wounded, or taken prisoner. The total number of Allied dead was about a thousand. The raid was a complete disaster. It was the only major Allied operation against the coast of France prior to D-Day on 6 June 1944.

were starting back for the South and he goes back tomorrow to rejoin his unit.

It poured all day so I have done very little but study, and listen to the wireless with its glowing news stories, how we have pierced the Gothic line in Italy, taken Vimy Ridge and are sweeping towards Belgium and Germany.

I have just been listening to an account of a Zeppelin raid in the last war and it brought back to me one or two memories of my own. I was born in 1913 and can still remember one or two isolated incidents. One I can remember clearly. My mother and I were staying with my grandparents in Buckinghamshire and one night we were disturbed by a great rattling of windows, doors, and china on the wash stand. I can remember leaning out of the window with my mother and seeing silhouetted against the sky this great sausage-shaped thing and my mother calling to a group of people standing in the road below. Another thing I can remember – my sister and I in bed, watching my mother dress, and the owner of the house where we were lodging, who was a nurse, coming in and taking her temperature and saying it was madness for my mother to get up and my mother replying she must go out – she had no food for us. This was during the flu epidemic [1918–19] and my mother has since told me the nurse in question was worked off her feet. How my mother managed during those years on 17s a week for herself, 2s 6d for me and 1s for my sister I cannot imagine.* It seems to me that things have been made much easier and better planned this time even though family allowances are still not anything to make a song about.

* The sum of money she cites for the family is almost exactly the same as that in the famous 1913 study of urban poverty by Maud Pember Reeves, *Round About a Pound a Week*.

Sunday, 3 September

We have now been at war five whole years and we are starting on our sixth year of war and to my idea these last five
years have immensely improved us as a nation. When I look
back and think how soft we were mentally and physically,
content to believe any reassuring words that were handed
out to us, and just going on our own indolent way – I do
hope this is over, that we shall not slide back with a few
patched up ideas to satisfy ourselves; that vigorous efforts
will be made to provide work for everybody; that our slums,
what are left of them, will be pulled down; that our health
services will be improved and also our educational system.[*]

   This evening I went to church. The preacher's plea that
we should turn to God as much in our hour of triumph as in
our hour of desperate need seemed almost unnecessary in
view of the fact that although there was a gale blowing and
rain pelting down, the church was even more crowded than
on any other Day of Prayer we have had.

Monday, 4 September

Brussels, Dunkirk, Antwerp, Boulogne – the names are stag-
gering in their significance as the Allied advance sweeps on.
Where are the Germans going to make a stand? Will it be
behind the Siegfried Line or will our soldiers be singing that
song that came out nearly five years too soon, about 'Hanging out the washing on the Siegfried Line'? I was in Town
this afternoon and saw shops with whole windows filled with

---

[*] Her list comes close to describing the core agenda of Britain's post-war Labour
Government, 1945–51, though most new houses were not put up until the 1950s
under Conservative Governments.

Union Jacks and placards advising people to buy early to be ready for the Peace celebrations.

For our part we have quite a ceremonial parade now. The Home Guard is providing guards for our prisoners-of-war and to watch the changing of the guard is one of the sights of the Infirmary at the moment. Four are on duty during the day and six at night, with fixed bayonets and some wicked looking guns in addition. It is funny when you think that for several nights there was one solitary night nurse on duty that side.

Tuesday, 5 September

On into Holland and Luxembourg. How much longer can our supply lines keep pace with this bewildering advance? Who will get to Berlin first? Will it be us or the Russians? At one time it seemed certain that it would be the Russians but now it seems more than possible that we shall be the first. Fighting in Germany will not be like France or Holland or Belgium where we are amongst friends. I think the fight will be hard and incredibly bitter but optimistic souls are seeing us in Berlin in a very short time.[*] Everyone seems to be infected with the wildest spirits, patients and nurses alike. Our convalescent patients think the war in Europe will be over before they are fit again. Burma Road next step seems to be their idea. One of the patients on the ward I am on was showing me some photographs in *Picture Post*, taken of the landing of some of the Royal Armoured Corps. He was

[*] The following week, on 13 September, Kathleen reported that 'one optimistic little man in the bus queue behind me was condescendingly explaining to a little woman how the war could not last more than a fortnight. He seemed to think we should nip round the Siegfried Line in a few hours and have a pleasant ride to Berlin.'

thrilled because he managed to identify his tank in a group of tanks parked in front of a large building. There was also a photograph of some of his 'mates' playing cards and a view of a bit of the port of embarkation taken from the interior of the boat before the huge gangway was drawn up. He said this was his last view of England before he left and it was his first view on his return.

Wednesday, 6 September

I read a scrap of news in a paper today which made me see red. It was that the Ministry of Pensions had ordered work to be started on standardized artificial limbs. I never heard anything so ridiculous in all my life, as though two people will be able to wear with comfort identical artificial limbs. Surely the least we can do for the unfortunate men who have lost limbs in this great struggle is to provide them with nothing but the best. What is the good of all the advances made in medicine and surgery and all the care and attention the patients without limbs are having if all they get at the end to carry them on in civilian life is a standardized limb which fits where it touches. It is of primary importance that they should be fitted individually by specialists and it is a very short-sighted policy on the part of the Ministry of Pensions. A man with a badly fitting artificial limb which is difficult to manipulate and may chafe and cause the wound to break down is not going to be a very useful member of the community.

Thursday, 7 September

Dwarfing all the war news today is the news on the Home Front that blackout restrictions are to be lessened [this came to be known as the 'dimout']. My mother will be very pleased about that as she has not so far made any serious attempt to blackout our new house. I don't know whether she vaguely hoped that she might not have to do it. Actually had the authorities been at all hot on the blackout we should have been fined many times over during the last week or two when the evenings have got darker earlier.

I came home this evening. Caught the 9.13 train from Blackburn. It was a dismal wet night and there was not a single light in the whole train. We sat in complete darkness during the whole journey. It was rather strange considering that everyone had been talking all day about the lessening of the blackout restrictions to travel without any light at all.

Friday, 8 September

My day off is about the only day of the week when I really get an opportunity to listen to the wireless and know just how far we have progressed. It seems we are expecting a stiff fight for the Channel ports and shall not be able to use Antwerp as a port until we have cleared the Germans from the other side of the river. I expect this bad weather we are having now will hamper things a bit.

I was talking to some of the evacuees and they are all thinking of going back next week. One woman talked of going home tomorrow. Her baby is only 3 weeks old and she has three other children. The baby was christened last Sunday and my people stood for the godparents. I think they find this dismal weather in the country very depressing and there is no doubt they do miss the pictures if nothing else.

Saturday, 9 September

Today was just one of those ordinary routine days when nothing in particular happened and I have been feeling rather jaded and not particularly bright all day. The reaction after all the exhilarating news we have had lately plus the fact that a particular friend of mine was transferred today to a convalescent depot, and with the Final examination looming ahead and I know so little. We have received our cards with our number for the exams. Mine is 128 and we sit the written part of the exam here. For the Practical part in October we have to go to Preston Royal.

Sunday, 10 September

A really beautiful day in contrast to last Sunday when it poured with rain. It was not my half-day so I sat and mended for the greater part of the half-day. We are usually fairly empty on Sunday as Sister tries to get as many patients home as possible on Saturday. Our Forces patients all went out directly after dinner, except two of them who are not out and about yet, and they had not returned when we came off duty. On Saturday and Sunday we get lots of people coming round the wards giving various things to the soldiers. This afternoon when I went into the ward about 5, on each bed there were a couple of packets of cigarettes, soap, matches, shaving stick, razor blades and tooth paste. Everyone seems to bring razor blades. They must think the Army spends its time shaving.

Monday, 11 September

I am very upset because I have lost my precious fountain pen. Have hunted high and low for it and have had to fall back on my old one again. There has been quite an epidemic of 'missing' things lately and I cannot remember where I last had my pen. It is a nuisance losing it just before the exams like this and my old pen I am using now is liable to suddenly flood the page.

We have had permission to take down the netting which has been gummed on to all the ward windows all these years. It does make a difference to the wards to be able to look out, as you could see nothing through the netting. We shall continue to have to put up the plywood blackouts each night but it is something to have more light during the day.

Tuesday, 12 September

There is a rumour going round that we are not taking any more wounded. I believe they are being kept in France and of course now that the flying bomb menace seems to be over [the Allies had captured most of the launch-sites] there will not be the same need to send them North even if they are brought back to England. We shall all be disappointed if this is the case as they certainly brightened up the Infirmary considerably – too much the powers-that-be consider. Our civilian cases go home in an ambulance and have to go back to bed as soon as they get home. Consequently they never feel well enough to get boisterous while they are here but the Service patients are up and about for weeks before they get transferred to a Convalescent Home. If it is a fine day and they can get out, the place is comparatively quiet but on a rainy day it is in an uproar.

Thursday, 14 September

Another beautiful autumn day and I sat out in the garden surrounded by text-books vainly trying to concentrate and knowing full well that it was my last chance before the exam. It will be a glorious feeling when it is over and I can just do as I like without feeling compelled to swat every free minute. At least [I] shall have a few weeks' breathing space before the results come out and I have to start again.

About 6 o'clock the weather changed and it started to rain and by the time I started back it was pelting down and I had no mackintosh. I had to bring out an old cape I bought in pre-war days at Marks and Spencer's when I was caught out in the rain somewhere. Got back just before 9 in time for another coaching class. What a life!! [Two days later, after another coaching class, she was 'wondering why I ever started nursing'.]

Friday, 15 September

Today I had a great argument with a friend of mine as to whether we were through the Siegfried Line or not. She said that we were but I did not agree so when we came back from tea there came a tap on the door of the ward and there she was with a paper in her hand to prove her statement. Unfortunately, though there was a map of Germany in it the Siegfried Line was not marked so I sent her back to her own ward for another paper to prove her statement. The wards we are in are on opposite sides of the corridor so I walked back with her to the door of her own ward and waited there. A few minutes later she reappeared minus the paper but with a great tall soldier in tow with his arm on an aeroplane splint which made him look taller. He proceeded to give me a great lecture on Allied strategy and said that we should outflank the Siegfried Line and that we should probably be beyond it as he was speaking. There was an

empty bed on the corridor and he proceeded to arrange the
Front Line on it with the various Allied armies in position.
Having got everything clear he suddenly turned to me and
said 'It will be all over before Christmas, nurse, and you can
give up nursing and marry the boy friend.' I had never even
set eyes on him before so I stared at him in amazement, but
before I could say anything the Sisters appeared back from
tea so we faded away to our respective wards. My friend told
me afterwards that he said that the only women who took an
intelligent interest in the fighting were those who had someone out there, or who had very personal reasons for wishing
the war over.

7

Stresses and Strains

September–November 1944

Sunday, 17 September

My half-day today, and a beautiful day it has been too. The trains and buses were crowded and I should never have got home had I not shown my [priority] card. I think these cards were originally issued to us so that we could get back quickly to the Infirmary in case of an air raid but we use them now to help us to get on the buses. I think it is a racket personally and don't use mine unless the need is fairly desperate but I wanted to get home fairly quickly so as to do some swatting and had I taken my place in the queue I should not have been home until long after tea.[*]

---

[*] The following year, on 11 March, she again made use of this privilege. 'It has been my Sunday half-day. A glorious day, but oh, the queues. I only managed to get on the bus for Clitheroe by showing my endorsement card, to the great disgust of the first people in the queue.'

The extra hour in bed this morning [clocks had just been turned back] was beautiful but it was not so nice to see it getting dark at 8 o'clock. When I went out to catch my bus there were all the cottages with just their ordinary curtains drawn showing little squares of light and the bus came in well lighted, by recent standards anyway. I had to go by train from Chatburn and the station there was very gloomy. The train was half an hour late and we sat in darkness in the waiting room. However when I got out at Blackburn and into the streets, what a difference. The streets were really well lighted and as I had to walk up having missed the last tram I did appreciate not having to fumble my way up, groping for the kerbs. I could never see anything in the blackout and used to envy those people who walked briskly along.

Monday, 18 September

The papers are full of the airborne landings in Holland and of the Americans piercing the Siegfried Line but I still think it will be quite a tough nut to crack and will hold up our advance considerably. Overriding all the war news for a few of us is the awful feeling that the day of the exam is drawing ominously near. My head seems in a whirl and I seem quite incapable of thinking clearly. I hope it straightens out a bit before Wednesday. Have never felt like this before an exam. I don't think I have been swatting too much but I certainly did not feel as bad as this before the Preliminary Exam.

Tuesday, 19 September

Have had the most ghastly headache all day and have had to take piles of tablets to keep myself going. Better to have the headache today than tomorrow but would rather have been without it altogether as I usually feel a bit dopey the following day. I was off duty at 6 and came off duty amidst cheerios of 'Good luck' for tomorrow. My headache had cleared somewhat by this time and as I had promised to go to the pictures I thought that maybe a change of surroundings and thoughts might improve matters so I went but barely remember what I saw. It was pouring with rain when we came out and as we had missed the last tram up we had to walk. We were very hungry but owing to the fact that Blackburn was having another holiday and our standby, the fish and chips shops, were closed, we could not get anything to eat and had to get some bread off one of the wards and fill ourselves with bread and jam.

Wednesday, 20 September

Well the dreaded day is over and what a day. It will take a miracle for me to pass on the papers I have done. If anyone had told me beforehand I could have done so badly I should not have believed them. The exam started at 10 and at ten minutes to we went into the lecture room and sat down at our respective tables. There were about thirty of us but only twelve from this Infirmary. The others came from various other hospitals.

The awful moment when the Sister Tutors come round with the question papers! We had an hour for the first paper on medicine and medical nursing. Then we had a break of ten minutes when we had a drink of tea and back again for the paper on Surgery. I made such a mess of that that when we came out for the mid-day meal I was in a fine state of nerves and so were a few more of us. The Sister Tutor gave us tea after the meal and then back again until 4 o'clock for the nursing paper. The trouble is that you are allowed ½ hour for each question which is never long enough for me. The result is I get behind so that I was starting the last question, which should have taken me one half an hour, at ten minutes to 4. I scrawled hastily through it but it was not very bright.

At last it was over and most of us went and had tea at The White Bull Hotel. We had ordered it beforehand and as it was quite a custom they gave us a decent meal.

After that we went to see *Let George Do It*, a film featuring George Formby, which at least made us laugh.[*] Then we came back and went to a dance we were giving here, which I quite enjoyed until the remembrance of the awful paper I had done crossed my mind and then I felt most depressed. In one of my moods of depression I was persuaded to go out for a drink and well-meaning friends plied me with drinks to cheer me up – to such an extent that I had to use all my powers of concentration when I got back to conceal the fact that I had [had] more than I should. What a day! I hope I don't have to put up with another like it.

---

[*] On 12 January 1946 Kathleen recorded a memory of the famous Lancastrian singer and comic actor. 'I have never seen George Formby on the stage but I remember when I was nursing in an Emergency Hospital at Poulton-le-Fylde seeing George Formby cycling round in his Home Guard uniform collecting paper salvage for some big Salvage Drive. He looked so exactly like he looks in his films that ever since I have had the idea that he is not acting but just being himself.' She also once wrote of Lancashire's most famous female film star and singer, Gracie Fields, after hearing one of her performances on the radio (13 August 1943), 'She seemed to be getting tumultuous applause from the munitions workers she was entertaining. Whatever she did I am sure she would always get a big reception in Lancashire. All true Lancastrians seem to have a soft spot in their hearts for her.' Both celebrities began their careers as children in Lancashire music halls.

More than a fortnight later, on 7 October, when she was preparing for the practical part of these Finals, she wrote again of exam anxiety. 'I have come to the conclusion that the worst part of the nursing profession is the Exams. We all get so worked up over them that we cannot even think straight when the time comes.'

As Kathleen's diary makes clear, nursing was a demanding job, involving high expectations, even putting aside the stress of exams. These demands were appropriately acknowledged in print shortly after the war by the authors of one of the volumes of the admirable History of the Second World War: United Kingdom Civil Series *(edited by Sir Keith Hancock). 'The work of a nurse is hard and exacting,' they wrote, 'even under the most favourable circumstances. It demands intelligence, physical endurance, discipline and a particular human quality . . . A nurse deals with people who suffer pain, fear and unhappiness. She must be able to bear the sight of ugliness and distress. She must show understanding for a variety of human reactions and moods. She must be kind and sympathetic and patient, whatever her own feelings may be at the time. Much of her work is an exhausting routine, demanding high efficiency, but at any moment she may be faced with emergencies and crises in each of which a life may be at stake.' They also pointed to the discrepancy between a nurse's responsibilities and the modesty of her financial rewards.*

Thursday, 21 September

I felt considerably brighter today than I have felt for weeks in spite of the thought of yesterday. I am not going to look at a text-book for the remainder of the week. But I am going

---

* Sheila Ferguson and Hilde Fitzgerald, *Studies in the Social Services* (London: HMSO, 1954), p. 285. Chapter 9, 'The Nursing Services', is an excellent survey.

to concentrate on doing all those odds and ends I have neglected doing the past weeks. I started off my period of relaxation by going to bed this afternoon to make up for not being in bed until the early hours of this morning. I had such a nice snooze that I had to go back on duty without my tea, which was a bit of a nuisance, and I had not done any of those odds and ends I meant to do.

We had a convoy in during the early hours of this morning, which seemed to come as a shock to some people who had apparently made up their minds that the war was practically over. After all the setbacks we have had during the past five years it amazes me that people still indulge in so much wishful thinking. When I attempt to point out that we are as yet only on the fringe of Germany and that we shall have a lot of hard bitter fighting before we get to Berlin, I am told I am a pessimist. They are expecting us to sweep into Germany at the same pace that we have swept across Northern France. Am afraid the airborne Army we landed in Holland is having a tough time of it.

Tuesday, 26 September [in Downham]

In the afternoon I went shopping with my mother [probably in Clitheroe] who wanted a few things and thought it would be a good idea if I went with her to help her to carry them. She bought a couple of stone hot water bottles, 6s 6d each, as a start and a couple of mop heads. Fortunately she went in for lighter articles later on as these hot water bottles seemed to weigh half a ton before I had got very far round with them. I was quite happy when the shopping orgy was over and we returned home for tea.

It does seem strange to have the blackout – or rather dimout – half-way through the evening and have to come back here [Blackburn] in the dark. Not that the dark evenings are so bad now with the streets fairly well lighted but coming back to the Infirmary on a dark winter's night and missing or not being able to get on the last tram and having to walk back to the Infirmary was something of a nightmare. It is only last winter that Blackburn adopted star lighting. Before then there was not a scrap of light in the streets and you have to walk through rather a roughish quarter to get to the Infirmary.

The war news was taking a turn for the worse. On 27 September 'On the 6 o'clock news bulletin came the information that our paratroops or rather what is left of them have been withdrawn [from Holland]. I did not realise that the situation was so critical. It must have been terrible for them. It made me feel quite depressed.' On the last evening of September Kathleen was at a cinema and the newsreel 'showed the people of Eindhoven frantic with joy as the Allies took the town, with their streets gaily decorated, and one knew that so soon after that news reel had been taken they were going to be heavily bombed [and over 200 civilians killed].'

Sunday, 1 October

So Calais has surrendered, or it would be more accurate to say the Germans defending Calais have surrendered and Dover and one or two other towns will no longer have to put up with shells from Jerry guns on the other side of the Channel. A year or two ago my brother got pneumonia on the white cliffs of Dover and spent several weeks in an underground hospital there.

Today was Harvest Festival Sunday in Downham and the little church was decorated with the usual fruit, vegetables and flowers and we sang the Harvest hymns, 'We Plough the Fields and Scatter the Good Seed on the Land,' etc. There is something rather comforting in singing these old hymns, which are so familiar to us from our childhood days, in this changing world of ours. Our own vicar is ill but we have been fortunate enough to find a missionary who is waiting to go to Southern Greece who is only too willing to deputise for him.

When I got in I found my mother with some bright green knitting in her hand pondering over a leaflet headed 'Clothing for liberated Europe'. Last time she was knitting socks for soldiers, this time a green jersey, and she is on so many committees for this and that that she could not remember which society was sponsoring the 'Clothing for liberated Europe'. It sounded such a grand name for a little green jersey [to be given] to a two-year-old.

Monday, 2 October

This evening I went with a friend to see *For Whom the Bell Tolls* [1943, starring Gary Cooper and Ingrid Bergman] and enjoyed it much more than I expected. I knew it was tough in parts and that I should not like to watch the part where the political prisoners have to run the gauntlet of the Republicans [in the Spanish Civil War] armed with wooden staves. Incidentally that part was almost unnecessary but the rest of it was very good and it was without the conventional happy ending.

Between the news and the picture itself the manager appeared and said they were holding a competition for a 'Cover Girl' and he had five girls from whom the audience was to choose by the volume of its clapping. This competition was going on for the whole week and on Saturday night the five winners were to be judged to see who was the Final winner. He then brought five girls on to the stage, none of whom looked at all like my idea of a Cover Girl for anything and after much clapping from certain sections of the audience the winner was picked out by the manager. I must say that we could have done much better at the Blackburn Royal Infirmary. Some of our 'glamour girls' are far and away better-looking than the winner.

Tuesday, 3 October

We have had a very easy day on duty. We discharged several patients and some who were supposed to have come failed to materialize. It was the staff nurse's day off and Sister was supposed to be off duty at 6 with her day off tomorrow. At 5.30 she decided to go and catch an earlier train home than she had intended and once I had done one or two dressings and attended to one or two out-patients I had nothing to do until it was time to write the report. Our civilian patients consisted of four elderly ladies, three small boys and four deaf men all over 60 so I wandered up to the ward where we have our Service patients – only three left now – and did some jigsaw puzzles with them. We have a craze for them at the moment and we all have a try at putting a piece in whenever we go into the ward. All the bed tables have completed jigsaw puzzles on them which we are reluctant to break up.

Wednesday, 4 October

Today the Practical Part of the Preliminary Examination was held here and we had to turn out of our dining room for it and squash into the lecture room for our meals. It was such a squash at breakfast that as soon as we had finished we got up and went out so that someone else could have our seats. One of our Service patients and one of our small boys volunteered to act as models for the nurses to bandage etc. in the Practical Exam. As we were sitting at dinner we saw three grim stately matrons walk into the Examination room and I lost my appetite thinking that I should probably be confronting them a week today. I was off duty at 5.30 as we were so slack so had time to change into mufti at my leisure and catch the bus home.

Thursday, 5 October

I woke to a most beautiful autumn day. It was so lovely that it seemed a shame to stay in bed and I was soon up and out into the garden. The lovely weather brought everyone out and the buses were full of people coming for a stroll round Downham. I saw quite a number of the evacuees, mothers and small children, enjoying the sunshine. In fact I was quite surprised to find that there were still so many left in the village.

In the afternoon I went into Clitheroe to hear the verdict on my watch which I so carelessly allowed to fall out of my pocket. It was as I suspected – impossible to repair until the war is over – so what I shall do now about counting pulses etc. I don't know as I don't suppose my mother will lend me her watch indefinitely.

Sunday, 8 October

It has been really sunny today but I was off duty this morning and put in a last-minute bit of swatting. Our two Service patients had been invited to tea but one of them had I regret to say a hangover from last night and the other one said he did not feel capable of dealing with four elderly ladies on his own so I was asked to ring up and make some excuse for them. But I could not get them on the phone which was perhaps a good thing as I am not particularly good at excuses so later on in the afternoon one of the ladies rang up to find out what had happened. Fortunately Sister answered the phone and she got one of the men down to make their own excuses. It is very kind of people asking the Service patients out like this and while the men do appreciate the thought behind it, to be quite candid they don't always enjoy it very much. They feel they are expected to talk about things in Normandy and they don't always want to. In fact a great many of them want to forget about it as much as possible.

Monday, 9 October

As a diarist at the moment I am hopeless. What with a personal matter which is occupying my thoughts quite a bit and the exam looming ahead on Wednesday I am going round in a dream. I just glance at the headlines of the patients' newspapers and then forget the details of what I have read. I have grasped enough to realize, though, that it is a ding-dong struggle we are having at the moment and that the great breakthrough we were hoping for will not come yet. I try not to go round saying I told you so to my various friends who accused me of being such a pessimist when a few weeks ago I foretold the present state of affairs.

Tuesday, 10 October

Some of the Finals went to Preston today for the Practical part of their exam and were eagerly greeted by the rest of us who plied them with questions as to how they got [on]. We got the usual mixed bag of replies. Some seemed very satisfied with themselves, others most dissatisfied, but they all agreed that the examiners were very nice.

I spent my off-duty getting my uniform ready for tomorrow. Putting clean collars and cuffs on my dress, making up a clean cap etc. as we have to go to the Practical part of the exam in uniform. I felt rotten tonight and am afraid I am in for a cold.

Wednesday, 11 October

The dreaded day is over and what a day. When I woke up it was blowing a gale and pouring with rain for one thing, and another – I had a rotten cold. My head ached, my throat was sore and I felt hot one minute and cold the next. My friend brought me an enormous breakfast, which I could not eat, and then I got up. Four of us had an early dinner consisting of stew and lukewarm rice pudding, after which we set off for Preston. Eventually we reached the Royal Infirmary and were conducted to the cloakroom, where we got into uniform, and went quaking down to the waiting room where we sat round waiting for our turn to be examined. At 4 o'clock my ordeal was over, having forgotten everything I knew when I confronted the examiners. I was not in a very happy frame of mind but at least it was over. We went and had tea and then went to see *Pin-Up Girl* [a 1944 musical comedy with Betty Grable] just to cheer us up. I felt like nothing but my bed but lacked the necessary energy to come back on my own. When we did eventually arrive at Blackburn we were unable to get on a tram and had to walk back to the Infirmary in a torrential downpour. We were drowned rats when we did reach the Infirmary and tumbled into a hot bath and so to bed. A most ghastly day.

Thursday, 12 October

What a wonderful feeling of relief to feel that the exam is over with – for the time being, at all events – and it is possible to enjoy one's off-duty without that guilty feeling that you should have a text-book in your hand. In my off-duty this afternoon I was frankly lazy. I wrote one letter, which I was obliged to write, and then I read some copies of women's papers such as *Woman's Own*, *Women and Beauty* etc., completely frivolous but what a change, and then I dozed.

Friday, 13 October

I feel that it is time I turned my attention to my holidays, which I start next week. The first step towards them appeared to be a new costume and I made up my mind to go out in my off-duty this afternoon and get one in spite of it being Friday the 13th. Accordingly in spite of the fact that it was pouring Heaven's hardest I started out just after 2 with two or three other nurses. I did not find it at all easy to get a costume and went in and out of so many shops that eventually my friend refused to accompany me into the shops.

I found there was not a costume to be had between Utility ones up to about 5 guineas and costumes of 15 guineas and over. The latter I could not afford and eventually ran to earth a fairly decent Utility costume in black for about £5. It was not really the type of costume I had in mind but it is not too bad and fits me fairly well.

Monday, 16 October

Tonight I went to see Charles Boyer in *Murder in Thornton Square*. It was very good but totally unlike his usual parts. In this film he is very cleverly insinuating to his wife that she is becoming insane and he nearly succeeds in making her lose her sanity. The [late Victorian] period they were living in made it seem possible that such a thing could be done. The tall London house and the rooms so cluttered up with furniture and drapery that there was little or no daylight, and then the life of a married woman at that time, so secluded if her husband wished it to be, all helped to make the right atmosphere.* Give me 1944 with all its disadvantages great and small.

Tuesday, 17 October

This afternoon in the teeth of a howling gale I went on another shopping expedition. I seem to have got the

---

* This 1944 film, titled *Gaslight* in the United States, is a creepy psychological thriller in which an abusive man works systematically to manipulate his wife into believing that she is losing her mind, including through the mysterious dimming of gas lights. Lighting is, indeed, used to impressive cinematic effect. The film, adapted from a 1938 play by Patrick Hamilton, also starred Ingrid Bergman, who received an Oscar for Best Actress, and Angela Lansbury, who made her first film appearance.

pre-holiday spirit which always seems to entail buying
new clothes. I collected my black costume which had to be
altered, bought a red woollen blouse to wear with it and then
set off in a search for shoes. To find the size, colour, style
and to be comfortable seems an impossibility these days and
I find these Utility shoes don't grip your heels. The heel
grips on the market just now are worse than useless too. I
tried several shops and could get nothing I liked or that fitted until eventually I decided to try to 'walk the Barratt way'
and there I found a pair of shoes which really did fit, though
they were lighter than I had intended getting for the winter.
Now I am left with two coupons to last me until the end
of February and if I have to give any coupons for uniform
between now and then, well I guess I shall just have to go
to gaol.

*While she was on holiday, the war came to her mind in different
ways. On 20 October she was glad to hear of the capture of Bel-
grade. 'One capital after another is being liberated but still unfortunate Warsaw is in German hands. It must be the most tragic
capital in Europe.' Hopes that the war would end this year were,
she observed, largely dashed (24 October). The following day she
thought that 'the Russians seem to have got going once again' and
'the Allies seem to be making slow progress everywhere'. Closer to
home, women's work in aid of others continued unabated (22 October). 'My mother is knitting furiously to get some jerseys finished
for this "Clothing for Liberated Europe". I was roped in to knit
up some oddments of wool into something for a sale in aid of the
Women's Institute. Whenever I come home my mother seems to be
making something. At the beginning of the war it was clothes for
evacuees. Then came Comforts for the troops, Navy, Army and Air
Force. Now it is Clothing for Liberated Europe. The wool seems*

*quite decent, much better than you can get in the shops.' As she noted
the following day, not everyone was happy with this situation. 'I see
in the paper today that women are complaining of the good quality
of the wool used for these things for Liberated Europe compared
with what they can buy in the shops for their own children. As a
matter-of-fact I have not seen any wool in the shops lately. Nothing
but yarn.' On the last day of October 'the local organiser of the knitting for Liberated Europe came in and presented my mother with a
pound of wool to be knitted up. She said the response had been very
poor this time and she was left with 4 lbs to knit up herself.'*

*Kathleen had two deaths to remark on during this fortnight. On
26 October 'It was a decided shock to learn that the Archbishop of
Canterbury was dead [William Temple, b. 1881, Archbishop since
April 1942]. Only last night I was listening to one of his short
addresses to the Forces. So many public men seem to be dying suddenly. It must be caused by the high tension at which they live. Better
to die suddenly, though, than to live on to a decrepit old age and die
slowly and painfully as I have seen so many old people die.' On 31
October she listened to the broadcast of the archbishop's funeral and
thought 'what it must feel like to come to the end of a well-spent life'.
The other death was also of a clergyman – Charles Gamble, aged
64, the Vicar of Downham (29 October). 'He had only been here
about three months and preached his last sermon on September 3.
Am afraid I have never even seen him.' (The preacher she heard on
the evening of 3 September – see above – must have been a visitor.)
His body was lying in the church overnight on 31 October, with the
burial the following day.*

Wednesday, 1 November

This afternoon my mother and I went to the Vicar's
funeral. Though I have seen death many times it was the

first funeral I have ever attended. It gives you a different aspect on death from the one we get in the course of our work, with the wreaths, the velvet covers, the coffin bearers and the simple and yet quite impressive service. We get such a materialistic view of death when we see just the pitiful body, devoid of all trappings, without the spark of life. There was quite an impressive array of clergy at the funeral, including the Bishop of Burnley who conducted the Service.*

In the evening we went to Clitheroe to see Deanna Durbin in *The Butler's Sister* [1943 romantic comedy]. It was quite amusing but broke down half-way through. They got it going again after a time and apparently it is quite a common occurrence. I heard a girl behind me remarking that it invariably happened when she came to the pictures.

Thursday, 2 November

The laughable muddle over the standing down of the Home Guard does not seem to abate and I very much doubt if half the uniforms will be available for handing in. Since that misleading statement that the Home Guard was to retain its uniform I have seen various articles of the uniform being worn on different occasions. My father at one time was a member of the Auxiliary Fire Service in common with several other men in the village but it is quite a long time since they were disbanded. They still have the bits of uniform

* Charles Gamble had been inducted on 1 July 1944. 'The Bishop of Blackburn conducted the ceremony and hordes of parsons and their wives descended on the village in taxis and by bus. I did not go to the Service but I understand that there are some quaint customs connected with the induction such as locking the new Vicar out and he has to knock before he is admitted.'

with which they were issued – the cap, overalls, and boots. No one seems to know what they are supposed to do with them and the last time I saw the boots my father was digging potatoes in them.

It looks as if we shall soon be able to use Antwerp with the new landings going so well around there.

Mr Churchill's speech regarding a General Election seems to have met with most people's approval.* Naturally far more interest is taken at the moment in the possible date of the ending of the war rather than the possible date of the next General Election. I wonder who will get in in America, [President Franklin] Roosevelt or [Thomas Dewey] [the Republican Party's candidate]. I hope it will be Roosevelt.

Friday, 3 November

We arrived back [from shopping in Blackburn] in time for tea and later on in the evening we went to a 'Hot-pot Supper and Entertainment' in aid of the Red Cross. It was the first one I had been to, though they are very popular up here. The 'hot-pot' supper consisted of rabbit-pie, followed by jam tart and a cup of tea and after that came the entertainment. This took the form of singing and a comic turn. The comedian produced some very broad jokes which went down very well

---

* Churchill thought that the Coalition Government should not be ended before the defeat of Nazi Germany and that no General Election could be held before around mid-1945 (Robert Rhodes James, ed., *Winston S. Churchill: His Complete Speeches 1897–1963* [8 vols.; New York: Chelsea House, 1974], vol. VII, pp. 7020–24). He ended with the words: 'I should deprecate strongly the over-emphasizing of party differences now, and recommend that we all bend ourselves with unflagging energy and unbroken union to the national task.'

with the type of audience who would not have enjoyed anything very subtle.*

Saturday, 4 November

It has been a very stormy day. I went into Blackburn to meet a friend. I was lucky enough to be able to walk down to the station in a dry interval but it started to rain again almost as soon as I got there. In spite of the weather, when we got to Whalley the platform was crowded with 'hospital blues' from the military hospital at Calderstones [just outside Whalley]. At Blackburn I saw one of our nurses meeting one of them. He was originally at the BRI and they became engaged before he was transferred to Calderstones.

The person I was meeting is at a Convalescent Depot in Blackburn waiting for his 'medical'. From what I am told about this place it is more of a kill-or-cure depot than a convalescent depot. There is no heating of any kind in the huts. The only place where they can get warm is in the recreation room and a fire was not installed there until November 1. They have to walk from one end of the camp to the other where there are a limited number of washing facilities (cold water of course). Some of the men are arriving at the depot minus overcoats as they have not been issued with them on discharge from hospital as they do not issue kit at this place. They will have to wait until they rejoin their unit before getting one. Fortunately my friend has one of a kind – an ATS one which must have been made for a giantess as he is almost 6 feet tall. When they

---

* 'Lancashire humour,' she once observed, 'is on the broad side' (30 November 1943).

are issued with clean laundry they have to take off their underclothes, socks, etc. and parade in just their top uniform and boots while the clean things are given out. As my friend says, some of the boys have come straight from hospital to this depot and coming from one extreme to the other they find conditions there very trying. He had a period of three weeks at a Convalescent Hospital between the discharge from the BRI and coming to the depot so he had time to get a bit hardened.

During the morning he took a party of the boys up to a mill which they are having to clean up for the Americans who are coming in. I cannot imagine convalescent Yanks cleaning up a mill for a company of able-bodied Britishers to occupy. Needless to say, it does not lessen the feeling of hostility, which in spite of all the sentimental nonsense written about the friendship between our men and the Yanks, does exist, at least on the part of our men. I have never heard a Yank say anything about how he felt towards the British soldier but the majority of our men seem to dislike them intensely. I have a feeling it may be because they are so popular with the British girls but whatever its cause the dislike is there.

Sunday, 5 November

Guy Fawkes Night here is celebrated as 'mischief night,' during which night the boys of the village roam around doing as much mischief as they can. Last year they took the Vicarage gate and put it on the top of the school chimney. Consequently we were not very surprised this morning to find that our gate had been taken off its hinges and put across on the other side of the road. Strictly speaking today is Guy Fawkes

Day but I suppose they thought it had better be celebrated
Saturday night rather than Sunday night.

*That week Kathleen spent four days visiting friends in Cleveleys and
Fleetwood on the Lancashire coast and paid a visit to Blackpool
(7 November). This seaside city, she wrote, 'does not seem to change
much except to look a bit shabbier each time I see it. It still seems full
of men in uniform of every description and plenty of glamourous
girls. After the grim realism of smoke-grimed Blackburn, Blackpool
always seems to me a place of "froth and bubble," where nothing is
taken seriously.' When she returned to Blackburn two days later she
stopped at its train station for a cup of tea and 'several railway
men came in and started discussing Churchill's speech at the Lord
Mayor's Banquet. One of them said he was sure that Churchill must
have been "lit-up" as he had never heard him stammer so much and
repeat himself.* From that they went on to express their satisfaction
at Roosevelt getting in once again [for a fourth term].'*

Friday, 10 November

When I woke up this morning I wondered for a brief second
or two why I felt so depressed and then it dawned on me this
was the last day of my holiday.

At last Mr Churchill has officially claimed what we have
been hearing rumour of for the last few weeks – the V-2
rocket-bomb, which travels through the stratosphere faster
than sound but which so far does not appear to have been
used in any great numbers against us. I presume that it will
have a greater range than the flying-bomb so that it will

---

* Churchill's hesitant speaking prompted comments from around a quarter of Mass
Observation's diarists, some of whom thought he was tipsy, others just finding his
delivery rather bumbling, perhaps because of fatigue.

penetrate further than Southern England, which means that even up here we shall not be safe from them.*

I was much more concerned with my own personal feelings of disgust at the prospect of work again, I must confess, than at Hitler's V-2 weapon, and arrived back at the Infirmary about 9 o'clock feeling disgusted with life in general. I am not one of those very adaptable people and always take a few days to get accustomed to new surroundings so that I never view a change of ward with much delight, added to which I have been whisked away to another bedroom in my absence so that I began to feel almost as bad as I did when I first started.

Saturday, 11 November

I was none too pleased when at breakfast time this morning I heard myself read out as staff nurse in the Annexe to the Women's Ward. It was just the very ward I was dreading going on but as the Sister is away on a week's holiday I shall get a breathing space before she comes back. This Annexe was originally an old Army hut erected during the last war and though I gather there has always been talk of pulling [it] down and rebuilding a more permanent affair, somehow it has survived to see another war. It holds about twenty-four beds and is extremely cold at this time of year.

It is Remembrance Day and we all forgot about the two minutes' silence at 11 o'clock. I remember when I was at

* The V-2, a ballistic missile, had a long range and could not be defended against, unlike the V-1, most of which were shot down before they detonated. The first V-2 had fallen on London on 8 September. The existence of this new and lethal German weapon was not officially acknowledged by the government until now, and Churchill, with some reason, downplayed its importance (*Complete Speeches*, VII, 7029–30).

school [in the 1920s] what a solemn moment it was, and how I used to think of those who had lost their lives in the Great War – not that it meant anything personal to me but I thought it was the right thing to do. I remember too being at the last Service at the Cenotaph [in London] and wondering as I stood in the crowd how long it would be before we were fighting again.

The following day, the 12th, she made note of a change in her attire. 'I wore for the first time today the blue belt showing that I am now a fourth-year nurse. Looking back, these three years seem to have passed with incredible speed and though undoubtedly I have had my bad moments, I am thankful that I pulled myself out of the Civil Nursing Reserve and have done something worthwhile with these three years.' (The CNR, part of the Civil Defence Services, employed mostly auxiliary and assistant nurses, many of them part-timers.)

Monday, 13 November

Today I disgraced myself thoroughly. I got up in the morning with a headache and soon after breakfast I started to be sick and this continued on into the morning. The nurse who is in charge of the ward in Sister's absence sent me off to lie down about 11 o'clock as I was worse than useless. My sickness should really have been reported to the powers-that-be but as I knew it would only last a few hours that was the last thing I wanted so I stuck a day-off notice on my door so that the Home Sister would omit my room when doing her daily round. It worked very well; no one disturbed me and I got up about 4 o'clock feeling much better though my head ached still. With the usual perversity of things it cleared just about the time I came off duty so we decided to go in for supper. I was glad I did as otherwise I should probably have missed my phone call from the boy friend of the moment who rang up unexpectedly. If you get a phone call and you are not around, people are not very eager to come up to the second floor to look for you.

This 'boy friend of the moment' is never named, nor does she offer further information about him. This is typical of her feelings when it comes to men who (one imagines) interested her: she is reticent about recording these feelings in her diary. This man was likely the 'friend' whom she spent time with on Saturday, 4 November; almost all the other friends she mentions are clearly women. It is probable that in later 1944 the fact of having two boy friends, at least one of them unknown to the other, was the 'personal matter', mentioned five weeks earlier, on 9 October, that was causing her to worry.

Tuesday, 14 November

A quiet day but quite enjoyable, especially now that I am getting used to my ward-full of female patients. I really think I like nursing women better than men. They are more understanding and reasonable than most men, who often behave like spoilt children when they are ill; and they are often more grateful. I know lots of people would disagree violently with my last remarks; lots of nurses, especially, think looking after women rather a bore, particularly those of a 'glamour girl' type.

We have a new cook and the food has definitely improved. We had some apple tart today and the pastry just melted in our mouths. Even the stew was not quite so bad, which just goes to show that the war is blamed – and quite wrongly – for lots of things.

Wednesday, 15 November

I had quite a pleasant day and came off duty at 6. I met a friend in Town [probably the 'boy friend of the moment' mentioned above] and we went to see a film, *Jack London*. I had never realised that Jack London was such a national figure in America, or at least I should say a person of such importance that his life story was interesting enough to be filmed. It seemed to me, though, that the film was made more as propaganda against the Japs than anything else.*

It was after half past eleven when I got in and I suddenly realised that I was very hungry and had eaten nothing but a slice of bread at teatime since my mid-day meal. I crept on to the baby ward where I got a couple of slices of bread, and the night nurse informed me I was quite safe. 'They' were all in the theatre. Lulled into a sense of false security by this statement, I marched boldly up three flights of stairs to my room and proceeded leisurely to get ready for bed. I was blithely cleaning my teeth when my door opened and there stood the Senior Night Sister who informed me that I had been here long enough to know that lights should be out by 11 o'clock. Accordingly I put my light out until I heard her footsteps retreating downstairs and then put it on again.

* This 1943 film is loosely based on the life and adventures of the very popular writer Jack London (1876–1916), whose Yukon-based *Call of the Wild* was widely admired. A ship named after him begins the film. Towards its end, set at the time of the Russo–Japanese War (1904–5), when Japan was an ally of the United States, the narrative is manipulated to portray Japan as a nation with aspirations to world domination, 'even if it takes 50 to 100 years,' as a Japanese military leader in the film is made to say.

Thursday, 16 November

Today is my birthday [she was 31] and my day off as well. I arrived home to find my brother and his wife there. He has fourteen days embarkation leave but he feels he has had good innings as though he was called up on the day war was declared his Army travels have only taken him in Sussex, Surrey and Kent. He came from Huddersfield where he will be stationed until he goes overseas. It was a pleasant surprise to see him at home but not so pleasant to learn that he was on embarkation leave.

Friday, 17 November

I had a letter today from my fiancé who is a POW in Germany. He is very worried because he has not heard from me for months and is afraid something terrible must have happened to me. I imagine he must be thinking that I have been killed by a flying-bomb or rocket as I expect the Germans give *them* to understand that these things are causing more damage over here than is actually the case. It is two or three months since I heard from him and he says he writes every other week. I sent him an Air Mail letter-card right away but don't suppose he will get it before Christmas now.

Saturday, 18 November

Today I was off duty at 6 again and went to the pictures again. I seem to have been to more film shows in the last two or three weeks than I usually go to in as many months. Fortunately my friend had the forethought to book or we should not have got in anywhere. The cinemas are always crowded on a Saturday night. The best picture in Town is *The Song of Bernadette* [who reputedly experienced eighteen visions of the Virgin Mary in 1858], and my friend said he was too late to book for that – all the seats were taken – but I have an idea he was secretly rather relieved. I don't think that type of picture appeals to him. So we went to see Charles Laughton in *The Canterville Ghost*, which, considering how ridiculous was the whole story, turned out to be surprisingly amusing and we quite enjoyed it.*

Sunday, 19 November

Today was my half-day and as my friend is departing for Scotland on Monday we arranged to meet early with the idea of going into the country for a long walk and having a nice tea somewhere. It was a fine morning but sad to relate it started to rain about 2 o'clock so we decided to go into Preston and go to the pictures in the evening. When we got to Preston the only café we could find open was a little café in the bus station so we went in. Here we were offered egg and chips, which I was sure would turn out to be dried egg, but I was wrong. It was a real egg with a great plateful of chips. There were no pots of tea, just cups of tea poured out of a great jug, and there was a great tray of bread and butter standing on a sideboard from which the waitress slapped a few pieces

---

* This 1944 film was a delightfully wacky wartime distraction – 'a comedy that puts you in the best of spirits,' according to an advertisement. A troop of US Rangers is billeted in an aristocratic castle that is haunted by a 300-year-old ghost (Charles Laughton). A series of unlikely plot twists determines that one GI (played by Robert Young) is a remote relative of de Canterville and able to dispatch the ghost by performing an act of bravery, but not before a party in which the troops display the latest in American dances (such as the boogie-woogie). The cast includes the child actress Margaret O'Brien.

on a plate for you. Both the waitresses and the tables were surprisingly clean, though, and the place was crowded with Forces and their girl friends. There were even a few officers in there too. I suppose they were all in the same plight that we were – could not find anywhere open.

Later on in the evening we went to the pictures and saw *Andy Hardy's Courtship* [1942]* after standing in a queue which seemed miles long. When we came out the last bus, which leaves at 8.25 for Blackburn, had gone so we had to come back by train. We stood in a queue for tickets and were packed like sardines in the last train from Preston to Blackburn on a Sunday night.

Monday, 20 November

I woke up this morning, my day off for the week, to find that it was pouring with rain. The various noises in the Nurses Home prevented me from sleeping but somehow I did not feel inclined to get up and get downstairs in time to have a lukewarm cup of tea before setting off to catch the bus home. I was a bit early and as there was no possibility of a queue – the rain was sweeping across the pavement in great gusts – I went into the station buffet for a cup of tea and a sandwich to fortify myself.

Once I got home I did not venture out again except to go to the Free Library. It is held in the village school every Monday night and the librarian blithely allows one family five or six books at a time to keep as long as you want them. There is quite a good collection down there to choose from and I can usually find one or two books worth reading.

---

* This was one in a series of sixteen Andy Hardy films, starring Mickey Rooney, that were vastly popular at the time.

I said goodbye to my brother as I knew I should not be home again before he went back from his embarkation leave. I do hope he does not go to Burma.

I reached the Infirmary feeling more miserable than I have felt for a long time. I missed my friend who had gone to Scotland and did not feel exactly elated about my brother. I dread the thought of Saturday [when the final exam results are to be announced] and don't feel very happy about meeting the Sister of the ward who is due back on duty tomorrow.

Wednesday, 22 November

Tonight we had a dance. It was absolutely crowded out, mostly with Yanks. We have another batch in the mill but I don't suppose they will be staying long. However, they generally stay long enough to penetrate to the Infirmary. It was quite good fun though I find the Americans don't seem to care much for anything except 'jive,' which does not appeal to me in the least. Some of the nurses are quite expert at it, I noticed. We have a radiogram for the dances now instead of a band and it is better in a great many ways. The radiogram does not want so many intervals for refreshment as the band seemed to do. Our own refreshments were not of the highest order, I must confess – a cup of watery coffee and a piece of that all too familiar yellow slab cake. I was 'relieving' the night nurse from 9.30 to 10.45 but got into mufti afterwards as our uniform is by no means glamourous.

After the dance came the usual round of sweeping the floor and getting the dining room ready for breakfast, for which the volunteers were rewarded with a drink of tea before going to bed. Lots of the staff had of course gone to see the Yanks off the premises, which seemed a very lengthy business in some cases, but my bed was calling too urgently.

Thursday, 23 November

When one stops to think about it, it is alarming the number of cancer cases one gets in and unless it has been diagnosed in its early stages how little can be done for it. It is tragic the number we have returned from the theatre with the information that the abdomen has been opened and the growth is inoperable, which means that it has invaded most of the vital organs and death is inevitable. Curiously enough after the abdomen has been opened people often seem to improve a little and go home with the firm conviction that they are on the road to recovery. Whether it is just a short-lived triumph of mind over matter I don't know but soon the inevitable relapse occurs, and there is no hope. In some cases, of course, radium and deep X-ray therapy are beneficial and the growth is arrested if not killed, but the success of these two methods depends so much on the type of growth and its position.

Friday, 24 November

The results of the exams are expected out tomorrow and those of us who sat are hovering between dread and anticipation. For myself I am so sure that I cannot have passed that I have broadcast the fact that if I fail I do not want any sympathy. I can only imagine one thing worse than failing and that would be to cry about it.

Today after dinner Matron sent the Sister and domestic staff out of the dining room and we all wondered what we

were going to be lectured about. Then she informed us that
the Ministry of Information had rung up to say that an American dance was being held tomorrow week and they were
sending twenty tickets along for the staff and would Matron
see that they went to the 'right type of girl'. She then gave us
a little homily about upholding the good name of the Infirmary and remembering that we were on our own ground and
the Yanks were a long way from home etc.

Saturday, 25 November

The great day is over. Great for us at least who have passed
our Finals and can now call ourselves State Registered
Nurses. That I am amongst this happy band seems nothing less than a miracle to me. The air of tension amongst
the nurses was terrific this morning. The first question on
our lips was 'Have the results come through?' as soon as the
postman had arrived because the date of the results coming
out does vary from time to time. When we heard they had
come we felt we could not bear to wait until 9 o'clock to
know our fate. Just after 8.30 I was on my way back to my
ward with a bottle of sterile water when another nurse who
sat with me and is on the same ward rushed out, grabbed
my hand and said we could go to the Sister Tutors' room.
We were the first there but we had to wait outside the door
while the two Sister Tutors had a discussion and by the time
we were allowed in all the Finalists and Prelims had arrived.
Then came a moment of agony while the Sister Tutor read
out the list of passes and my name was incredibly amongst
eight of us passed, four failed. Not a very good result. And
then the Sister Tutor handed out the individual notification
to each nurse and mine was missing. I was assured it would

come by a later post but I did not really feel happy about it until I came in at teatime and found it on my bed. Every little while I feel inclined to read it just to assure myself that it is really true [she was now one of some 27,000 State Registered Nurses employed in English hospitals].*

Monday, 27 November

A quiet day both on duty and off. I see from the glimpse I get at the newspaper headlines as I rush around the ward that we are still making slow progress towards Germany. Some of the patients have husbands or sons who have been in the East for several years and they are getting very excited at the prospect of seeing them again. Naturally they are all expecting or hoping that 'he' will be on the first boat load.

I have had one or two telegrams of congratulation today and a letter addressed to Nurse Johnstone SRN. It is all very exciting and the most surprising people stop you and congratulate you – people who you think are barely aware of your existence let alone knowing your name. When I think of how truly miserable I felt this time last Monday night – my friend having gone to Scotland, I had said goodbye to my brother for goodness knows how long, the Sister of the ward was expected back that night and the forthcoming results when I was quite certain that I should have failed – all combined depressed me extremely. It just goes to show that the old saying about the worst never happening is often true.

* Ferguson and Fitzgerald, *Studies in the Social Services* (1954), p. 335.

Current Facts, Future Prospects

November 1944–February 1945

Tuesday, 28 November

After a very stormy night it was comparatively calm this morning when I went into the Town. I went round leaving my belongings in various places to be cleaned and mended and am sure I shall be calling for them on the wrong dates. My coat, the only warm coat I possess, I just had to leave to be cleaned and I was told it would take a fortnight. I hope we don't get a really cold spell during that time. My watch I left at the jewellers and was told to call back in two months. My umbrella which I left to be recovered would not be ready until February, which seems so far ahead that I may forget about it altogether.

This evening we were presented with our hospital badges and everyone made a great fuss of us. One of the patients presented me with a lovely bunch of bronze and yellow chrysanthemums she had just been given to her, which are now adorning my room. This evening we had a Nurses Christian Movement meeting and the new vicar of the Parish Church gave us a very good address on 'pilotless lives'. Matron put in an appearance and there was a very good attendance. There is no doubt that it is a more flourishing and vigorous affair than it was even a year [ago].

Wednesday, 29 November

Today was a day of peace on duty. It was Sister's day off and what a difference it makes to the atmosphere of the ward. She had the staff nurse on WS [probably Women's Surgical] cooking a chicken for her during the morning and the savoury smell made our mouths water. As far as I could gather she was spending her day off in bed, eating, and whether she intended to eat the whole of the chicken herself was a matter of much speculation amongst the staff.

It was visiting day and I noticed most of the patients had been given tripe by their visitors. One woman had three lots brought to her and she was offering it round to the staff but as none of us were Lancastrians it was not very popular. It is strange how fond Lancashire people are of tripe. The long queues outside the tripe shops testify to that.

Thursday, 30 November

[In Downham]. I slept soundly this morning until 10 o'clock which surprised me very much as I usually wake round about 7. I felt better for it, though, as I was beginning to feel a bit 'drawn' after the tension and excitement of the past few days and now that I no longer sleep directly opposite to the Home Sister my light does not go out so promptly. It was a typical grey, wet November day so I hardly ventured outside. Instead I finished my renovation, turning a coat into a dress, and did a bit of 'Knitting for Liberated Europe' to help my mother on a bit.

So Mr Churchill is 70 years old today. What a man! However one disagrees with his political views, there is no doubt in my mind that he will go down in history as one of the most outstanding personalities of all time.

Friday, 1 December

I was never so thankful to get off duty as I was this evening. Had anyone asked me what I thought of nursing as a career, I should have said that it was the most heart breaking of all careers and should have advised anyone against taking it up. I have had the most nightmarish day on the ward, nothing but one thing after another. The morning was fairly quiet but after dinner the fun began.

To begin with a woman collapsed and died within about ten minutes. She was one of those cancer cases I mentioned a day or two ago and it was a most merciful end, though I must say that it came as a shock to me. Sister had disappeared for the moment and when she came back, though I had tried all the methods, heart stimulants, oxygen etc., the patient was breathing her last. Sister seemed to hold me personally responsible, though she admitted there was nothing else to be done for her. Later on in the afternoon we disagreed fiercely over some morphia for a case of burns admitted from casualty. She was a girl in the Land Army and had thrown some paraffin on a fire to light it. I guess it is a thing she will never do again.

Sunday, 3 December

My Sunday half-day and what a day, pouring with rain and
blowing a gale. I was very undecided whether to go home
or not but decided to go when I saw a slight lifting of the
clouds round about 1.30. I managed to catch an early bus
down and so bad was the weather that there was not even a
queue so I stood in the shelter of the Station entrance waiting for the bus to come in. There were lots of Americans
standing aimlessly around. One was taking snaps though of
what I could not imagine as all there was to be seen were a
few buses and one or two dejected little queues consisting
of people huddled in mackintoshes or buried under umbrellas. A few of the Yanks were with girls and they obviously
had no idea what to do with themselves. Blackburn on a wet
Sunday afternoon is one of the worst places to while away a
few hours in. There is not a single place open where you can
pass a bit of time away in the dry.

Arriving in Clitheroe I saw an unusual number of people
sheltering in the doorways from the rain and in the middle
of the Market Square was a stand covered with some drip-
ping wet Union Jack bunting. I was informed by one of the
onlookers that some Army officer was expected to take the
salute of the Home Guard at 2 o'clock but that he had not
turned up yet. While I was waiting for my bus he arrived in
a car and for a few minutes the sun peeped out and three
platoons of the Clitheroe Home Guard marched stolidly past
the stand and up the hill to the Castle. They had barely disappeared from sight when it started to pour with rain and
the officer who had taken the salute and was talking to the
Mayor leaped into his car and drove away. Simultaneously a
lorry arrived and a couple of men dismantled the stand and

took it away. The whole episode took less than ten minutes from start to finish and I began to wonder whether I had not imagined the whole thing, so completely had everything disappeared from view.

This stand-down of the Home Guard was accorded almost two full columns of coverage in the Clitheroe Advertiser and Times *(8 December 1944, p. 6), and the weather did not go unnoticed. 'Considering the climatic conditions, which varied with depressing frequency from being just poor and unpleasant to utterly vile, there was an impressive turn-out of men and the parade was witnessed by quite a number of their fellow townsmen.'*

Monday, 4 December

I went to see Matron this morning to have a talk with her about staying on or not. She can appeal for six months' deferment for so many newly State Registered Nurses and after thinking things over I decided that it would be a good idea if I could stay on here for six months, and save a bit of money, and incidentally get a little more general nursing experience before I started to train for another certificate. This idea of pushing you on to take further training as soon as you have become a State Registered Nurse seems most unfair to me. Matron said she would put in an appeal for me though she could not promise I should get deferment. It depended on the Appointments Committee at Preston how many nurses she was allowed.

Tuesday, 5 December

We have been having a lot of talk today about pensions for nurses and the superannuation scheme. I put forward the suggestion that hospitals should be State-controlled and nurses should have pensions on retirement like civil servants. Some agreed about the State control, others violently disagreed, but all agreed about pensions for nurses. Of course the superannuation scheme provides a part-solution on the subject of pensions for nurses. You pay in for a certain number of years and then at a given age you can draw out a weekly annuity amounting on an average to about £1 a week or a lump sum. I think you pay 15s a month and the hospital pays 15s but not every hospital has this superannuation scheme in force. In some hospitals you start as soon as you begin your training. In this hospital you have to be State-Registered before you can pay into it.

Wednesday, 6 December

Today we heard a lot about the All-Alliance dance thirty of the nurses (we hope they were the right type of girl) went to last night. Most of them seemed to be disappointed in it. They said the walls were lined by Yanks, few of whom danced, and those who did dance only wanted to 'jive'. They found it difficult to dance to the music of the Yankee dance band even when it was supposed to be playing a waltz. And the refreshments consisted of cocoa, and cheese and chicken sandwiches – and we had been imagining them consuming quantities of ice cream and tinned fruit.

Thursday, 7 December

Today a great many of our wounded went on leave and I understand they are going to hospitals nearer their own homes when their leave is up. There are a greater number of amputations in this last convoy from Italy than in those we have had previously from France. I suppose the reason is that those who are not seriously wounded are kept in Italy to go back to the Front Line when they are better whereas at one time they were sending all cases from France, seriously wounded and otherwise, and some of the cases we got from France were very trivial. It was pathetic, though, to see some of the men with only one leg starting off down the drive on crutches, trying to balance their kit bags and haversacks in addition. It seemed to us very inhuman that they would not all have been taken down in a bus to the station instead of having to struggle down on the trams with their kits. The ruling was, though, that only those capable of travelling off their own bat could go on leave and I suppose they were naturally all so anxious to go on leave that they said they could manage, whether or no.

Kathleen undoubtedly kept up with news on the progress of the war, though she mentioned it only from time to time. 'It does seem terrible', she remarked on 8 December, 'that now that the Greeks are liberated they should have started fighting amongst themselves, and what's more that our men should have to go to the Government's aid and get killed in the process.' (Greece was on the verge of full-scale civil war.) Three days later she 'sent some duty-free cigarettes – through a tobacconist of course – to my fiancé in Germany'; and his existence came up again the following day when she was mulling over her future and thinking about District Nursing. 'Actually I think I should like it had I not been thinking of getting married but what is the use of going in for a lengthy training if you are not seriously considering carrying on with it? I really think things would have been simpler had I not passed.'

With Christmas approaching, gifts had to be thought of, though
the choices were very limited. On Wednesday, 13 December she was
in Downham and 'Before settling down for an evening in front of
the fire I went to collect the present that Father Christmas is bring-
ing my little nephew [Peter, aged 2]. It is a most substantial engine
made of wood by a local man who lost an arm in the last war. I
don't know how he manages to turn out such intricate work. He
has already made a doll's bed with some fancy carving at the foot
and head for my niece and he is only charging 12s 6d for each toy
which, when you consider the trash that you get in the shops for £1,
is very cheap. Needless to say he is loaded with orders for toys for
Christmas and does not see how he can get them all made.'

Thursday, 14 December

The person from the Appointments Committee at Preston has been today and interviewed all the new SRNs. We
have most of us got six months' deferment until the end
of May. We had to make some sort of statement as to what
we were going to do in the 'special fields' when one's six
months' deferment was finished. I decided on the spur of
the moment that I would take the first part of the midwifery
training and on being pressed as to where I said in or near
London – so that was that. By taking the first part you get
a working knowledge of midwifery and you are not obliged
to practise it afterwards like you have to do if you take both
parts.

I had a letter today from my brother at Huddersfield. He
said they appeared to be making a move on Sunday but it
was cancelled.

We have nine of us recovered from the shock of having
four chocolate biscuits each for tea today. The most we

usually see of biscuits are a few slightly musty ones at supper occasionally.

Saturday, 16 December

Today has been beastly cold, driving rain and wind. I dashed out in between the storms to see what I could do locally in the way of Christmas cards and managed to get enough at not too exorbitant prices.

I had a letter today from my fiancé in Germany. He said he was just receiving letters from me posted in May and June. His letter was dated the end of October. He said that the time seemed to pass more slowly than ever now that the end is in sight. It seems to me in my moments of despondency that the war will go on for years and years. I cannot rid myself of the horrible thought that Germany may yet pull herself together as we did when all seemed lost and as the Russians did at Stalingrad and that we may plug away for years at the German frontiers. Thank goodness I never really took any notice of the optimistic people who said that the war would be over for Christmas.

The following day in Downham, after hearing the news about the German offensive in Belgium, Kathleen lamented that 'My forebodings about Germany's recovery are getting stronger than ever.' The next day, the 18th, 'My mother and I listened to practically all the news broadcasts today, hoping to hear that they [the Germans] had been pushed back. I must say there is something to be said for the absorbing life in hospital. We have no wireless now so when we look at the patients' daily paper we only vaguely realise what is going on. Consequently, we get saved a lot of anxiety.'

Friday, 22 December

Everyone seems to be scanning the morning papers each
morning now and reading of the Germans advancing 10, 15,
20, and this morning in one of the papers 35 miles into Belgium. Most of us are saying, except those with Yankee boy
friends, if the British had been holding that sector the Germans would not have got through. I daresay we are being
unfair to the Americans as the odds seemed to have been
against them. One cannot but help admire the skill and
marvellous powers of recovery of the German Army. They
are making superhuman efforts to prevent the fight being
waged on the sacred German soil. If only all their brains
and skill and fanatical determination could be directed into
doing good instead of evil, what a power they would be in
the world. If only they had our good intentions – because I
am convinced, however we thunder, our intentions are good.
With their 'drive' the world would be a much better place.

Sunday, 24 December

We had a very rude awakening at half past five this morning.
I had been awakened by an attack of coughing and was just
settling down for another sleep before the bell went when
I heard what I took to be a plane approaching. It was very
low and I held my breath as it soared over the roof, shaking
the Nurses Home by the vibration of its engine. For a few
seconds it continued on its way and then there was silence
followed by a terrific crash, which nearly shook me out of
bed. The whole corridor sprang to life and as I was getting
out of bed to join the others I heard the sound of the air
raid sirens in the distance and then several more crashes but

further away this time. There was no more sleep for any of us and everyone was arguing fiercely as to whether it was a flying bomb or an aircraft that had crashed. The Night Sister rang up the police to see if we were to prepare for casualties but they said nothing had dropped in the borough. On the 9 o'clock news in the morning we heard that flying bombs had landed for the first time in the North so that those people who had said they were flying bombs in the first place went around preening themselves. Later on we heard they had dropped at various places between here and Preston but had caused very little damage.*

It seemed such a contrast to the early hours of the day when we went round the darkened wards tonight singing carols. We went in a long crocodile two by two, with torches or candles, singing all the way. The patients always enjoy it and I must say when I stopped singing, to give my tired throat a rest, and looked round at the procession, there did seem something about the whole thing that gave one an unearthly feeling, as though it did not quite belong to this world. There was no light in the quiet ward except the dull glow from a fire. The only illumination was from the torches and candles of the nurses, which only gave enough light to show the absorbed faces of the nurses as they walked slowly round, looking at their copies and singing, concentrating so wholeheartedly.

Monday, 25 December

Christmas Day. At 6 o'clock the C of E's were roused by a knocking on their doors so that they should rouse themselves

---

* One of the V-1s fell on the village of Tottington, near Bury, killing seven people and injuring another fourteen (Nick Dunnachie, *East Lancashire at War* [Stroud: Alan Sutton, 1995], pp. 38–9).

and go to the 6.30 Communion Service. The RC's had mostly gone to Midnight Mass – the first to be held, I believe, since war started – so they were able to roll over in bed with a clear conscience. We were a motley looking crowd which assembled in the waiting hall to walk up to the church, some in full-dress uniform, some in half-uniform, half-mufti, others completely in mufti. It was bitterly cold and dark when we stepped outside and we were glad when we got into the warmth of the church. There was no one present but nurses, other more fortunate people being able to stay in bed a bit longer and attend a later one. We were ravenously hungry when we got back in time for breakfast when we had grape-fruit and an egg.

We did not do more work than absolutely necessary but just as the patients were being served with their Christmas dinner a bad 'burns' came in. The back of her dressing gown had caught fire with disastrous results. The patients had turkey, plum pudding and mince pies [and later the soldier patients enjoyed carolling by the nurses: *Northern Daily Telegraph*, 27 December 1944, p. 5] but we do not get our Christmas dinner until later in the week so we had pork-chops followed by mince-pies.

As soon as I got back from dinner I set to work on dressing the burns, which took me a full hour, and by that time it was more than time for me to go off duty. There was a Christmas tree on the children's ward during the afternoon and the Mayors and Mayoresses of Blackburn, Darwen and Clitheroe came and gave out the children's presents and made a few speeches. I thought I would go down and have a look but had to come away before the speeches as I knew there would be all the routine work of the ward to get done before we went to 'high' tea at 5.30. We had a jolly good tea, ham and tongue and salad, trifle, mince pies, marzipan, fruit, Christmas cake with plenty of fruit, almond paste and thick icing. We hardly knew how to stagger back to the ward.

The Rotary Club were going to give a concert to the wounded on the Men's Surgical ward so at 8.30 when we came off duty we went up and arrived at the interval, when we had more refreshments including ice-cream. The concert, which was very good, was over about 10 and after we had helped to put the ward to rights we came back to the Nurses Home where there were numerous bottle parties in progress. I only had time for a glass of cider because a friend of mine who normally does not drink at all had had some brandy put into some beer she had been drinking earlier in the evening and was absolutely haywire. The minute I took my eyes off her she wandered off to do some mad thing and nothing could persuade her to go to bed as she sleeps on the third floor and had got the flying bombs on her mind. Eventually she calmed down, and we left her sleeping on someone else's bed and went to bed ourselves.

'We lived on the fat of the land yesterday', Kathleen wrote on 26 December, 'but today we have come down to earth with a bang and have practically starved. It is a pity we cannot be like a camel and have a little reserve stored away to draw on when times are bad.'

Sunday, 31 December

The last day of 1944. It was my half-day too so I was able to go home and naturally the talk turned to the changes and events for the family in the last year. We have had our ups and downs and for myself I think I shall remember 1944 as on the whole a good year. I have become a State Registered

Nurse and though I worked quite hard for it I have had some good times as well. If 1945 turns out as well I shall not grumble. My mother and father have moved into a different house during the year, my sister has had a premature baby which died, and my brother has gone overseas, so we have all of us in some way had fresh experiences, though not all were pleasant. To go from the personal to the things that have happened in the world, how vastly our position has improved during the past year makes one realize how much we should be thankful for instead of moaning about the reverse we are now experiencing on the Western Front.

To finish the Old Year really well and to start the New Year a crowd of us went to the Watch-Night Service at the Cathedral and when we came out there were still lots of people about wishing everyone a Happy New Year and all over the place we could hear people singing 'Auld Lang Syne'.

The following evening, the first of 1945, Kathleen and some fellow nurses 'went into the sitting room to listen to the news before going to bed. There are short spells when we have the wireless in the sitting room for a few days and longer spells when it is away being mended, which run into weeks. The Jerries don't seem to be making much headway in the offensive now. If only we could muster up sufficient strength to sweep them right back to Berlin and have done with this war.'

Tuesday, 2 January 1945

A very sad thing happened today. Amongst one of the earlier convoys there was a soldier with a badly smashed arm. His wife came up to lodge in Blackburn so that she could be near him. As she was expecting a baby and had arranged to go into a Nursing Home in Blackburn for the event, he was not put down for transfer so that he could be near her. She had a baby boy about three weeks ago which was admitted to the children's ward yesterday evening and died this morning. A post-mortem was done on the baby and it was found to be suffering from double pneumonia. The father is most upset about it. He was so proud of his son and lost no opportunity of displaying him. In fact it is our private opinion that the baby has been exhibited too much. The father is only 20 and the mother 19 and I guess they just did not understand much about babies. We are all sad about it because he has been here so long and everyone knows him and likes him.

Wednesday, 3 January

Things seem very flat at the moment. Christmas is over and the New Year has begun. The war news is depressing. It is not very bad nor yet very good. I am faced with the fact that I have committed myself to do Part One of my midwifery training, a prospect which does not appeal to me in the slightest. There seems no prospect of the war being over this year or next as far as I can see and I can almost imagine myself a grey-haired matron before my fiancé comes home again. We are working hard, we are short staffed and altogether life seems grey.

I need some new pyjamas desperately but with my two precious coupons I can do nothing about it. I have, though, optimistically sent for a pattern of some but what use the pattern will be to me without material I cannot really say. I am, though, like that famous character of Dickens [Wilkins Micawber in *David Copperfield*] hoping that something will turn up.

Thursday, 4 January

It has been bitterly cold today. My poor patients have been huddled beneath the [bed]clothes with only the tips of their noses showing and even with hot water bottles have not been warm. The two inadequate little electric fires we have on each side of the ward have not warmed the ward at all and the radiators have only been lukewarm. This ward, which I think I have mentioned before as being only an Army hut from the last war tacked on to the end of the Women's Surgical ward, is terribly draughty, [and] the windows don't fit properly so that any heating arrangement has not a fair chance. It is very inconvenient too. To get to the ward kitchen from the Annexe you have to walk along a short corridor, then through a small ward along the main corridor and through another small ward, so that is pretty heavy going at meal times to carry trays as far as that for twenty patients. Matron always tells people she is taking round that had it not been for the war it would have been rebuilt, but they had twenty years to rebuild it in and there was nothing concrete planned when war started.

Friday, 5 January

Coming back [to Blackburn from Downham] on the bus I sat in front of two women, one of whom obviously from the way she was talking had a son who was a prisoner-of-war. She was telling the other woman how she had received a visit from a POW who had escaped and who had been in the same camp as her son. They were in a working camp near the Yugo-Slovak frontier and eighty of them were on their way to their work when the guards were overpowered by some Yugo-Slav partisans and they marched for days in the mountains with the partisans before they made contact with the Allied forces. It was an interesting tale and I was glad the women did not get off the bus until after she had finished it.

Tuesday, 9 January

When I got back on duty after my morning off I was told that there had been some shooting affair in Clitheroe and that several people were killed. I supposed that maybe there had been some accident to some soldiers practising or something but was horror-struck when I heard the true story. A man and his little son were brought in seriously wounded by a humane killer. His wife and two little girls had been killed with it and they belong to Downham. It is the family who used to live in the house we now occupy. The man and little boy both died before 8.30 this morning so I suppose no one will ever really know what happened in that farmhouse in the early hours of the morning. The general idea is that the man must have gone mad and killed his family and then himself but the doctors say he had three wounds, one above his heart and two on his temple, and it seems hardly possible that they could be self-inflicted as a humane killer has to be reloaded after each shot.

Wednesday, 10 January

The sole topic of conversation seems to be the shooting tragedy. It is in the daily papers and patients and nurses alike, knowing I come from Downham, are bombarding me with questions. There are long arguments as to whether the husband or wife could have done it or whether it was an out-side job. Seeing that the whole family are now dead one can only hope that one of them did it, as it would be too horrible to think that there may be a maniac at large who could do such a horrible thing. It seems incredible that such a com-plete and apparently happy family could have been wiped out in such a way. It would not have been quite such a ter-rible thing if they had been killed by enemy action or in an accident.

Thursday, 11 January

The inquest on the shooting tragedy was held in Clith-eroe at 11.30 so the reporters, who my mother said had made such a nuisance of themselves yesterday in Down-ham, transferred their attention to Clitheroe. The verdict was that Cornell had murdered his wife and children and then committed felo de se. Nothing was said of the pos-sibility of his being of unsound mind. In fact the general idea seemed to be that the whole thing was too deliberate for that to be the case. No one could throw any fresh light on the motive for the murders. There seems no motive. A young healthy man with a pretty wife to whom he appeared devoted, three lovely children, a well-paid job and employer who thought very highly of him. He seemed to have the kind of life that millions of men all over the world would have envied. His people, who are staying with us, cannot provide any clue, so that it seems it will be an unsolved mystery.

Unsurprisingly, this family tragedy attracted a great deal of pub-lic attention. It was reported in The Times of London *and of*

course was a major story locally. The apparent killer, Edward
Cornell, aged 30, was the farm bailiff to Mr Ralph Assheton, MP
and Chairman of the Conservative Party and the owner of the
Downham estate. Cornell's wife was 31 and their three children
were all under the age of 7. Months later, on Sunday, 24 June, when
there were crowds of visitors in Downham, Kathleen and a friend
were having tea on the front lawn of her parents' house 'and heard
one or two passers-by say that this was the scene of the shooting tragedy early in the year. Of course the unfortunate family did live here
for the greater part of their time in Downham. They had only been
at the farm a few months. The village people say that farm [West
Lane Farm] is unlucky and it certainly seems so. The new farm
bailiff is ill at the moment with pneumonia.'*

Sunday, 14 January

Sunday and my half-day. Had a busy morning, admitted two
head injuries, one an old lady who had fallen downstairs
and pierced her head with a remarkably long hair grip, the
other a girl brought in unconscious, found on the roadside
in a pretty poor state. It turned out later she was a farmer's
daughter delivering milk and had fallen out of the back of
the milk float. It is surprising how often this happens, especially to older women.

I was undecided whether to go home or not as we still
have the relatives from the shooting tragedy staying with us
so I went into dinner. Was glad I had done so because we
had Christmas pudding. It was such a fine afternoon and it

---

* *The Times*, 10 January 1945, p. 2 and 12 January 1945, p. 2; *Northern Daily Telegraph*,
11 January 1945, p. 5. Unsurprisingly, as the *Clitheroe Advertiser and Times* reported (12
January 1945, p. 4), 'the whole district was shocked and mystified' by the tragic events.

seemed a waste of a free afternoon to stay in so I got changed
and caught the train home arriving just in time for tea.

Monday, 15 January

The farmer's daughter we admitted yesterday morning died
during the night, quite suddenly. They had not even time to
notify her people. What a shock it must have been for them.
She was only 22, and though I knew she was pretty bad I
did not expect her to go so soon. I have seen 'head injuries' which appeared much worse recover. We have a custom
amongst ourselves of referring to our patients by the nature
of their complaint or operation, which must sound strange to
other people. For instance, anyone could often hear us make
statements such as 'The "head injury" is restless' or 'The
:appendectomy" has a lot of pain'.

*An almost constant fact of life this month was 'the intense cold' (22
January) and the efforts, many ineffective, to deal with it. 'All the
patients have been huddled down under the bedclothes.' On the 23rd
'The ward was even colder than yesterday, only 48°F'; on the 26th
it had sunk to 43°F. That day 'I asked the Sister if we could wear
cardigans [the nurses wore short-sleeved dresses] and she gave us
permission. I might say that it is practically an unheard of thing
for nurses to wear cardigans on duty but once our ward had started
the ball rolling, by teatime the greater part of the nursing staff had
appeared in cardigans of every colour and shape.'*

*Few houses in Blackburn and district had central heating
(including her parents' home in Downham), so water pipes had
frozen, and coal was in short supply. 'We are beginning to think
ourselves fortunate in living in a hospital,' Kathleen wrote on
the 27th. 'We have at least an adequate supply of hot water and*

radiators in our bedrooms and sitting room which, though the atmosphere is never exactly over-heated, at least it is never icy cold. My own bedroom would be fairly warm but for the fact that last October a gale broke my window and it has never been mended. I have a large piece of match boarding nailed over it but there is a 2-inch gap at the top through which the wind is whistling merrily at this very moment.'

There were a few (but not many) brighter moments in January 1945. On the 19th she remarked on the advances of the Russians towards Germany. 'Hope of a speedy end to the war seems to be reviving and I have been asked if I will not alter my forecast of the war ending in October to an earlier date but I am sticking to it.' More prosaic but still noteworthy was the occasional treat. On the 12th 'Everyone in the building has been issued with a couple of oranges, patients and staff alike, so we shall get a little fresh Vitamin C. We have plenty of Vitamin tablets on the ward but they never seem to me as though they can possibly do anyone as much good as a nice juicy orange.' Two weeks later she and others enjoyed more fresh fruit. 'All the staff were given three oranges and two lemons today. A pile came up for the patients too, but I don't know exactly how many they got.' One day (the 16th) she was enjoying reading a book – Yeoman's Hospital *(1944), by Helen Ashton, about life in a provincial hospital. 'It is one of the few stories of hospital life which is anything approaching reality and must have been written by someone who has been a member of the staff in a provincial hospital. It does not emphasize the sordid side, nor does it glamourize hospital life. Many of the incidents could have happened here – and have for that matter.' (This novel, authored by a woman with a medical degree from the University of London, portrays realistically the work and staff relations in a hospital in the town of 'Wiltchester' during twenty-four hours in December 1943, with romance, gossip, back-biting, class-resentment, and the like added in.)*

Thursday, 1 February

The chief topic of conversation is the wonderful progress
of the Russians towards Berlin. It does seem incredible that
they should have got so far in such a short time when we are
in the same position as we were months ago.

There is quite a big gathering of the nurses for the
9 o'clock news in the sitting room after supper now. As I
looked round tonight at the nurses sitting there waiting for
the news, I was reminded of what a soldier said to me last
summer, 'that unless a girl had some personal interest in the
war such as a fiancé or husband at the Front she never bothered how much progress or the reverse occurred.' His words
seemed true. Every nurse there had a boy friend in the fighting line or overseas or a POW, and each of us are hoping to
get married as soon as the war is over.

Monday, 5 February

We had 2 deaths on the ward today. One, an old lady, died
in the early hours of the morning before we came on duty,
the other died at dinner time. We had a really frivolous conversation at the dinner table and came back on to the ward
talking and laughing. It seemed such a sharp contrast to go
straight to the bedside of the dying woman surrounded by
her sorrowful relatives. Only a matter of seconds elapsed
before she died. There was nothing I could do to save her.
It had all been done – Ceramine [injection], radiant heat,
blood transfusion – we had worked hard all the morning
to save her but all our efforts were useless. The ward was
so quiet you could have heard a pin drop when she died.
None of the other patients spoke a word and several of them

were having a little weep. They had cheered up by teatime
and the discharge of a couple of patients and the admission
of a new one gave us an opportunity to rearrange the beds
so that there was not the depressing spectacle of an empty
bed standing where there had been an occupied one this
morning.

Wednesday, 7 February

I had a letter this morning from my brother [in India], obviously written en route, in which he said that my remark
about outposts of the Empire in the last letter I wrote him
before he embarked seemed to be true and that I had better
get a stock of notepaper and write often.

There are various references in the paper to POW camps
the Russians have over-run but they never give them a
name. Have not heard from my fiancé since November. He
is in a working camp attached to Stalag VIII B and in a way
I hope it is in some remote part of Germany which will be
untouched by war. I would rather wait a few more months
as I have already waited five years than have him caught up
in the fighting and perhaps get wounded or even killed. It
would be wonderful, though, to know that he was out of
German hands. Sometimes I get very despondent and think
that he will never get back safely and that I have waited all
these years for nothing.

Monday, 12 February

It was pouring with rain when I woke this morning [in
Downham] and I just spent a peaceful morning in bed
reading a peaceful little book which I had given to me at

Christmas called *The Silver Ball* [1943], written by Lady [Susan] Tweedsmuir. A tale of pre-war country life in a village and it was really very soothing.

I scan the newspapers every day to find news, however small, as to what is happening to the POWs in camps which have now been over-run by the Russians. I find that the famous Stalag VII B is probably amongst them and as my fiancé is in a working camp attached to VII B I am wondering what will have become of him.* Of course the Germans are supposed to have transferred some of them to camps nearer the interior of Germany and he may be amongst them. The last letter I had from him was written on October 28 so goodness knows what may have become of him since then. I just cannot imagine him getting safely back to England.

Friday, 16 February

We have a girl on our ward who came in with burns a week or two ago. She is married and has two children. Her husband is in Italy and up to this morning she had not heard from him for a month. Yesterday she had a visitor who informed her that her husband had probably gone to Burma as her husband and the visitor's husband had always been together and the visitor's husband had now been sent to Burma. This upset the poor girl terribly and she sobbed the rest of the day. Today after reading a letter from her husband she was almost hysterical with delight. She has not seen her husband for three years except for forty-eight hours' leave in Edinburgh when he flew over from Sicily with some Army

---

* Since she wrote Stalag VIII B on 7 February, an error of some sort is evident. She returns to the identifier VIII B below (23 February) and later.

bigwigs. Their second child is the result of that forty-eight hours' leave and of course her husband has never seen him. She was hoping her husband would get some compassionate leave owing to her accident but I don't think her condition is bad enough to warrant that.

Saturday, 17 February

We often get asked by patients how to set about getting compassionate leave for relatives in the Forces and today I got asked by two men who wanted extension of their compassionate leave. At least one of them did. The other has got a temporary release from the Army and had got his papers for a 'medical' prior to rejoining. I don't quite know on what grounds he got this temporary release but he has been in a civilian job for some time now. His wife is not in for any serious complaint, and though she is only 31 she weighs 20 stone and owing to her enormous weight her wound had to be re-sutured. But I don't think the Army would release him just because his wife is over-weight. He wanted a letter from the Infirmary about his wife's condition so that he could apply for an extension and he wanted the letter today. It is hopeless sometimes to get hold of the Resident Surgical Officer who is supposed to write these letters, but I sent a nurse round the building with notepaper and primed with particulars, to find him. Eventually she returned with the blank sheet of notepaper except for the RSO's signature, and I was told that he could not possibly spare time to do it now – I must write it. Which I did, after much anxious thought. I wanted to be truthful but I also wanted to give the man a fair chance of getting his extension.

Sunday, 18 February

Sunday once again. I was off duty this morning and while I was getting ready for church I saw with amusement three small boys charging round the grounds, one brandishing a miniature Tommy gun while the others made appropriate noises. The enemy was a large dog who seemed to be thoroughly entering into the game. During the afternoon I saw the same small gang tearing along the main corridor complete with Tommy gun and uttering blood curdling yells with Matron in hot pursuit. The children in the neighbouring streets regard the Infirmary grounds with its ever-open gates as their legitimate playground and look most amazed when they are ordered out. During last summer bigger numbers than ever invaded the grounds and it was not until some small boys lit a fire under the Annexe (the ward I am on now) one Sunday afternoon, causing panic amongst the visitors and patients, that any vigorous steps were taken to stop them. The police stuck up large 'Trespassers will be prosecuted' notices too, and no children were seen in the grounds, but they are gradually creeping back.

Monday, 19 February

We had a terribly busy day on the ward and I was thankful when 6 o'clock arrived and it was time for me to go off duty. The weather was unusually warm too and coming so soon after the icy spell it made me feel really tired, though I must say it is pleasant not to have to go around feeling like a block of ice.

I managed to make the final spurt when I came off duty to catch the bus into Town which would enable me to get the 6.35 home. I always think that standing in a bus queue gives you a feeling of being invisible and I find myself staring at people as they pass in a way that I would not do if I was just standing alone. The square in front of the Station is always very busy at this time of the day – people pouring into Blackburn by train and bus from the various war factories in the vicinity. There are always a lot of members of the Forces about too, looking round for a way of passing the evening. I was watching three comical little Americans, in their big unpolished boots and little leather gaiters and those queer little short mackintosh jackets they wear (they are no objects of beauty) and thinking to myself that even the slovenliest of our own men in battle dress look much better than they do, when a man in the queue next to me suddenly said 'Some Scotch Guards' !! in a tone of great disgust. He then went on to say that he could tolerate the Americans if only they did not brag so much. He then said he was in a carriage full of Americans a night or two ago and they were boasting so much and running down this country to such an extent that he changed carriages at the next station in order to avoid a stand-up fight.

Tuesday, 20 February

I see in the paper that relatives of POWs are petitioning their MPs for authentic news regarding those men who were in camps now over-run by the Russians. I must say that I think by this time some sort of list could have been issued by the Russians or Poles, giving names of liberated prisoners. I read of POWs thumbing lifts for Warsaw or Moscow. I can just imagine the poor things, cold and hungry, not knowing friend from foe, trying to get somewhere for food and shelter. After being prisoners, some of them for as long as five years, it must be very bewildering to suddenly have to fend for themselves. The more I think about [it] the less likelihood there seems to be of my fiancé getting safely home.

Wednesday, 21 February

More and more nurses seem to be getting married from here. In pre-war days they would have been obliged to resign but Matron is allowing them all to stay on if they want to whether they have been here for a few weeks or have nearly finished their time. The majority, of course, are getting married on their boy friends' embarkation leave or sometimes the boy friend has been abroad for several years and is now on leave. Some of them met their husbands here, casualties from Normandy. What a sorting out there will be when the war is over.

9

Endings

February–June 1945

Friday, 23 February

Today I had a letter from my fiancé written on the 12th of December and though I was glad to get it I should have liked a bit more recent news. He was still in the labour detachment attached to Stalag VIII B when he wrote and I am hoping that he may be amongst those taken to Odessa. I don't suppose he will be but one can always go on hoping.

I went tonight with some of the staff to see *Till We Meet Again*. It was very sad and I really like a more restful type of picture. I am afraid I am an escapist where pictures are concerned, and I prefer pictures that do not show Nazi brutality. In fact I hate seeing brutality on the screen at all and always close my eyes at these points. I try to avoid pictures where I know there will be beatings and tortures, even though the rest of the picture may be good. There was, however, very little of that sort of thing in *Till We Meet Again*, and I did not have to close my eyes.*

Sunday, 25 February

As I waited at the bus stop in Chatburn [on her way to Downham] I tried to visualise the house which used to stand in its own little garden, opposite the bus stop, before it received a direct hit by a bomb which literally did not leave one stone standing on another. But so short is human memory that I could not remember one feature about it. Behind me stood a row of ruined houses, a grim reminder that however remote and quiet the village, that is no guarantee for safety. It was in the early afternoon that a German plane swooped down in the summer of 1940 and unloaded a stack of bombs on Chatburn, aiming we imagined at a very small cotton mill, but it missed the mill and as most of the occupants of the houses were working in the mill at the time there were only four deaths, and a few minor injuries.

Tuesday, 27 February

At lunch time we had a fierce argument about the nurses from The Florence Nightingale [Hospital] at Bury, who are being prosecuted for fraternising with German prisoners-of-war. It is a fever hospital and apparently the POWs had

---

* This 1944 American film is ostensibly about a convent's Mother Superior and gardener helping prisoners to avoid recapture by German troops. However, it quickly turns into a Hollywood romance – chaste because the female lead is a novice nun tasked with helping an American airman escape (he is married). Two people are shot and killed in the film, the Mother Superior and the novice nun, neither involving visible shedding of blood.

been in with diphtheria from a local camp. Apparently it was after these Germans were discharged that this 'fraternising' took place, though how I don't quite know. When we had Jerries in here there were one or two of our nurses who were regarded as being too friendly with them; on the other hand there were some nurses who would have watched them die without raising a finger to save them. Personally I just cannot feel a hatred towards a whole race of people. I still cling to my belief that there are good and bad of every race, though I am often assured that is not the case. Perhaps had I been an unfortunate inhabitant of an occupied country I should know how to hate. But it is a strange thing that quite a few of these nurses who are so violently antagonistic to anything German have no close connections involved in the fighting, have never been bombed or suffered any of . . . [without explanation, she does not complete the sentence].

Friday, 2 March

We are all taking a keen interest in the case of the nurses from The Florence Nightingale Fever Hospital at Bury, who have today been fined for their friendship, or whatever you like to call it, with the German prisoners-of-war. Am sure in any other country but ours there would not be any opportunity for that sort of thing. Several of our nurses did their Fever training at the Florence Nightingale before they came here and they know the two Sisters in question, who are both Irish. We have an Irish element here whose sympathy with the Allied cause is questionable. Talking of Irish nurses, we have a very nice one on our ward and today she received a box of milk chocolates from her mother in Ireland. Our eyes nearly popped out in surprise and she assured us that boxes of chocolate like that were no rarity in Ireland. Am afraid the poor girl did not get many of them herself – by the time she had handed them round once or twice we had made a good hole in the box.

Sunday, 4 March

In the early hours of this morning when I heard the wailing of the air raid sirens I thought to myself of the old saying 'Be sure your sins will find you out' [she had been in Blackburn overnight at a party]. We had not had the sirens for ages, months if not years, and just the very night that I fail to return to the Infirmary they have to go. I could not hear any planes around let along bombs dropping so I decided to stay put and did not waken my friend, who was sleeping soundly. We arrived back at the Infirmary about 7 in time to get changed and go in to breakfast. We were relieved to find that in the confusion we had not been missed. In the early part of the war there was a rota for the nurses saying who had to dress and go on to the ward to be there in case of air raid casualties. But as Blackburn has had remarkably few air raids it was gradually dropped and consequently no one knew what was expected of them. When I first came here there was a big room in the basement containing tiers of bunks to which those not on call had to go in the event of an air raid. These have been moved now and the nurses congregated in the sitting room not knowing what to do as some of the administrative staff told them to stay there, others told them they could go to bed, and altogether it was a muddle.*

---

* This day's events prompted her the following day to comment on street lighting in Blackburn. 'There are still some side streets with gas lamps and when the sirens sounded yesterday morning the electric street lights were put out, but in

Wednesday, 7 March

So Mrs Jones has got her reprieve [from hanging for murder]. I never really thought she would be hanged. We just don't seem to do those sorts of things in this country. Personally I think the only justification for hanging a person would be if it brought the murdered person back to life and as that is impossible, well, it does seem pointless. We have had great arguments here for and against and there seems no doubt that she has been a really 'bad lot'. Still, it may be a lesson for other girls living the sort of life she was leading – that it does not pay.*

The war news Kathleen recorded was mostly encouraging. Changes were occurring quickly, almost all of them to the advantage of the Allies. On Sunday, 11 March she read in a newspaper that 'the first lot of prisoners-of-war released by the Russians had left Odessa by ship for a Middle East port. I don't suppose my fiancé is one of them but one can always hope.' Some war-related scenes were markedly mundane. On 12 March she travelled with a friend

rows of side streets dotting the hill side the gas lights were still burning merrily.' There must have been many scenes in wartime Blackburn that were little changed from the later nineteenth century. One woman (b. 1935) recalled that when walking through one part of the city as a girl at this time 'we passed houses, garages, corner shops, pubs, warehouses, foundries and [cotton] mills. Men in cloth caps, ladies wrapped in black shawls, whatever the weather, sat on chairs outside of their houses, knitting. Some of the ladies smoking pipes as well as the men.' (Joyce Fielding, *Little Me* [privately printed, 2013], pp. 78–9.)

* Elizabeth Jones, aged 18, along with her US Army deserter friend, Karl Hulten, had been convicted of the murder of a London taxi driver, and sentenced to death. He was hanged; her sentence was commuted to life imprisonment. Much had been made of her unsavoury and promiscuous lifestyle – she was a (self-described) striptease dancer – and the case, known as 'the cleft chin murder' (because of this feature of the victim's face), was widely discussed. The crime was a subject of interpretation in George Orwell's famous 1946 essay, 'Decline of the English Murder'.

*by train to Lancaster and 'In our carriage was a Canadian sol-
dier who seemed to have made a study of British railways. He
knew the local lines much better than a Lancastrian to whom he
was talking and as for the Southern Railway he seemed to know
every station, however small.' If Britain was full of foreigners –
and it certainly was – countries far away had become temporary homes to many British soldiers, one of whom was Kathleen's brother, Stanley, posted to the South East Asia Command.
He 'has written me far more letters since he went overseas than
ever I got in England [16 March]. I have had instructions to
keep him posted with any constructive post-war plans and what
people think of them. He seems specially interested in the housing
problem and thinks that he and his wife will be obliged to live in
a shanty town composed of Portal Houses [i.e., prefabricated;
named after Lord Portal, the Minister of Works 1942–44] when
he comes home.'*

Saturday, 17 March

We, or rather I should say the staff in the Annexe, had a nice
surprise when we came back from tea. An ex-patient had
been up to see us and had left us a pair of woollen gloves
each, in a Fair Isle pattern, which she had knitted herself.

I was off duty this afternoon and went into the Town
which was crowded with shoppers. On the market we saw
a stall with placards all round it asking people to sign there
for a constructive peace. Various famous people, such as
Professor [C.E.M.] Joad, Eleanor Rathbone [Member of
Parliament], the Dean of Canterbury etc., they claimed
had signed this petition. On either side of the stall was
a long queue of people which we stared at in surprise
as they did not look in the least like people who would

bother to sign a petition let alone queue up to do it and we were right. As we walked past the stall the mystery was explained. At the far end of the same stall there was someone selling ice cream.

Wednesday, 28 March

The sole topic of conversation seems to be the end of the war – how soon will it be? I am looking forward to it intensely and yet dreading it in a way. While it is still in progress I can go on hoping that my fiancé is OK but I don't know what I should do if the war ended and he did not come back. The last bit of news that anyone heard from him was the letter I got in February written in December and from bits you read in the newspaper anything could have happened to him since then. When he did not come back at the time of Dunkirk I felt I should never see him again and I may still be right.

Monday, 2 April

The news is really wonderful. No V-bombs over England since Thursday too, and the first weather bulletin since the war started.

I would rejoice so wholeheartedly if only I knew where and in what condition my fiancé is at the moment. I seem to be ridiculously obsessed about it. When I pick up a paper it is not the wonderful headlines I look at or how far the Allied armies have got, but I just skim through the paper to see if there is any news of prisoners-of-war. It is not very reassuring what I do see – items about 1,000 dying from malnutrition on a forced march from Poland, or being bombed and machine-gunned on a train, or bits of cheerful (?) news like that which do not exactly raise my spirits.

Friday, 13 April

The first words I was greeted with this morning were the statement that Roosevelt was dead. I am sure there will never be a man whose death is so universally regretted. Everyone seems to feel that we have lost a very good friend and it struck me this morning that though I had heard every other Allied leader criticised I had never heard anyone say anything against Roosevelt. Even when we stood alone and America seemed undecided whether to come in or remain neutral the general idea was that if it was humanly possible Roosevelt would persuade America to come to our aid.

Saturday, 14 April

I went out this morning into the Town to do a spot of shopping and buy my small niece a birthday present. After touring all the so-called toy shops in Town I bought her a set of dolls' furniture, price 12s 6d. It was more than I wanted to pay because even though I am now earning £100 a year instead of £30, £40 and £50 (my income for the past three years), it soon goes in replacing things I have not been able to afford for some time. I was so fed up with trailing round that I took it [the dolls' furniture] in sheer desperation. I broke the pin on the badge for State Registered Nurses a few weeks ago and it is still away getting a new one fixed. I was thankful to meet a friend and go for some coffee after being told that my badge is still away. Shall be lucky to get it back before I leave.

Sunday, 15 April

Another lovely Sunday. Too lovely to be on duty from 1 o'clock onwards we thought. We were very busy, though, so the afternoon and evening passed quickly – too quickly in fact. When I came off duty at 8.30 it was lovely so I decided to pay a call on an ex-patient who lives fairly near the Infirmary. I did not want to stay in as I knew I should be miserable if I did. One of my friends left on Friday to get married, one or two others had a half-day, and I thought it would be better to go out and not mope about by myself.

Monday, 16 April

I was informed today that I had to take my day off for the week tomorrow instead of Friday as there had been some muddle over the day off of one of the nurses who is taking the Practical part of the 'Prelims' on Friday. It was a beautiful evening, sun shining, birds singing, and it was lovely to get out of the bustle of the hot wards back to the peace of the countryside.

I did not feel so peaceful, though, after listening to the 9 o'clock news in which we were informed that two POW camps had been liberated containing some of the POWs who had marched from Poland in that awful weather with practically nothing to eat. There were awful descriptions of the condition of the men and the sufferings they went through on that march. How any of them survived seems to be a miracle. I can foresee that I shall go through days when I think I can hope that my fiancé is still alive and days of despondency when I can see no reason why he can possibly be alive. It reminds me of the time after Dunkirk when I looked forward so eagerly to every post, hoping I should hear he was back in England, and of course he never came. It was months later we heard he was a POW and I remember people consoling me and saying that at least he had a better chance of coming back alive than those on active service. Little did we know what the future would bring forth.

Tuesday, 17 April

We really indulged ourselves today [in Downham] and had a fowl for our mid-day meal. It was too old to call a chicken and we had to boil it but it made a nice change and we are not so critical these days as we used to be in pre-war days when a chicken was not a very unusual item on the menu. My mother and sister-in-law [now living with the Johnstone family in Downham] set off after lunch to visit the nursing home where my sister-in-law is going for her confinement so I retired to the garden in peace. The countryside did not sound so peaceful as usual because some troops were having manoeuvres on Pendle Hill and there was a great clatter of machine guns and despatch riders tearing about on their noisy motor-cycles.

Wednesday, 18 April

I arrived back on the ward this morning to find two of the nurses in a very miserable state. One of them, a Scotch girl – her fiancé is on embarkation leave – and she asked Matron for some holidays as they wanted to get married and Matron refused. The other girl was getting married on June 2nd and after an inexplicable silence on the part of her fiancé, she had received a letter saying he wanted to break off the engagement and as I was not feeling particularly cheerful myself we were a miserable two.

Friday, 20 April

Everyone seems very pleased at the idea of the raising of the blackout on Monday. I don't know why they should be so thrilled about it because we have had the dimout for some months now and even in peace time people usually drew their curtains when they switched their lights on at night. The street lighting is very adequate up here too. I very much doubt whether it is ever much brighter. I suppose it is more the thing that it stands for that people are so pleased about – the end of the war is in sight.

Ghastly things are coming to light in Germany. These terrible concentration camps make one think that a people who could allow such horrors to go on in their midst deserve no mercy themselves. Even though they may have taken no actual part in it themselves, they are morally responsible and are certainly not fit to govern themselves. It seems to me Germany should be occupied for many years to come. [The following day, these 'atrocities' were the main subject of horrified conversations.]

Sunday, 22 April

If the Russians were 14 miles yesterday [from Berlin], today they are in the outer suburbs of Berlin and shells are falling in the centre of the city. It looks as if Berlin will not surrender without a struggle. I always thought the Germans would fight to the bitter end, but it seems senseless as they are so obviously beaten.

I heard on the news at home today that Allied prisoners-of-war were being marched to the South where everyone seems to think Hitler will make his stand. In the paper it said today that 140,000 were still in German hands, 40,000 had been liberated. As we went along a street near the Infirmary in the bus this afternoon we saw bunting across the street at one point and someone remarked that it was in honour of a POW's return home.

Monday, 23 April

Though it seems extremely doubtful that the war will end on April 25th as so many people seem to think, it is quite possible that the Russians will be into the heart of Berlin by that date. I wonder if Hitler is in Berlin and whether he will stay there to the bitter end. When is the link-up happening between the Allies and the Russians? So much of such importance is happening that we seem to be taking everything as a matter of course. Looking back to those dreary days of 1940 onwards, when the Germans were triumphant everywhere, seems almost like looking back into another world.

Blackout has officially ended tonight but looking out from my window into the valley where so much of Blackburn lies, I cannot say that there are any more or any less lights than there have been for months. We are hoping that the two wards and the theatre, the windows of which are still bricked up, will be allowed to have the brickwork removed now. The hospital authorities asked if they could be removed when the dimout came but the powers-that-be said no. It is bad for the patients and staff to be in an artificial light the whole time.

Wednesday, 25 April

There was great excitement in the ward today. The son of one of the patients, who has been a POW for five years, has been repatriated and he came to see her today. Yesterday morning she received the official telegram saying he had landed in this country. He was taken at Dunkirk and has been in Stalag XX A since. He has done that awful march across Germany, and looks terribly thin and his hair is turning grey even though he is only 25. He looked very sunburnt which I think gave him a deceptive air of being in a better condition than he really is. He said there had been no ill treatment in his camp as far as he knew, that the worst part was the monotony, but he said nothing about the march through Germany except that it was 'frightful' and he obviously did not want to talk about it. He said the longest day he had ever spent was the last day in captivity when they knew the Allies were approaching. He was taken to Brussels and flown to a reception camp near London and was on his way home in a very short time. He said he had not come across anyone from Stalag VIII B, the camp my boy friend was in.

On the last day of this month Kathleen, like everyone else, was anticipating imminent victory. 'With Mussolini dead and Hitler dying or already dead I feel that we have been saved a lot of trouble of trying and condemning them when the war is over, and whatever punishment was meted out to them it would not bring back to life one person killed in this war, or repair in any way the terrible things that have been done.'

Tuesday, 1 May

I was so intensely interested in the war situation yesterday and the possibility of peace very soon that I forgot to hand in my resignation. So this morning I went along to Matron and told her that my six months deferment was up at the end of May, airily glossing over the fact that I should have put in an appearance yesterday. She did not appear to notice the omission and kept me talking for a long time on the 'direction of nurses,' which she is finding as great a nuisance as we are. It strikes me that they will not be needing any more recruits for the Civil Nursing Reserve if peace is declared so in that case I do not see what I shall be doing next.

A nurse has just rushed in to say that Hitler is dead, according to a German report, and a good thing too. There have been such conflicting accounts of Hitler and his health and whereabouts that one hesitates to believe it. It seems too much of a coincidence that he should die like that of cerebral haemorrhage just as the war is nearing its end [in fact he committed suicide].

Wednesday, 2 May

This evening the phone rang and I picked up the receiver expecting to hear 'How is Mrs So and So?' [Kathleen was still nursing on the Women's Ward] or 'There is a case coming in', but the voice at the other end said 'Is that Nurse Johnstone?' and then proceeded to say 'I thought you might like to know the war is over' – and my heart stood still until she added 'in Italy'. It was a very pleasant bit of information, though, and is a step nearer the end. Later on this evening, after we had listened to the 9 o'clock news and talked a bit, I came upstairs and was lazing in the bath when there came a loud bang on the door and I was informed that Berlin had fallen. Pleased as I am at all the good news, how much more pleased I could be if at the same time I knew my fiancé was safe. For several days after I have heard on the wireless that more POWs have been liberated, I wait hopefully for news but still none comes.

Sunday, 6 May

Today turned out to be really fine and warm and with the sun shining brightly. I managed to become more enthusiastic about Victory than I had thought possible – especially after going to bed in a really bad mood last night of deepest depression. It is annoying how one's own small troubles seem to dwarf to us events of national importance. I think one reason why I felt cheered was the information given to me by a girl I know whose fiancé is also a POW that there were several local boys in Stalag VIII B who had not as yet been heard of. One who is back from that camp fell out of the ranks as they were being marched south somewhere near the spot where the Yanks and Russians first met. So there is hope that he may still be alive amongst them.

The news that in a matter of hours or maybe a day or two and Victory would be announced raised my spirits still further and we started looking out [i.e., getting out] our Union Jacks.

Monday, 7 May

After listening to the 6 o'clock news when we were told that according to German reports they had agreed to unconditional surrender, I went out into the garden [in Downham] firmly convinced that at last it was over. The sun was shining brightly and we were all out in the garden when the news flash came in and it was not until I got on the bus at Clitheroe that I heard the glad news. The streets were already gaily decorated and one of the most gay was the little main street in the village of Chatburn.

I knew the conductor on the bus – his wife had been a patient of mine – and I asked him about his son, also a POW, but he had heard nothing. Then someone asked him with ill-timed levity whether he had got his flags out. He said that unless this boy came home his wife could not bear to put any decoration up. They lost their only other son on the Anzio beachhead. At this moment another man got on the bus and the conductor turned to him and said briefly 'Heard anything, Joe?' and 'Joe' shook his head. His son was also in Stalag VIII B and 'Joe' told me that the last letter they had from him was last July and the one before that January. There is always someone worse off than yourself.

Arriving back at the Infirmary I found a party in full swing and presently a little crowd of the 'boys from Burma' ['walking wounded' cases who had arrived two days before] and a few nurses including myself found ourselves at the local 'pub' to celebrate the great news.

Tuesday, 8 May

VE Day. I just cannot believe it. I keep on saying to myself – the Germans are licked; the war in Europe is over – but after 5½ years it is so difficult to grasp.

The first part of the day seemed very flat. It was pouring with rain for one thing and another we had several cases for operation and I was so busy and annoyed with the surgeons for coming in to operate on such a day.

After Churchill's speech, however, everything seemed brighter.* I managed to get hold of a wireless for the ward

---

* This victory broadcast was impressive for being brief, notably factual, understated, and lacking in triumphalism (*Complete Speeches*, VII, 7152-53).

so all the patients were able to hear it. It stopped raining and the sun came out and I went off duty at 4 o'clock for the rest of the evening. The question then arose how were we going to celebrate. I had been invited out to a party later on but had also promised to go to a Thanksgiving Service with my friend. So I went to the Thanksgiving Service at the same church we went to the Service on D-Day, and what a contrast in such a short time. Little did we know then that before a year was out Germany would be hopelessly beaten.

After the Service I rushed back to the Infirmary, changed and arrived at the party in time to hear the King's speech. It was a good party and I got the proper Victory spirit but left the party about 11.30 as I was offered a lift back to the Infirmary. My intention when I got in was to go to bed and with this idea in mind I got into my pyjamas but was lured downstairs by the sound of the wireless. In the sitting room I found a crowd of nurses and I suggested that we went outside to see the bonfires and a few fireworks, which we did. But suddenly everyone wanted a bonfire of our own and urged on by a couple of Sisters, we got one started and then someone suggested [that we add to the fire] the old blackout shutters made of plywood we have fixed up at the ward windows every night and taken down every morning during our stay here. As if by magic nurses appeared from all quarters rushing out with the shutters and by the time Matron appeared dancing with wrath we had got the best bonfire burning for miles round. Oblivious of spectators who had gathered from nowhere, Matron commenced to investigate the whole proceedings. We had been warned of Matron's approach and had recklessly thrown on every shutter in the vicinity so that by the time she arrived the blaze was at its height. Nothing could daunt us by this time and the arrival of the night porter with a small stirrup pump to try to put it out and the fact that the Night Sister tripped up and rolled down the grassy slope was just too much for us and we cheered wildly. Then we heard midnight striking and, leaving the bonfire which was dying down by this time, we went back into the sitting room to sing the National Anthem and so ended our VE Day.

Wednesday, 9 May

Last night Matron in her wrath threatened us with a Board Meeting but amended it later by saying that we must decide which of us should go to the General Office to report the wanton destruction of some of the good (?) plywood shutters. To be awkward we decided to all go, so accordingly this morning about forty to fifty of us invaded the General Office where the unfortunate man to whom we had to report looked most alarmed. Keeping his face straight with difficulty, he heard the tale and then pointed out those precious shutters were Government property. We are not unduly alarmed at this statement and think that it is unlikely we shall hear anything more about it.

After our mid-day meal, which consisted of cold chicken and ham, salad etc. followed by fruit salad and strawberry ice cream, we burst into song, 'Keep the Home Fires Burning' and 'We'll Make a Bonfire of Our Troubles' being two of the favourite ones. One enterprising person sang 'Pistol packing Momma, lay the blackout down', making a parody of the whole thing. A friend of Matron's, a missionary from China, gave us a lecture on her life in China this evening. This lecture had been arranged last week and could not be postponed. Some of the nurses wanted to boycott the lecture but our better nature triumphed and we attended in good force. Matron had hastily arranged a dance for us after the lecture, working on the principle that 'Satan finds mischief for idle hands to do'. It was good fun and finished at midnight, but oh my feet.

The celebrations were now winding down. 'Things have seemed a bit flat today,' Kathleen wrote on 10 May, 'after the exultation of the past two days. I can see the problems of peace being far more difficult than the problems of war. Someone has just looked in to tell me that 10,000 POWs have been flown back on Lancasters today. But as I told her that pleased though I am that so many are coming home, I am not really interested in 10,000, only one would be enough to satisfy me providing he is the right one.'

Saturday, 12 May

The chief topic of conversation seems to be the heat. In the North we are not accustomed to hot weather and most people seem to be wilting under it. It does not matter how hot the weather may be, few people venture out into the Town in summer dresses without coats and this morning I even saw some woollen jumpers.

People up here seem to have taken the news of Victory in a very matter-of-fact way. I think the fact that the war has hit them so little may account for it. We do not know what it means to spend night after night in shelters nor all the discomforts and dangers that air raids bring with them. In addition, with so many mills and factories all round here there are many young men and women in reserved occupations who in other parts of the country would have been called up. Consequently, aside from minor discomforts, such as blackout, rationing etc., their family life and way of living has not suffered such a great upheaval.*

Friday, 18 May

Gone are the great crowd of nurses who have been in the habit of assembling round the wireless in the sitting room. When I went in after supper tonight I found only one nurse in there and she was reading. The war with Japan, important though it is, seems too remote to take a keen personal interest in.

We are more interested at the moment in the fact that we have at long last received our nine stocking coupons. My coupon assets now consist of the afore mentioned coupons, 1½ on my own book and 5 loose ones presented to me by a patient a few weeks ago.

Tuesday, 22 May

Well it looks as though a General Election is almost upon us. Did anyone mention the word 'peace'? A General Election at home, quarrels over Trieste, Syria annoyed at the landing of French troops, Russia and the Polish question, and of course the war with Japan still on our hands. Am afraid we have far to travel before we can even begin to think about it, never mind enjoy it.

A world of perpetual peace would be very dull, though. Speaking for myself, often when I am in the middle of fuss and turmoil I think to myself how I should enjoy a peaceful life in the country, the only changes being the changing of

---

* Three bombs fell on Blackburn during the war, causing two deaths (Beattie, *Blackburn* [1992], p. 165).

the seasons, and yet after two and a half days of country life [during the just-concluded Whitsun Weekend] I was quite glad to catch an early train back to Blackburn and go to see *Frenchman's Creek* [a lavish technicolour adventure film] in a crowded cinema. A real escape film from the problems of today. I liked the book [by Daphne du Maurier, 1941], which I read a year or two ago, and the film seemed to me to follow the book more accurately than most films taken from books.

Wednesday, 23 May

Back to the daily grind and not feeling too lively either. I could not get to sleep until after 2 this morning, which was most unusual for me. Whether it was the tea I drank at a late hour or whether it was aching disappointment of finding no letter or telegram waiting for me I don't know. It amazes me in my sane moments that I can still hope after all this time that my fiancé should still be alive. It is true we have had no word to say he is not but I should imagine that all the POWs will have been repatriated by this time. Nevertheless tomorrow I expect I shall still be watching for the postman.

Churchill has resigned on the crest of the wave before the difficulties and disappointments of peace have become apparent. I think the Labour Party have done themselves a bad turn in the forcing the issue at such a time even though they don't want the General Election until autumn [see the Appendix for her observations on national politics].

Thursday, 24 May

Last night after I had finished my bit of writing I meant to go straight into supper and then to bed but somehow I found myself giving in to the dance we were holding that night. I was wearing an old blouse and skirt and did not even bother to powder my nose but somehow I had a lovely time and enjoyed myself more than I had done for a long time. It was our V-E dance and we had our dining room decorated with red, white and blue and crowds of soldiers from a major down to a private and the dance went with a swing from beginning to end.

Needless to say getting up this morning after about four hours' sleep was not so enjoyable but I have not felt sleepy all day which was a good thing as we have had a hectically busy evening with very ill patients coming back from the theatre. New cases coming in, every honourary [physician] doing a round and myself vainly trying to write the report.

These were days when Kathleen must have been thinking a lot about her future, and sometimes she wrote about these possibilities – or, more accurately, about her doubts and uncertainties. On 25 May she was coming close to making up her mind. 'As it seems most unlikely that my fiancé is still alive, though his people have not yet heard anything to the contrary, I have been thinking over very seriously what I intend to do and I have decided that if possible when I have got Part One of my midwifery, I shall join the Colonial Nursing Service and see something of the world, before I settle down to a staid middle-age.' *She was about to leave the Blackburn Royal Infirmary – her term of service was nearly over – and was preparing for departure.* 'It seems so strange to be leaving like this after 3½ years, especially as when I started I thought the war would be over long before I had finished my 3 years and sat for my Finals. Until these last two or three weeks I had never envisaged the prospect of leaving here with the war in Europe over and having to set off again and start in a new post. I always imagined that my fiancé

would be back, and that we should get married. I am finding it
difficult to adjust myself mentally to carrying on without him in the
background.' (27 May)

Four weeks later her uncertainty about Bill was definitively laid
to rest.

Friday, 22 June

With this sunny weather, broken though it is by thunder-
storms, I am getting really sunburnt and I mean that literally.
My arms are beginning to feel quite painful when exposed
to the sun. I suppose it is because it is years since I was on
holiday at this time of the year – not since June of 1940.
It was glorious weather then and everywhere one met men
burnt brick-red from Dunkirk. I was watching and hoping
then that my fiancé would be amongst them but he was not.
It was many months later that we heard he was a POW. Now
the latest news I have of him is in a letter received this morning from a friend of his who was in the same camp, saying
that he fell out as they were on their way across Germany.
He was too weak to go any further and the rest of them were
too weak to help him along. He was very big, 6 feet 4 inches
and broad and would be quite a heavy weight. So that is that
and only confirms what I have felt for a long time.

Ten days before this, on the evening of 12 June, she had gone to a
card party and reflected on her fortune in life. 'It was a good thing
the stakes were low because I lost the maximum amount of money
possible. I had the most atrocious cards and was consoled by the old
saying about being "unlucky at cards, lucky in love". Unfortunately
I seem to be the exception who is unlucky in both.' Months later,
on the last day of the year, at a quarter to midnight, as she was

*'waiting quietly with my father and mother to let in the New Year',
she thought back on the previous twelve months. 'In spite of the
ending of the war, 1945 has not been a very good year for the family
on the whole and I have no regrets that in a very few minutes it will
be behind us. I cannot help remembering that in the last letter I had
from my fiancé [23 February], written at the end of 1944, he said
that next year we should be letting in the New Year together.'*

Epilogue

Kathleen's time at Blackburn's Infirmary was ending in late May, with her future still in doubt. She was starting to apply for admission to midwifery training hospitals. Matron signed a document concerning 'my moral character' (30 May) and she 'went to say goodbye to one or two people whom I am not likely to see again. I think Lancashire people are very generous and hospitable. I have never found such friendliness and pressing hospitality as I have found in Lancashire and I have lived in various places from the North of Scotland to the South Coast. I came away with all sorts of little presents, tea, lemon cheese, honey, handmade leather handbag and purse, all from people I have come in contact with through my work.' ('I think that Lancashire people are some of the most hospitable people to be found in this little island of ours,' she had written a few weeks earlier, on 8 March 1945.) On 31 May, her last day of work in Blackburn, she was collecting all the things she needed to take with her – and saying a sort of goodbye to a place she had come to know well over three and a half years. 'I had a look into the baby ward, now empty in order to have a spring clean after the bricks had been taken down from the windows. It looked so light and airy that it was difficult to imagine that it was the same ward which for five years had been bricked up with artificial lighting all day.' She wasn't off duty until 6 p.m. Then she left 'in such a rush I had very little time to feel upset and I was barely ready when the taxi arrived at 6.45. I had another taxi to meet me at this end [perhaps Clitheroe] and the driver informed me that he had taken my sister-in-law to the Nursing Home this morning. When I got home I found I had got another little niece [to be named Geraldine] born at 2 o'clock.'

It was not long before Kathleen learned what her next stop in nursing would be (8 June): taking Part One of the midwifery course at a hospital in West Bromwich, Stafford-shire, starting the first of July. On 16 June, after a week's holiday, 'I had a very energetic day at home, washing, iron-ing and altering my old uniform dresses in readiness for six months' hard labour. They advise pupil midwives to bring their own uniform if possible in case they have none in stock to fit and as I am not stock size [she was on the thin side] it is unlikely they will have a ready-made uniform to fit me.' She had little enthusiasm for these new studies (26 June). 'I don't really want to do midwifery and try to console myself with the thought that it is only for six months and that I should be home in January. I have made up my mind that I am taking no more exams after this. Life is too short to spend the greater part of your time studying.' Still, training in midwifery it was to be. On 30 June she arrived at the Hal-lam Hospital in West Bromwich – she left home in the rain and arrived in the rain. Her room in the Nurses Home there already had her name on it.

Kathleen was to spend the rest of 1945 in West Bromwich, before moving in mid-January to Manchester, where she worked for most of the following four months in the radium unit attached to the Christie Hospital. During her time off she often returned home to Downham by bus. Then, from 1 June, she was attached to the General Infirmary in Salisbury, Wiltshire, training for Part Two of her examination in midwifery. Sometimes she was less than pleased with her life. Midwifery, she wrote on 13 July 1946, 'is a most heartbreaking profession'. The work was hard and 'if things go well you get no thanks; if things go wrong you get all the blame . . . Not one woman in 10 bothers to say thank you when she goes out, unlike ordinary patients in hospital who are usually most grateful.' Still, there were more upbeat moments, such as when she wrote her in diary on the last day of August 1946. 'I think these past three months have been some of the happiest I have spent in hospital. The Sister on the ward said she hoped I would practise midwifery when my six months' training was finished. She said I would make a good midwife and that my method of delivery could not be improved on. I must say I thought the latter statement was not very accurate but it does give you a boost up to get a bit of praise, for a change.'

Kathleen was still training for midwifery in Salisbury, the first of her three months in district nursing, when her diary suddenly ends on 30 September 1946. No explanation was given for this abrupt ending, and she offered no concluding reflections on the thirty-nine months she had spent as a diligent keeper of a diary. The few records and family memories of her life after 1946 reveal that she qualified in mid-1947 as a member of the Queen's Institute of District Nursing and was listed on a roll of midwives in 1950. She worked for many years as a District Nurse and later Health Visitor in Lancashire, employed by the County Council, attending especially to the welfare of mothers and their young children at home.

She had a special interest in deaf children, their families and their education, and took special training for this work.

Shortly after her father's sudden death in 1952 at the age of 64, Kathleen left Downham and continued to live with her widowed mother, mainly in Longridge, Lancashire. When she was 55 years old, in September 1969, Kathleen married one Thomas Edmondson (b. 1893), a widower and retired quarry blacksmith, in Longridge. They had met while she was caring for his late wife. Nurses, as Kathleen had remarked in her diary, often met their husbands through nursing work (though usually at a younger age). Tom and Kathleen lived together, in modest comfort, in the house in Longridge that she had been sharing and continued to share with her elderly mother. Kathleen's retirement from nursing probably happened not too long after her marriage, perhaps around the time she turned 60 (in 1973). These years of retirement did not last long. On 9 October 1982 she died in the Ribchester Hospital, a few weeks before her 69th birthday. While the immediate cause of death was apparently bronchial pneumonia, she had probably been in failing health for some time. Her work as a wartime diarist was probably unknown to anyone in the 1940s or later, aside from the few staff members at Mass Observation who would have received and perhaps looked over her writing, and of course the staff and researchers at the post-1975 Mass Observation Archive, now housed at The Keep in Brighton.

Kathleen's surviving relatives (nieces and nephews) have varied memories of their aunt. (None of them knew of her wartime diary before 2021.) Peter King (b. 1942), the first of Kathleen's nephews and who appears as a toddler in her diary, reports that his mother, Phyllis, 'always spoke with awe about her [Kathleen's] capabilities' and, especially when they were young, 'regarded her as a knowledgeable authority figure' (14

September 2021). 'I understand that Kathleen was a kind support to my mother' when she gave birth to a premature baby in August 1944, recalled Phyllis's third daughter, Mary (b. 1947), in mid-2021. Kathleen's eldest niece, Elizabeth (b. 1939), who is mentioned several times in the diary, wrote around the same time that 'My mother admired Kathleen and said she was highly intelligent and had many skills and deserved a more formal education.' 'Conscientious', 'thought-ful', 'encouraging' – these are words Mary used in remember-ing her aunt. Phyllis's family 'looked forward' to Kathleen's visits to Wiltshire and (recalls Elizabeth) 'loved our holidays in Downham' (September 2021). Kathleen stood out as an independent woman with a career and her own car (a new Morris Minor in the early 1950s). She was respected for the care she gave Ellen, her elderly and ailing mother, who out-lived her husband by twenty-one years and became increas-ingly dependent on her elder daughter. And, of course, as a District Nurse and then Health Visitor, Kathleen must have provided important support for many families and distressed people in their own homes in East Lancashire. In September 1951 the Vicar of Downham sent her (along with a gift) a note to express the villagers' 'appreciation of the good work you have done amongst them as their District Nurse'; on an ear-lier occasion this help was publicly acknowledged.[*]

* * *

Finally, to speculate: What reasons might Kathleen have had for such a serious commitment to diary-writing? Readers may have already come to their own conclusions. Our view is that

---

* Letter of 21 September 1951, in the possession of her nephew, Philip Johnstone; *Clitheroe Advertiser*, 21 July 1950, p. 8.

diary-keeping for Kathleen was one way of keeping busy, of occupying her mind, of minimizing those 'idle' moments when she might be prone to ruminate and ponder the worst. Writing gave her opportunities to reach out, to engage with listeners (that is, people at Mass Observation, and perhaps future generations), and to function as a kind of reporter on the world she inhabited. This busyness helped to keep worry at bay, or at least to muffle its impact. To write was to act creatively, to leave a kind of mark, to exercise her intelligence in ways different from those associated with nursing. To write helped her to avoid becoming too overwhelmed by personal troubles. And writing was a very different kind of task from the acts she performed at work and at home and while out and about in Blackburn and Clitheroe and the East Lancashire countryside. Perhaps her diary was a sort of anchor in tumultuous times.

History has been full of voices that will remain unheard. Kathleen Johnstone stood out as a person who kept a record – often a vivid record – of her everyday experiences and her observations on the lives of others. Like most good diaries, hers captures the immediacies of living, written within hours after thoughts and feelings and actions have occurred. This record of her world – small in a sense but linked to a much larger world – can now, fortunately, be enjoyed and appreciated by later generations. A thoughtful and observant diary is a work of lasting value.

Appendix

Politics 1945/46

*As the United Kingdom embarked on its first election campaign since 1935, Kathleen took an interest in what was going on and occasionally wrote about these public events. On Monday, 4 June 'I listened to a part of Mr Churchill's speech this evening but as all he seemed to be doing was pouring scorn, in no very dignified manner, on the Labour Party, and not putting forward any very concrete proposals, on behalf of the Conservatives, I disappeared to iron a blouse.' Kathleen was not the only voter who disliked what Churchill had broadcast that evening.**

Tuesday, 5 June

After our visit to the nursing home I came back into Blackburn and had tea with some friends of mine. The talk turned on the General Election and I asked them what they were going to vote. Even as I asked the question I knew what the

---

* This was Churchill's notorious speech in which he foresaw a Labour Government instituting some sort of 'Gestapo' state. Almost everyone agreed that the speech did nothing to aid the electoral prospects of the Conservative Party (*Complete Speeches*, VII, 7169–74).

answer would be – Conservative. They run a hardware shop of their own and naturally do not want things nationalised. I am beginning to think myself that with the war with Japan still in progress and foreign affairs needing so much attention it is hardly the right moment to start a big scheme of nationalization.

The following evening, Kathleen 'heard Viscount Samuel's speech in support of the Liberal Party and his refusal for the Liberal Party to throw in their lot with the Conservatives. I cannot help wishing that the Liberal Party was stronger but according to the last set of figures I saw they are only putting up 300-odd candidates against the Conservative and Labour 600.'

Thursday, 7 June

I have been listening to Sir John Anderson [Chancellor of the Exchequer] speaking on the wireless tonight. He calls himself a non-party man but he plumps down heavily on the side of private enterprise which I think gives him a decidedly Tory bias. As far as I can gather from the Conservatives I have listened to, private enterprise and freedom go hand in hand, and nationalization and slavery. I think private enterprise may be a good thing in its way but surely the primary consideration of any person or persons, company or share-holders, engaged in private enterprise is profit to themselves, not the good of the community they are serving, and this freedom – where did it lead a great many people in pre-war days? Into everlasting dole queues from which the war saved a great many. If there had been no war I guess a lot of these people would still be there and may even yet drift back unless something decisive is done about it. Sir John

Anderson said there is no one cure for unemployment. How often did we hear that in pre-war days.

Thursday, 21 June

My sister-in-law and I were saying this morning that with the General Election in front of us the daily papers are very confusing. My people take the *Daily Mail* because they have always taken [it], not because they approve of it politically. My father has definite leanings towards Labour and my sister-in-law takes the *Daily Mirror* which she sends on to my brother in Burma. According to both papers, whether Tory or Labour get in, the country is heading for ruin. I must say Labour seems to be managing very badly. Professor [Harold] Laski [Chairman of the Labour Party] seems to be putting his foot in it properly [by appearing to align his thinking with that of the Soviet Union].

In the early summer of 1945, Churchill was widely seen as a great wartime leader, including by voters ill-disposed toward his party. In later June, as historian Paul Addison has said, Churchill 'undertook a triumphal tour through the country, greeted by cheering crowds from Birmingham to Glasgow.'* Over two days (26/27 June) he was met by enthusiastic, sometimes enormous, crowds in Yorkshire and Lancashire, the latter including Manchester, Oldham, Burnley, Accrington and Blackburn (the last reported in extraordinary detail in the Blackburn Times, *29 June 1945, p. 3 and the* Northern Daily Telegraph, *27 June 1945, p. 1 and 28 June 1945, p. 4). He finished in Preston, greeted by 'Miles*

---

* Paul Addison, *The Road to 1945: British Politics and the Second World War* (London: Pimlico, revised edition, 1994), p. 266.

of Cheering Crowds' – *'We are proud in Preston to have had the chance of acclaiming him,'* *according to the* Lancashire Daily Post *(28 June 1945, p. 2)* – *with Kathleen in attendance.*

Wednesday, 27 June

As we [she was with two friends] wanted to see Churchill we went to the square in front of the Town Hall. It is a most imposing building and ideal for this kind of purpose as at the bottom of the main steps leading from the entrance the speaker is so far above the heads of the crowd that everyone is able to get a good view. We thought Churchill was speaking at 5 o'clock and got along there at about twenty minutes to 5 and then gradually the news got around that he would not be speaking until 6.15. In the meantime we were entertained by speeches from the Conservative candidates for Blackpool, Chorley Lancaster, The Fylde, and one or two others whose names I did not catch – also by Mr Hudson, Minister of Agriculture. The member for the Fylde had brought along a bag of fish for Mr Churchill from the fishermen of Fleetwood. There was a certain amount of good-natured heckling from parts of the crowd; and one little man kept on chanting 'Tell us the old, old story'. Six fifteen came and went and still no Churchill appeared and any person with speaking ability sitting up there on the platform was brought to the microphone and in between the speeches a loud speaker blared away 'She's my lady love'. Why they chose that to fill in any lull I don't know. It was so inappropriate that there was a wave of laughter every time it started.

Then just after 7 there was a stir in the crowd. A lady with a red, white and blue bouquet dashed up the steps and presented it to Mrs Churchill who appeared at the entrance with Mr Churchill. There was a great burst of clapping and cheering and much waving of little Union Jacks as Mr Churchill came down the steps bareheaded and smoking a cigar. He was accompanied by his son Randolph Churchill and the other Conservative candidate for Preston, Captain Amery. I am afraid that we only had time to listen to the few opening sentences of his speech as I had visions of having to walk home from Clitheroe and having already endured eight speeches on the Conservative policy I did not think that even Mr Churchill could add anything new. As he started his speech someone from one of the housetops started to shout 'Vote for Labour,' and there were indignant murmurs from the crowd who had previously laughed at the Labour efforts at heckling. What a pity he ever took over the leadership of the Conservative Party. He should retire at the height of his fame before his achievements are dimmed by Party politics and squabbles.

The following day in Downham, 'I was so busy [preparing to travel to West Bromwich] that I did not even have time to look out of the garden gate to see who was speaking outside the "local". My virtue was rewarded, though, by catching a glimpse of a van and hearing a voice saying as it drove slowly down the hill, "This is Reginald Fast's broadcasting van – Vote for the Conservatives" etc.'

Thursday, 26 July

I am utterly amazed at the Labour Party winning the election with such a good majority but I felt terribly pleased about it in spite of my forecast being wrong. My sympathies have always leaned towards Labour though I must confess I wavered somewhat before the election. I should not be a bit surprised if they make a mess of things but I am convinced that a Conservative Government would have made a worse one.

I could not help a feeling of regret when I heard the formal announcement on the wireless that Mr Churchill had resigned as of course he had to do. Even though he was the leader of the Conservative Party it always seemed to me that his popularity was for himself alone, not the Party he represented. This struck me very forcibly when I saw him at Preston on his election tour and he is leaving office with his popularity undimmed, at the height of his success.

Friday, 27 July

I had a couple of letters today, from my friend who is a staunch Conservative, and my brother in Burma who is a red-hot Labour man. He said his papers arrived in time and he got his vote but he should think there were roughly two-thirds who did not. He estimates that about 90% of Servicemen are Labour and if that is the case then they should be satisfied with the result whether they got a vote or not. He says that Churchill is not popular with the Forces out there but as I should imagine that none of them are exactly enjoying themselves, they are not under the circumstances able to take an unbiassed view of those in authority who have sent them there.

Kathleen's final comments on politics were recorded in the following year, on 25 March, after she had returned to Downham for a few days from her nursing job in Manchester and her brother, recently returned from Burma, and his wife and baby daughter were also there as visitors. Kathleen arrived at 11 that morning.

I went to bed about 1 o'clock and slept soundly until my mother called me just after 5. The sun was pouring into my room. It was such a short time since it was almost dark at this hour when I was getting up. We had gin and tonic this evening and a most heated argument on politics. My sister-in-law is a definite Labour [supporter] and in spite of everything Russia has done still pro-Russian. My brother was Labour but since the Labour Party got in he seems to have become Conservative. My mother is Conservative but strangely enough anti-Churchill. I am Labour but I think quite a bit of Churchill. So between us we had a glorious argument, everyone becoming very heated and nobody succeeding in convincing anyone else. I think the unaccustomed gin helped to increase the heat of the three female members of the party as we had each been given a generous helping by my brother.

A Note on Editing

The most important decisions rendered by editors are found in the selections they make from the primary source to put into print. Occasionally a diary has been published in its entirety; much more frequently, though, decisions have been made *not* to publish portions of what the diarist wrote. This is rarely for reasons of censorship but mostly because the diary is too long, or full of repetitions, or packed with detail on subjects of little interest to most contemporary readers. We have selected around half of Kathleen Johnstone's diary between June 1943 and June 1945 for publication – she wrote almost every day during these two years – and have made these selections with the following considerations in mind.

We have highlighted passages of descriptive merit, usually when she is being observant about some scene of incident or human relationship. These are passages that draw the reader into her experiences of the moment. We have also reproduced most diary entries that are ruminative or reflective or in some way psychologically sensitive. While we have left out a lot of what she says about the weather and public transportation and shopping and other routine matters (many of them repetitive), we have included, we think, enough of these passages to give the reader a sense of her daily life, which of course varied from month to month and depended on whether she was on duty as a nurse or at leisure. Finally, since the diary exhibits more of a narrative thrust from the summer of 1944, as she dreads her upcoming final nursing exams and as the war looks to be heading for victory, with the prospect of a reunion with her POW boyfriend and a new post-war life, our selections from later 1944 and 1945 are particularly attentive to these hopes and fears for the future and less concerned with documenting everyday events.

Since Kathleen's handwriting is legible and her writing largely free of errors, there is no need for much tweaking of her diary. Our interventions are limited mainly to two issues: capitalization and punctuation. Kathleen capitalized many words that would now not be capitalized (this was the style at that time); moreover, she capitalized inconsistently. We have for most part retained her liking for capitals and tried to ensure that this practice is observed as consistently as possible. As for punctuation, since Kathleen – indeed, most wartime diarists – wrote in haste and may often not even have reviewed what she wrote for errors, slips in punctuation were virtually inevitable. We have altered her punctuation, where appropriate, to enhance clarity of expression while maintaining for the most part her light use of commas (in places where others would have used them). Any misspellings – and there aren't many – we have silently corrected.

Acknowledgements

Most of what we learned about Kathleen Johnstone's life before and after the Second World War came from her nieces and nephews, and we are very grateful for their advice and informative replies to our questions. Elizabeth Newton Price, Peter King, and Mary Jefferies are the children of Kathleen's sister Phyllis, and Dene Shaw and Philip Johnstone the children of her brother Stanley. We corresponded with all of them and had the pleasure of meeting four of them, along with Mary's husband Peter Jefferies, in Clitheroe and Downham in October/November 2021 (Peter King lives in California). Through them, we were able to learn more about the Johnstone family and inspect various photographs and documents that were new to us, especially those supplied by Phil Johnstone. We greatly appreciate the cooperation and help of all these family members. We also owe thanks to our friend and family researcher Ann Stephenson, whose sleuthing tracked down Dene Shaw (Geraldine Johnstone), born on 31 May 1945, as Kathleen reports in her diary, which led to our connections with her and other members of the family.

Mary Painter, Community History Librarian at the Central Library in Blackburn, was a key supporter of our researcher. She answered numerous enquiries by email and when we were working in Blackburn advised us on primary sources, showed us material we would not have discovered on our own, and discussed matters relating to Kathleen's wartime experiences in Blackburn. We are very grateful to Mary for her assistance throughout this project. While we were in Clitheroe Shirley Penman kindly gave us access to the *Clitheroe Advertiser* – and had given us valuable advice on local matters before our visit. She also introduced us to Tom McLean, an expert on the history of Downham. Tom guided us and family members on a tour of Downham, arranged for all of us to meet Lord and Lady Clitheroe and their son Ralph Assheton, and spent the better part of a day later that week driving the two of us around East Lancashire, including Nelson (our home town on another continent bears the same name) and the countryside around Pendle Hill. We also wish to acknowledge the help of various other individuals: Jessica Scantlebury at the Mass Observation Archive; Helen Blum and Lindsay Forsythe at the Public Library in Nelson, British Columbia; staff members at the Lancashire Archives, the Bodleian Library, and the BBC Written Archives Centre; and Gordon Wise, our literary agent at Curtis Brown, who found us us a happy publishing home at HarperNorth.

Nelson, British Columbia,
May 2022